AMERICAN LAWYERS AND THEIR COMMUNITIES

REVISIONS
A Series of Books on Ethics

General Editors

Stanley Hauerwas and Alasdair MacIntyre

American Lawyers
and Their Communities

Ethics in the Legal Profession

THOMAS L. SHAFFER

(with Mary M. Shaffer)

University of Notre Dame Press

Notre Dame   London

Library of Congress Cataloging-in-Publication Data

Shaffer, Thomas L., 1934–
    American lawyers and their communities : ethics in the
legal profession / Thomas L. Shaffer, with Mary M. Shaffer.
        p.   cm. — (Revisions ; v. 10)
    Includes bibliographical references (p. 240) and index.
    ISBN: 978-0-268-00640-2
    1. Legal ethics—Social aspects—United States.   2. Lawyers—
United States.   3. Italian Americans.   I. Shaffer, Mary M.
II. Title.   III. Series.
KF306.S45   1991
174'.3'0973—dc20   90-50974
                                                         CIP

FOR ROBERT E. RODES, JR.

Contents

Acknowledgments

Much of the material in this book first appeared, in a different form, in periodical articles. I am grateful to the following publishers for permitting me to use this work:

"The Legal Ethics of Belonging" (the 1988 Law Forum Lectures), 48 *Ohio State Law Journal* 703 (1988). Copyright © 1988, Ohio State University

"Legal Ethics After Babel," 19 *Capital University Law Review* 989 (1990)

"Professionalism as a Moral Value," inaugural Howard Lichtenstein Lecture, Hofstra University, 1989, published at 26 *Gonzaga Law Review* 393 (1990–91), and used with the permission of Monroe H. Freedman, Howard Lichtenstein Distinguished Professor of Legal Ethics

"Rispetto as a Virtue in the Tradition of Italian-American Lawyers," 64 *Notre Dame Law Review* 838 (1989). Copyright © by *Notre Dame Law Review*, University of Notre Dame

"Lawyers as Assimilators and Preservers," 58 *Mississippi Law Journal* 405 (1988), inaugural Overton and Levona Currie Lecture, University of Mississippi, 1989

"The Gentleman in Professional Ethics," 10 *Queen's Law Journal 1* (1985), Willis G. Cunningham Memorial Lecture, Queen's University, 1984

"The Tension Between Law in America and the Religious Tradition," in Richard John Neuhaus (ed.), *Law and the Ordering of Our Life Together* (William B. Eerdmans Publishing Company, Grand Rapids, Michigan, 1989)

* * * * *

The special joy of this book has been working with my daughter, Mary. She shared with me the research, interviewing, thinking, and writing that went into Chapters Five through Seven. She also read and re-read, criticized and re-criticized the rest of the text, worked on the documentation, and prepared the index. She is not responsible for all of the speculation, of course, which is why I preserved the first-person singular in those chapters. My wife, Nancy, advised on and corrected the entire thing, as she has done with almost all of my work, for nearly forty years, with incisive generosity. Our son Ed the sports journalist and our son Andy the vet student helped with research and criticism.

Robert E. Rodes, Jr., has been my teacher and friend for more than thirty years. He is the first lawyer I met, when I came from a lawyerless mountain town in Colorado to the Notre Dame Law School, in the fall of 1958—and he is, I think, the best, in all senses, and particularly in the Aristotelian sense. He has always been generous in putting aside his own important work to help me with mine. He read, revised, and corrected the material in this book—in most cases twice, once when it was done in lecture or essay form, and again in the manuscript for this book. And he balked at some of it; his lucid disagreement means that all errors of perception and reason here are my own; he has done all he could. . . .

If I avoid appearing as crippled as I am in theology (see chapter one), it is because friends and colleagues in theology are patient and attentive. I am grateful to John Howard Yoder, Stanley Hauerwas, Louis W. Hodges, and Harlan R. Beckley for helping me with my theology— and for their friendship. But for Stanley Hauerwas, especially, my theology would be, more than it is, suspended between my Baptist boyhood and my curious present. Many others, from callings as various as Talmud and small-town southern law practice, have been helpful. Thanks to John Acuff, Frank S. Alexander, John Attanasio, Louis Auchincloss, Mark H. Aultman, Milner S. Ball, Joseph P. Bauer, Francis X. Beytagh, Jon W. Bruce, Walter Brueggemann, Robert A. Baruch Bush, Teresa S. Collett, Roger C. Cramton, Overton Currie, Anthony D'Amato, John DiPippa, Fernand N. Dutile, Thomas Eisele, Philip Faccenda, Anthony J. Fejfar, Roberto Ferrara, Monroe H. Freedman, Pier Massimo Forni, Elizabeth D. Gee, Michael Goldberg, Roger D. Groot, Mark H. Grunewald, Linda Harrington, Emily Fowler Hartigan, Steven H. Hobbs, Thomson Irvine, Janis L. Johnston, Carmella and Ken Kinslow, Duane LaRue, Lewis LaRue, Sanford Levinson, David T. Link, Burt Louden, Denis Magnusson, James Wm. McClendon, Jr., Andrew W. McThenia, David K. Millon, Martha Morgan, Brian C. Murchison, Richard W. Nahstoll, Peter T. Noone, Stephen L. Pepper, H. Jefferson Powell, Kevin Rardin, Robert S. Redmount, Robert Eli Rosen, Carole C. Roos, Richard Sandy, Dan Semmens, Joan M. Shaughnessy, Michael S. Slinger, Gregory M. Stanton, Kathleen Sullivan, Michael I. Swygert, Joseph P. Tomain, Dennis J. Tuchler, Margaret Williams, and Thomas Williams, Jr.

I am grateful, finally, to Marion Short and her late husband Robert for their generous support to the University of Notre Dame, support that includes an endowment for my chair in the law school.

T. L. S.

CHAPTER ONE

Legal Ethics After Babel

> We are hesitant to articulate our sense that we
> need one another as much as we need to
> stand alone, for fear that if we did we should
> lose our independence altogether. The ten-
> sions of our lives would be even greater if we
> did not, in fact, engage in practices that con-
> stantly limit the effects of an isolating individ-
> ualism, even though we cannot articulate
> those practices as well as we can the quest for
> autonomy.
>
> Robert N. Bellah et al.,
> *Habits of the Heart*

Legal ethics owes as much to Richard M. Nixon as it
does to the American Bar Association. Interest in legal
ethics in the last decade is one of many consequences of
the burglary in 1972 at the Watergate Hotel. The criminal politics that destroyed Mr. Nixon's presidency summoned American lawyers to a serious, systematic
curiosity about the morals of their craft.

A distressing number of the Watergate villains, including the President, were lawyers: John Dean, John Ehr-
lichman, G. Gordon Liddy, John Mitchell, Robert C.
Mardian, Richard Kleindienst, Herbert Kalmbach. The
bar-association committees that tend professional image
were not consoled by the fact that many of the Watergate
heroes were also lawyers: Senator Sam Ervin, Representatives Barbara Jordan and Caldwell Butler; Archibald Cox,
James St. Clair, Judge John J. Sirica.

By the end of the 1970s, at about the time the Watergate lawyers were being paroled from their relatively comfortable cells in minimum security federal prisons, the American Bar Association established a committee of eminent lawyers and law teachers to prepare a new statement of legal ethics for the American legal profession. The Association's accreditation standards for law schools had by then been amended to require instruction in ethics, or, as it had come to be called, "professional responsibility," and thus to require instruction in ethics as a condition for the license to practice law. "Law Day" ceremonies for a few years sounded less triumphant than they had in the glory days of the Cold War. Speakers spoke less of the menace of communism and more of the home-grown menaces of hubris and greed. They asked, or hinted at sympathy with those who asked, "What is the matter with lawyers?"

The answer when it came was no more triumphant than the Law Day speeches: There is nothing the matter with lawyers that is not the matter with everybody else. The "problem" from Watergate was not simply that lawyers failed to demonstrate character, but that they had failed to deliver on claims to exceptional character they had been making and that the country by and large accepted. As Harry Jones said, "Men of large affairs do not select their legal advisers entirely or principally for ethical insensitivity." The solution to the problem was for lawyers to stop making the claim.

This lawyers-are-not-noble answer has given comfort to law students over the last decade; it probably explains why law teachers no longer fuss over Watergate very much. Generally American lawyers in the making see no reason to be morally distinct; the distinction they think lawyers should have is distinction in knowledge and craftsmanship, and that distinction is understood to be technical, not moral. There is nothing new in this. It is the way nineteenth-century American lawyers came to terms with taking fees from the robber barons. In both cases skill at manipulating an esoteric access to coercive power overshadowed a "republican" tradition of civic virtue.

But there is a remnant from Watergate as there was a remnant from the Babylonian Captivity. The remnant from Babylon came back to Jerusalem and rebuilt the Temple. They saved the Torah for us. After Watergate, many hearts and some few minds see possibilities in an old American aspiration that lawyers should be persons of heightened moral sensitivity. The realization that evil among the lawyers in the Nixon White House was as banal as evil anywhere else did not entirely dampen speculative curiosity about what lawyers' morals should be. A remnant keeps the curiosity alive, and its service to the curiosity revives American legal ethics.

I do not claim that Americans were uncurious about their lawyers' morals before 1973. Our popular American lawyer stories are stories of moral lives in the profession: Lawyer Gavin Stevens is protagonist through a generation of William Faulkner's stories of southern gentlemen; Atticus Finch, in Harper Lee's *To Kill a Mockingbird* (1960), is better known to the average American twenty-year-old than King David is; network television has never been without one or more popular series of lawyer stories. America is steadily interested in the morals of lawyers.

Nor do I mean to say that there was not, before Watergate, a subject of study and practice called legal ethics. Since the early nineteenth century, lawyers in America have had both a normative tradition and a set of procedures for casting out the morally unfit. At least since the middle of the nineteenth century the latter, gate-keeping tradition has been called legal ethics. It occasionally proved interesting to a few scholarly lawyers, and led to study, generalization, bits of teaching, and some slight sequential discussion that was not about procedure and not about law. The Philadelphia lawyer Henry Sandwith Drinker was deservedly eminent for his efforts to give intellectual substance to the profession's exclusion and

expulsion procedures. In 1953, supported by a foundation grant, he published the only treatise on "legal ethics" that was generally available when I was a law
student. He was a gentleman; he knew what made a person morally unfit to practice law.

So, when the Watergate lawyers were disbarred, there
was a tradition of scholarship and discussion on the morals of American lawyers. But it was a small and unimpor-
tant thing: Drinker was thought to be expert in the
subject, but he was not employed by a university and his
work in legal ethics was a part-time endeavor. No one I
went to law school with *read* Drinker anyway. Most law
students of the 1950s and 1960s were not given instruction in legal ethics and were not examined on the subject by either university or court. The extent of my
consideration of the subject was a handwritten paragraph
I was asked to include in my application to be admitted
to the Bar of the Indiana Supreme Court. I was told to
explain what the A.B.A.'s Canons of Ethics of 1908 meant
to me. I do not remember what I wrote. I doubt if anyone read it.

Before Watergate, a few law schools offered courses in
which students could study appellate opinions in cases in
which someone who had been denied admission to the
profession pointed to a legal argument against exclusion;
or in which an ex-lawyer claimed he had been thrown
out unlawfully; or in which a lawyer complained about a
sanction less than disbarment. Those casebooks served
the ancestor of a different and now vigorously positivis-
tic discipline. It was not *ethics*. It was and is a rationale
for sanctions that good lawyers impose on bad lawyers.
The broader subject as Henry Drinker presented it con-
veyed conventional notions of professional propriety and
in places hinted at moral aspiration, but the moral aspiration was equally conventional. There was faint evidence in Drinker's discipline of a community of thinkers
whose common concern was to ask how a good person
goes about being a lawyer, or how a lawyer goes about

being a good person. Watergate brought a body of *law on lawyers* into relief, as it gave us lawyer after lawyer who, faced with the public fact that he had done something manifestly disgusting, said, "I did not commit a crime." It seems to have become necessary, after Watergate, to separate the law on lawyers from legal ethics *as* ethics. I will use this distinction and these two phrases as if they are thus separated: (i) the law on lawyers, and (ii) legal ethics as ethics.

Most of the legal profession's effort in the last decade has been to clarify and enforce the law on lawyers. I am interested in the other part, the neglected part of the separation, legal ethics as ethics. My concern is legal ethics as it rose to the top of the swamp, and in what remained after the continuation of the tradition and practice of excluding bad people from the profession and throwing scoundrels out.

The Law on Lawyers

In 1817, a truculent Baltimore law teacher named David Hoffman published "A Course of Legal Study," a systematic recipe for legal education. At the end of the "Course," Hoffman put an appendix on lawyer "deportment." In 1836, Hoffman revised his "Course" and expanded his appendix on ethics into a set of "Fifty Resolutions on Professional Deportment." Hoffman's 1817 and 1836 appendices are where legal ethics (in both senses) began in America.

Half a century later, as American lawyers were being identified with the robber barons of the industrial revolution, and as they began to found the earliest of the modern bar associations to defend themselves, it became first prudent and then routine for lawyers in association to express formal agreement with statements such as Hoffman's. The statements themselves were academic, not bar-association pieces of work; they originated as instruction, including large amounts of etiquette and mercantile manners, to law students who were not asked whether they agreed with what they read or heard. Hoffman's "Resolutions" were too Jeffersonian to be useful for the new bar associations. He thought pleading defenses such as the statute of limitations was immoral, and that no legal argument was sound unless the construction argued for would benefit the community as much as the client. Such doctrine was too restrictive; Hoffman's understanding of the ideals of American lawyers did not work for lawyers who advised the robber barons because Hoffman depended on the republican theory that lawyers are responsible for justice. The more popular source for proposed consensus was an amiable set of lectures given in 1854 by the founding dean of the University of Pennsylvania Law School, Judge George Sharswood, which could be read to make the *government* responsible for justice; in Sharswood's system the lawyer was only a player.

Between 1880 and 1908, these academic statements, garnished with adoption by local bar associations, were worked into (or at any rate called) a code. The most famous instance of codal translation was the Alabama Code that Judge Thomas Goode Jones worked out in the 1880s. (Jones was not an academic; he was then a circuit judge, a Confederate war hero who would become governor of Alabama and, later, a United States district judge.) In the twenty years after Judge Jones finished the Alabama Code, his draft for the Alabama Bar was adopted either as court rules by the supreme courts of several states or as statutes by state legislatures. The translation from statement to code and from bar-association code to court rule or statute meant that these statements had become sources of *law*.

The mainline twentieth-century tradition with which Henry Drinker is identified begins with the adoption by the American Bar Association, in 1908, of the "Canons of Ethics," a model legal code for state courts and legislatures to follow. The Canons were for the most part Judge

Jones's Alabama Code, and the judge was a member of the A.B.A. drafting committee. The aspiration was that the A.B.A. model would become general and the codal system therefore uniform. The tradition continued through half a century of interpretation and amendment (much of it presided over by the durable Mr. Drinker). It entered a period of revision in the postwar (World War II) profession, issuing in the A.B.A.'s "Model Code of Professional Responsibility" of 1969—also a model for courts and legislatures to adopt; and it reached its current definitive expression when the A.B.A. adopted its proposed "Rules of Professional Conduct" in 1983. About half the states now follow the 1969 Code, and half follow some version of the 1983 Rules.

This is the law-on-lawyers tradition in America; it continues now in a project of the American Law Institute to "re-state" the law on lawyers. If that restatement is approved by the majority of those attending a meeting of the Institute (a by-invitation-only organization of prominent judges, law teachers, and practitioners), it will become to the law on lawyers what the Restatements of Torts, Contracts, Property, and Trusts are to those parts of the law-school curriculum—an influential generalization of American common law on the coercive regulation of lawyers' behavior.

The modern development that is relevant to my project—and which I trace to the Watergate Hotel in 1972—is the moral aspiration that has gradually been excised from American lawyers' professional consensus. The Canons of 1908 (and their nineteenth-century antecedents) had mixed morals and law, just as law and morals were mixed in the minds and law practices of the legal gentlemen who produced the Canons and their antecedents. The 1969 Code retained both but separated them, so that the coercive part of the Code, called "disciplinary rules," was graphically separate and printed in bold type. But before the reader reached the bold type, the Code presented, under each of nine broad principles on lawyers' behavior, a consensus statement of moral aspirations called "ethical considerations."

The 1983 proposed Rules eliminated the ethical considerations, as it eliminated traditional words of moral assertion ("right," "wrong," "good," "bad," "conscience," "character") in favor of the words of etiquette and regulation ("proper," "permitted," indicative verbs of description rather than conditional or imperative verbs of moral duty and, in the basic text of the rules, "shall" rather than "should," as if the rules were the words of a statute). The 1983 project substituted, in its proposed title, "Rules" for "Code" and "Conduct" for "Responsibility." It declared independence from legal ethics as ethics.

Legal Ethics as Ethics

What the law on lawyers removed from its tradition is now the work of a small sub-fraternity of law teachers; I am one of them. In the early 1970s my law school (Notre Dame) assigned my colleague Fernand Dutile and me to teach legal ethics. Dutile was and is a criminal-law teacher who also writes on, edits materials for, and teaches the law of education. I brought to the task ten years of teaching wills and trusts and some relatively eccentric adventures in legal interviewing and counseling. We found for teaching material a couple of casebooks containing edited appellate opinions in admission, discipline, and exclusion cases. The path of least resistance, then and now, when one is assigned such a course, is to teach this body of law on lawyers, and that is what we did at first.

I found some fragmentary information, and came to hold the vague hope, that there were or might be law teachers who were interested in ethics in the way Socrates was—or even in the way the Rabbis were. Tex Dutile and I taught for a couple of years out of the casebooks and out of a problem book by Dean Norman Redlich, and I wrote, in a Festschrift for Louis M. Brown, an article called "Christian Theories of Professional Responsibility." It was a clumsy essay, but I think it was the first of its kind. Most of my friends in the law teaching fraternity spoke of it politely but as if I had compared the Internal Revenue Code to the Book of Revelation. A few kindred spirits read my essay, and some of them thought it was interesting. I began to get concrete information from them about law teachers becoming teachers of ethics.

Other law teachers had similar experiences. Thus in the last half-generation, university law schools have seen the growth and even early signs of the maturity of an academic subdiscipline and a fraternity whose principal interest in teaching, scholarship, and practice—one, two, or all three—is legal ethics, meaning *ethics*. It is a curious fraternity (as much a sorority as a fraternity, by the way; I think of Emily Fowler, Deborah L. Rhode, Susan Martyn, Mari J. Matsuda, Nancy Moore, Carrie Menkel-Meadow, Judith Maute). Members of it are people (i) with one leg shorter than the other; (ii) in the Tower of Babel; (iii) who are prepared to hear that they belong somewhere else.

Legs. Legal ethicists are not like their counterparts in medical schools. Few teachers and scholars of medical ethics are physicians; almost all legal ethicists are lawyers. Those who "do" medical ethics are philosophers and theologians—scholars who have given extensive, disciplined attention to the deepest and oldest sources of moral thought. (I am thinking of Stanley Hauerwas, Richard McCormick, James Childress, William F. May, Gerald Dworkin, et al.) Few legal ethicists are formally trained in philosophy or theology; most are, as I am, academic lawyers who seem to have tired of reading law. We read philosophy and theology, novels, anthropology, and humanistic social science. When we talk and write we depend on and exploit those who write what we read.

We *are* lawyers, though; we have been put through the black boxes that elders in law school and law firms put novices through. We have paid our dues, and graduated from boot camp. Many of us have even had to think about supporting our families with fees from clients. We are in a better position to talk about the morals of law practice than most scholars and teachers in medical ethics are to talk about the morals of practicing medicine. We can demand attention from former students and other practitioners as professional colleagues. Medical ethicists can rarely do that: They (figuratively and often enough literally) walk last in the procession of white-coated people who make rounds in the teaching hospital.

But medical ethicists have more confidence than we do when they write and talk about traditions of thought that support professional ethics as an academic discipline. They have paid their dues in the fraternities of the humanities, as graduate students, teaching assistants, learners of language and of argot. Many of them have been in the clergy and have endured the labyrinthine hierarchy and cruel bureaucracy maintained there, since the days of King Solomon, by the Children of God. Most of them have also been tortured by an academic tenure process that is uglier and cruder than the ones we have in professional schools. In a way that is analogous to our black-box conversion to "thinking like a lawyer," scholars in medical ethics have gained a confidence in the use of ethical literature that is, I suppose, like the confidence we American lawyers have with appellate-court opinions. Students of legal ethics lack this confidence in ethics; we have to gain confidence in the traditions of academic ethics, if we ever do, uncertainly and dependently. We bluff a lot, but in fact, with each of us, one leg is shorter than the other.

Babel. I manipulated the title for this chapter from Jeffrey Stout's book *Ethics After Babel*. Stout's book was a response to Alasdair MacIntyre's *After Virtue*. Both are parts of a conversation among students of ethics that includes Robert N. Bellah and the other four authors of *Habits of the Heart*. These three recent, impressive, apparently influential books on ethics enjoy a wide readership among academics, including lawyers who teach jurisprudence and public law, and each of them has become modestly popular among other educated readers. They and the conversations they provoke describe what we lawyers found when we proposed to be serious about ethics and to exploit our colleagues in the humanities.

We found chaos, disarray, and a stately argument over whether the chaos and disarray could again become useful. I say "again," because one thing those in academic ethics seem to agree about is that there was a past in which academic ethics was useful. They do not agree about when that past was, or on what sources in the past were useful. I say "stately argument" because the chaos and disarray do not alarm the debaters as much as we lawyers, who value orderly progress, might expect. The ethicists are less passionate about the mess their discipline is in than we lawyers are likely to be about our messes. They seem to have less at stake than we do. Maybe that is because their discipline is practiced in the Tower of Babel and we do not want ours to be. The thesis of Stout's book is that moral coherence is possible within and despite the chaos. Bellah's book says the chaos is more academic than cultural—that our habits of the heart (Alexis de Tocqueville's phrase) are healthier than professors such as MacIntyre may think.

In a sequel to *After Virtue*, MacIntyre claims that academic ethics apprehends the chaos: "Modern academic philosophy turns out by and large to provide means for a more accurate and informed definition of disagreement rather than for progress toward its resolution. . . . [Philosophers] succeed in articulating the rival standpoints with greater clarity, greater fluency, and a wider range of arguments than do most others, but . . . little more than this." Stout minimizes less than MacIntyre does, but that is because Stout expects even less from his colleagues; he argues that progress toward resolution is possible without the conceptual agreement MacIntyre says he cannot find. Stout argues that progress is not necessary, that we can act together without it.

The authors of *Habits of the Heart* report significant moral consensus in America, significant survival of the moral traditions of community and of biblical faith that Tocqueville noticed in David Hoffman's America, but they report that the students of ethics have failed to put a common language to these survivals, and so we (including us academic lawyers) do not know how to talk to one another about moral questions or how to introduce our students to their own ethical heritage.

Thus we lawyers of the remnant from Watergate did not find as much guidance as we had hoped to find when we turned to mainline academic ethics. What we seem to have concluded is that legal ethics should formulate for itself what its modern pioneers might have hoped to find elsewhere. We have to define our ethical questions as much as other legal scholars have to formulate contemporary questions about the law of property or the function of the fault doctrine in torts. We can exploit the students of ethics in philosophy, theology, and the humanistic social sciences, but we have to do it in the way other legal scholars exploit judges: We couldn't get along without the philosophers; if we didn't have them, we would have to invent them; but they will not hand us anything that is ready to wear.

We Belong Somewhere Else. The promise of moral philosophy is that it will give us a language that we can use to talk to one another about morals. Moral philosophy fails us entirely when we find that its language does not communicate. It fails us significantly when, although we find that we can communicate with its language, we cannot talk about what is deeply important in our moral lives. We could end up with a set of lowest common denominators instead of what Socrates gave the youth of Athens. MacIntyre argues that moral philosophy has failed in the first way; words such as "justice" and "reason" do not mean the same thing to a lecturer in philosophy as they do to the rest of us. The language of liberal democracy, which is the language of American legal education, fails in the second way (and lawyers cannot blame the moral philosophers for this): We lawyers are able to sit down with our students and talk about "rights" in the law, but the language of rights is purposely shallow—made to be shallow, so that it can serve a legal order that claims to be free of values, free of traditions, free of the horror and charm of human life. The language of rights does not communicate well when the subject is how to be a good person.

When lawyers who teach legal ethics—they of the uneven legs—move discourse from law to morals, and retain the language of rights, what they have to say is abstract, rarefied, and often perceived as trivial. (A value-free ethical system is about as interesting as a value-free poem would be.) Rights language in legal ethics may also be wrong, but, before that issue is even considered, it is shallow. When I attempt to contribute to such conversations I *feel* shallow; when I listen to them I feel that I belong somewhere else. My purpose in this book is to suggest what it looks like there, in one of the other places where we belong.

Choosers and Good Persons

Socrates went around Athens telling law teachers and law students that their highest concern should be to be good people. He said their next and consequent concern should be to show the citizens of Athens how to be good people. For Socrates, as for virtually all of the giants of classical moral philosophy and much of Hebraic[1] moral

---

1. I learned from Will Herberg to say "Hebraic" rather than "Judaeo-Christian." The advantage is the suggestion of a single theological ethical tradition: The ethics of Jesus are the ethics of the Jews. The argument is developed in Schnackenberg and in my essay on Hebraic jurisprudence.

theology, ethical discussion is discussion about being good persons and helping others to be good persons. When moral philosophy talks about Aristotle's "man of practical wisdom," or when literature tells us about heroes in our culture, or when the religious tradition tells us about saints; when we talk about paragons, role models, professional exemplars—about Catherine of Siena, or Atticus Finch, or Leland McKenzie of "L.A. Law"—*it is the good person we are talking about*. The ethical speculation that supports such moral talk is founded on disciplined curiosity about the good person.

This concern for the good person is the way classical moral philosophy informed those who proposed to teach the young; it was the context for Socrates's admonition to law teachers. Moral philosophy showed teachers how to point to the good person as a coherent object of admiration, a coherent source of moral standards, providing with his life a scheme for the moral formation of young people and, especially in the *Gorgias*, of apprentice lawyers. Goodness among apprentices who would soon be lawyers was, in Socrates's argument, a goal in itself; virtue and good character are goals in themselves. But as Socrates applied the idea to the lawyers of Athens it became also a means to a civic goal—the goodness of the *clients* of lawyers, the goodness of citizens. The lawyer-client relationship was a collaboration in the good.

If you trace that argument into the modern division of American legal ethics, into (i) the law on lawyers and (ii) legal ethics *as* ethics, you won't find evidence of Socratic influence anywhere. Not in the law on lawyers; not in the remnant's post-Watergate legal ethics as ethics. It has become a novel proposition, believe it or not, to say that if we want communities of good people we need lawyers who are good people. In moral discourse, as in political and legal discourse, we don't talk about good people; we talk about rights. The assumption in discussions of rights (in politics, law, or ethics) is that what citizens want for one another, or lawyers for their clients, is not goodness but independence. The purpose of the lawyer-client relationship is isolation from moral influence.

The focus on rights—on isolation from moral influence—brings a new assumption to the law on lawyers. Behavioral influence runs, not as Socrates thought, from lawyers to clients, but in the other direction: from clients to lawyers. And that influence is bad. It corrupts lawyers. Clients want lawyers to do the wrong thing; lawyers act as agents for their clients and do for their clients things they would never do for themselves. That's why, in 1983, we got a new beginning for the law on lawyers; the law on lawyers is now concerned with whether lawyers are obliged to refuse to do the wrong actions clients want them to do. The law on lawyers has been purged of concern for the goodness of clients. It treats clients as threats, threats to the rights—that is, the isolation and independence—of lawyers. What is to be hoped for with regard to clients is that the law will neutralize them as threats. The law on lawyers says it is goodness enough if lawyers can require their clients to obey the criminal law.

Neither is legal ethics as ethics concerned about good persons. Most of those who labor in legal ethics use the language of rights and accept the liberal premise that what makes a moral rule binding is that the moral actor chooses it. If that is so, it is both legally and ethically necessary to secure the isolation of the moral actor, so that his choices can be his own and not somebody else's. Rights provide the isolation. Most of post-Watergate legal ethics thus focuses on rights, as much as the law on lawyers does, and that means that legal ethics is *choice centered*, rather than *relationship centered*. To use the old words, legal ethics is concerned with autonomy rather than with character.

Rights language would probably, in any case, have become the principal language of legal ethics (and of jurisprudence)—out of habit. When the remnant of

Watergate established legal ethics in the minds and mouths of law teachers, our habitual liberal discourse was in place in law-school courses and legal scholarship and we naturally began to use it as a way to talk about moral questions. Most of us went on talking about rights, which means we talked about autonomy, freedom, acts, and choices instead of about people, about isolation instead of about relationships. I think this has been a mistake. It has been a mistake for us to write, study, and teach about the acts of abstract, depersonalized (inevitably *male*) lawyers. It has been a mistake for us to ask whether certain hypothetical choices are right or wrong and to neglect to ask about the people who make the choices. It has been a mistake for us to think of people as if they were insulated from one another and then to discuss them as we learned to discuss landowners in the law of property ("*A* conveys Blackacre to *B* and his heirs, who leases to *C*").

The mistake we were led into by the language of rights in the law led to other mistakes. If the choice, rather than the person, is raw material for ethical discussion, we are required by logic to concentrate on the acts of the actor: An act is the product of a choice. If thinking about acts leads to thinking about choices, then we have to think about the issues that lead us to choices. We think about issues, rather than about lives and persons and cultures. An issue, in law or in ethics, is a set of facts presented to a choosing psyche in the way a casebook legal issue is a set of facts presented to an appellate judge (who must decide the issue). In ethics, choices are what emerge from these issues, problems, puzzles, quandaries, or—as it is most usually put among lawyers and judges—"ethical dilemmas." So common is the presentation of the dilemma as a device for discussion in our subject that the phrase "ethical dilemma" is spoken as if it were one word.

Consideration of persons (lives, relationships, cultures) proceeds differently—as I hope I can show. The fundamental difference is anthropological: Deep down, *a person is not just a chooser*. There are things about persons (or, as moral philosophy often says it, moral agents) that are more interesting than the choices they make, or the sum of all the choices they have made.

Choice-based ethics turns on the significance of quandaries, but it has shown less interest than we might expect in how quandaries come about. (That is probably why discussions of rights in ethics seem shallow and are usually trivial. Moral philosophers know, as much as teachers of the law of future interests do, that the way to keep hold of a trivial subject is to make it complicated.) What would be interesting would be to locate what it is that makes one person see an occasion for moral choice where another person would see something else, but legal ethics mostly leaves that question to the poets.

Crimes and Misdemeanors, Woody Allen's curious film about guilt, large and small, shows what I mean. It is a story about filmmakers. An old philosopher has somehow interested the less confident of two filmmakers, and this lesser filmmaker, played, of course, by Mr. Allen, takes the unpromising course of shooting thousands of feet of film of the old philosopher talking into a camera. Then the old philosopher kills himself. The lesser filmmaker goes back to look at the hours he has of the old philosopher speaking his wisdom into the camera, perhaps to see if he can salvage something for commerce, but probably he wants to see if he can understand why what struck him as marketable moral wisdom ended in self destruction.

The filmmaker finally focuses on a piece of film in which the old philosopher says that human beings are defined by their choices. We are choosers, he says, and what any of us has turned out to be is the sum total of his choices. I took an early opportunity to talk to one of my law-teacher friends about that philosophy. I found it amazing, in general and in particular. My friend did not. He said he thought the old philosopher's observation fit the principal story in Mr. Allen's film—the story of a physician's *choosing* to murder his mistress—as it seemed to fit the philosopher's *choosing* to kill himself.

My friend may be right. I don't think so. If he is right, the fit is odd, even for a Woody Allen movie. The physician, an ophthalmologist, has murdered his mistress and he is tortured by guilt—he is tortured, rather than merely fearful of being found out, *because he is a Jew.* I don't mean that one has to be a Jew to feel guilty for murder, but that this person feels guilty as a Jew feels guilty. He feels guilty *because* he is a Jew. We know from Philip Roth and Bruce Jay Friedman and *Bye Bye Birdie* that there is something unique about Jewish guilt. Jewish guilt is a recurrent theme in Woody Allen's films, although this is the first time he tells a story about it that does not make us laugh.

The torture the physician suffers when he cannot sleep at night or pay attention to his patients during the day, and even his view, mostly after the fact, that the murder was a fateful choice (as if he had been Adam in the Garden), are products of his growing up in an observant and pious home, of hours spent in the synagogue and reading the Torah. The old philosopher says of us human beings that each of us is the sum of his choices, but *the doctor did not choose to be a Jew.* What is special and interesting in the story is that a Jew has done something evil—how that came to happen and what happened then. Certainly he did not choose to suffer from Jewish guilt, but that is what the story is about.

The last scene in the movie shows the doctor in improving emotional shape. He is still bothered, a little bit all the time and occasionally a lot, but he is getting by. He reveals this in a one-on-one conversation with the hapless filmmaker, in a corner, during a Jewish wedding celebration in the Waldorf Astoria Hotel. Maybe the doctor has moved his guilt to a new and even more sinister place—where the amazing thing is that he does not feel guilty anymore. (If so, that process is less choice than it is decay.[2]) Maybe he has figured out a way to live with his guilt. If so, his way is the way of Jews in America who can finance weddings and bar mitzvahs in the Waldorf, who want to be prosperous, esteemed Americans with Father-Knows-Best families more than they want to be Jews. The old philosopher would say that who the doctor is becoming, there in the quiet corner in the Waldorf, is the sum of his choices, but *the doctor did not choose to be a Jew in America.*

The film's most touching scene is also at this wedding celebration. The father of the bride is one of the doctor's patients, a rabbi who has gone blind. In the scene I am thinking of, he dances with his beautiful daughter, the two of them alone in the middle of the dance floor. The rabbi is an exemplar of courage. He is a modern man trying to understand and interpret both fate and Torah to himself and others. He is all of that and also a blind man who loves his daughter. He is a good Jew, but he did not choose to be a Jew, any more than the physician did.

I suppose one could say that, in a sense, the rabbi chose to be a Jew and the physician, in murdering his mistress, chose not to be a Jew, but that argument would be false. If the doctor chose not to be a Jew, his choice is no comfort to him when he wakes up in the middle of the night, tortured by guilt—Jewish guilt—for what he has done. If he chose not to be a Jew, what is he doing at the wedding of the rabbi's daughter? What is he doing in a Jewish family? The rabbi did not choose to go blind. His daughter did not choose to be a Jew or to have a father who would be such a good man, and would go blind.

I think Woody Allen is giving us a dose of *irony*; the irony is the old professor being admired for saying we are choosers when the language of choice explains so poorly

---

2. Mary, who understands the symbol of dancing better than I do, says: "I don't exactly agree. It's more of an extraordinary human capacity in the brain, in the heart. It's developing strength in the wrong direction—like strengthening the muscles already involved in bad posture, a dance teacher's nightmare."

the important things about the people in the story, and doesn't explain the old philosopher at all. I think Woody Allen saw this and set out to show it. If he did not, irony was an inevitable consequence of his theme. A poet cannot write poems about the people described in the ethics of autonomy, and the hapless filmmaker will never make a coherent movie about what the old professor said about choices—that is why the hapless filmmaker is so hapless: The only other film he made was a documentary on leukemia. The ethics of choosers could not explain to the blind rabbi why he should give his daughter a wedding in the Waldorf. The old professor's ethic does not account for his killing himself; we do not know any more about that after we hear his theory than we knew before. If we want an ethic for *that*, we have to tell his story, get into his *life* and into the lives of people he loved and lost and the lives of people who loved and lost him.

The ethics of autonomy needs people who can be described without relationships (or, at least, without the earthy things about *organic* relationships that would interest a poet), because the dogma is that the individual should choose his own morals; he should not get them from anybody else, as the doctor and the rabbi did, as we all do. This ethics of choosers says that what gives authority to morals is that we have chosen them. The rule is that each of us should choose his own morals; and if that is the rule, ethics has to be careful not to describe any of us as significantly related to other people. If a person's relationships are significant to her, then her choices might not be her own. The ethics of choosers thus describes excellence as separation: Each of us is a self-ruling, free chooser. In those attributes lies our excellence, and so the ethics of choosers treats each person as alone—a choosing machine that runs itself.

What I am suggesting, of course, is that it is useful in legal ethics to focus on the good person instead of on the chooser. Focus on the good person will imply a prominence for relationships in ethics—putting people back together again, or, rather, putting people back into ethical theory, noticing that we people are connected to one another, connected radically (at the roots). Connected organically: We belong; we are creatures who belong with one another. It is not that we belong because of our choices, but that we make the choices we do because we are connected to the people we are connected to. We belong before we make choices; we make the choices we make because we belong.

I mean to argue here, as Saul Bellow's Augie March did, that first we are, and then we can, if we want to (and after we happen to think about it), *choose* to be what we are. (To some extent, never entirely, we can even choose to be something else.) This is the human condition. We are primarily members, not choosers; we are primarily connected, not alone. "All the influences were lined up waiting for me," Augie said. "I was born, and there they were to form me, which is why I tell you more of them than of myself." Augie was a poor Jewish boy of my generation; he spoke of growing up in Chicago. He said: "I know I longed very much, but I didn't understand for what.... Friends, human pals, men and brethren, there is no brief, digest, or shorthand way to say where it leads. Crusoe, alone with nature, under heaven, had a busy, complicated time of it with the unhuman itself, and I am in a crowd that yields results with more difficulty and reluctance and am part of it myself."

Choosers and Good Persons in Law School

Legal education, more than any other kind of professional or graduate education, places high value on discussion in large classes—discussion rather than lecture because of our claim that our method is "Socratic," and large classes because large classes are essential to the economics of the enterprise. When Tex Dutile and I taught legal ethics with Dean Redlich's dilemmas, twenty years ago, I found that discussion needs different premises in ethics than it has for me when I teach law. In legal discussion there is an analytical discipline involved that we call "thinking like a lawyer." It depends on the understanding that law is the imposition of coercive power—law as what the courts will do, as Justice Holmes said, and courts are backed by force. Closure in an ethical discussion (at least in a discussion of ethics as ethics) depends on persuasion and insight, where closure in a discussion about law (including a discussion about the law on lawyers) depends on power. Someone has to be persuaded in the law, but unless the person persuaded is the person who can invoke coercion, the legal discussion is not closed.

Those of us who teach legal ethics as ethics are not satisfied to close off discussion of legal ethics by invoking coercion, as the law on lawyers does. That means discussion in legal-ethics classes will be discussion governed by insight and persuasion rather than force. My first method for this sort of teaching, using, as I did at first, quandaries, "ethical dilemmas," was to seek expressions of choice and opinion. I used, for example, a situation that was part of my own limited law practice in those days—the draft-eligible young man of the late 1960s who had been conscripted into the army and who wondered what would happen to him if he went to Canada.

In one such case my client had sought and been denied conscientious-objector status from his local draft board, and appeal was not promising. The basis for my client's conscientious objection was that he believed his country's military adventure in Southeast Asia was an unjust war, and according to his beliefs (traditional Roman Catholic beliefs) he could not fight in that war. He did not object to all war; his "selective objection," about which he had, unfortunately for his lawyer, been candid when he talked to his draft board, is not provided for in American law. His choices were to be inducted for combatant duty, prison, or to become a fugitive from the Selective Service system, a fugitive, the law said, from justice. He wondered what he should do; he asked his lawyer. His lawyer's quandary was between advice to disobey the law and flee and advice that would respect the law but require the client to go to prison. This was a *lawyer's* quandary because the lawyer noticed it. It was not a quandary for the client. What the client asked for was advice on power: Would the Canadian police arrest him and send him back?

In the classroom: Student *A* raises her hand and says she would never advise a client to disobey the law, that such professional behavior would be like a physician advising suicide. Our client, she says, has *no right* to disobey the law and so I have *no right* to tell him to disobey the law. Student *B* raises his hand and says, "Why not? He got a raw deal. How is it that a Quaker, who objects to all war, has a *right* to conscientious objection, but a Catholic, who opposes unjust war, does not?"

Student *C* raises his hand and says our client is confronted with a summons to limited martyrdom. (Judges in the United States sent evaders such as my client to federal prison; our law did not provide for capital punishment as, say, the law of Nazi Germany did. The martyrdom was limited, but five years in prison is significant enough to justify the metaphor.) With answers from *D*, *E*, and *F* to add to these three, I would have, in about fifteen minutes, produced an array of reactions to my quandary. With a bit of pressing to clarify positions, I satisfied what I at first thought to be a sufficient "Socratic" agenda for a large class of law students talking about legal ethics as ethics—and moved on to the next quandary.

The implication of my procedure was that legal ethics is a matter of choices. Once our hypothetical lawyer manages to keep herself out of trouble (the law on lawyers), what she does to herself and her client with her professional power and skill depends on what she chooses to do. When someone presses her to explain her statement about rights—and no one did—what makes her choice moral is that she chooses it. My legal-ethics

classroom, with a lot of help from voluble students, produced a moral smorgasbord from which students could
select what struck them as the moral thing to do. What
was selected would take its moral authority from the fact
that it was selected. Persuasion and insight were not
ruled out, but I hardly saw anyone who looked as if he
were being persuaded, and what students said seemed
less like insight than what people say when they explain
why they order beer by brand name.

I grew out of that way of teaching legal ethics by depending, despite my grumbling about them, on scholars
in academic ethics—mostly on Stanley Hauerwas, who
declared war on democratic-liberal ethics and politics at
about the time I started thinking that I was not doing a
very good job with my legal-ethics classes. (We were
both teaching at Notre Dame then.) The vestige of insight
I remember most prominently from those days, though,
came not from Hauerwas but from Christina Hoff Sommers, who teaches philosophy to undergraduates and
who inveighed against "ethics without virtue." Her argument was that the sort of ethics teaching I was doing un-
dermines common sense. After a semester of it, she
wrote, "In a term paper . . . one of my students wrote that
Jonathan Swift's 'modest proposal' . . . was 'good for
Swift's society, but not for ours.'

"One comes up against a grotesquely distorted perspective that common sense has little power to set right,"
Sommers said. "When a sophomore was asked whether
she saw Nagasaki as the moral equivalent of a traffic ac-
cident, she replied, 'From a moral point of view, yes.'"
Sommers concluded that the ethics she saw reflected in
these student responses demonstrated that the students
lacked the mental equipment to make a negative moral
judgment on behavior—their own or anybody's.

Sommers's broader concern was that her students' responses to moral questions indicated no sense of culture—no sense of where they had come from or of the
community they were being prepared for. That concern

seemed right and it seemed to suggest an approach for large-class discussion: I needed to dig *deeper*. When student *A* said a lawyer cannot advise clients to disobey the law, I needed to find out where in her personality and her life that answer came from. When student *C* talked of my client's martyrdom to a liberal jurisprudence of conscientious objection, I needed to find out more than that the source of his point was (as I guessed) his reading Jacques Maritain in college; he liked Maritain because of something that was older and deeper than college.

The anthropologist Carol J. Greenhouse, in her study of how Baptists in Georgia do justice, discovered something about the way people work when they think about morals. As nearly as I can tell, we discovered the same thing, although my discovery was the result of halting classroom experiment, and hers was scientific and supported by a foundation grant. The discovery is this: People show what their morals are by claiming where they come from. Greenhouse describes ethics as accounting for where a person belongs.

Greenhouse studied how members of a Baptist congregation in a suburb of Atlanta deal with their disputes; hers was a study of justice and of the home life of those who do justice. Her premise (or, to describe it as it seems to have happened, her conclusion, her discovery) is that people tend to explain their morals by claiming membership in a community—a family, an ethnic group, a region of the country, or, in the case of her Baptists, a congregation. We account for our morals—unintentionally—by naming what we belong to. I found the same sort of thing when I started pressing law students a bit about what seemed to be their moral choices. When I pressed student *A* about this, when I was lucky and would not let her get away with shrugging her shoulders and saying, "That's how I feel," she would add, "I feel that way because of where I come from."

Student *B*, when I pressed him to see if I could understand how he explained his reaction the other way, said (when I was lucky): "I was brought up to believe that an unjust law is no law at all." Really? Is that "principle" something he learned at his mother's knee? Well, no, it isn't. He learned the *principle* in college, from a political science teacher he liked a lot. The principle he says he remembers is one he learned relatively late in his young life. It expresses something he thinks, he says, but it really—now that he thinks about it—does not explain why he thinks as he does. When he thinks about explanation, the reaction of student *B* resembles what his immigrant Calabrian grandfather felt about refusing to kill Ethiopians for the Italian state. When I am lucky, student *B* will mention to me after class, or a month later, or ten years later, that the discussion led to his deciding that he felt as he did about the draft board because he is an Italian American. When he had figured out his ethic he had also figured out the importance of where he came from. And vice versa.

Greenhouse argues as an anthropologist. Her work is revealing for a discussion of the legal ethics of autonomy because that school of thought is weak in its anthropology. The critical feature in her explanation of behavior is that the explainer claims to be in a community: His accounting for himself is revealed in a claim of membership. He explains his morals by telling you where he belongs. He comes up with one explanation rather than another, "and thereby identifies with one group over another." Tocqueville said that America is "a society built not on obedience," not, that is, on principles such as the one student *B* came up with at first; not on choice, "but on participation."

Greenhouse did not claim that this process of explanation was as evident and handy as how one of her Southern Baptists might have explained his aversion to tobacco or dancing. Often the realization that I react as I do to a moral question because of where I belong marks the end of (or at least a stopping place in) a search. Greenhouse asked one of her Georgia Baptists why he did not stand

up for himself in a family quarrel. He did not say at first
that it was because he is a Baptist. He quoted a principle
or a bit of scripture, or he identified a habit he noticed in
himself. It was only after he talked a bit, and Greenhouse
helped him along, that he realized and said that his explanation was *membership*: He feels as he does about being
assertive in quarrels because he is a Baptist. Both the inquiry (which in an ethics class would have been stated as
a quandary) and the moral explanation relate to a "we-
feeling," a feeling this person gets when he looks to the
left and to the right and says to himself, "I am one of
these. When I speak of this people, I can say 'we.'" It is
not that he belongs because he made the right choice,
but that he is right because he belongs.

Ethnic membership as a way to understand morals often lies at the end of such a search; the first-person accounts Mary and I use later in this book read like
exercises in personal discovery.[3] But the moment of discovery is not at all like the moment of choice Sommers
noticed and decried as "half-baked relativism." Michael
Novak, focusing on the ethics of the late immigrants to
America, explained that their saying "we" in this way is
not a choice so much as it is a return, not joining up so
much as noticing where I already am—what I am—and
thereby gaining an understanding of my moral self.

I may even say, "I have come home." The event I might
have called a quandary or an "ethical dilemma" has
ended up giving me a sense of being at home. There is, I
suppose, some exercise of will involved in membership,
in this psychological homecoming. First we remember
that we are members; then, in some way or other, sometimes, we choose to be members. But choice is secondary, sequential and consequential, and it is the product of
an effort to see. Influences, as Augie March said, are at

---

3. Mary adds: "The authors of these accounts often seemed
thrilled that we asked the questions we asked—as if they had a lot to
say but, until then, hadn't the occasion or the audience for saying it. It
was like opening a flood gate."

work here, whether we see them or not. They are prior,
in time and in potency, to quandaries, choices, rules,
principles; they are prior to deductive reasoning, or
logic, or scripture, or threat. Belonging explains reality.

* * * * *

There comes a point in which Jem Finch, age twelve,
in rural Alabama in 1935, understands that his lawyer father is not, after all, an effete and book-bound old man
who can no longer play softball for the Methodists, but is
the sort of person Jem is going to *become.* Jem says, "Atticus is a gentleman, and so am I." Harper Lee said her
novel about Atticus was the story of a conscience. In
chapters two, three, and four of this book, I propose that
the community we American lawyers, men and women
in a modern profession, will find, when we explain ourselves as belonging, is the community Jem noticed, a
community of gentlemen.

Robert Viscusi, the social historian, turned to his fellow Italian Americans, at a conference of the American
Italian Historical Association, and said, with obvious emphasis: "We Italian Americans of professional rank are in
danger ... of respectability. Perhaps it is no great harm
that we have taken to bringing useless chafing-dishes instead of flexible cash as wedding presents. But it will
have been very great harm indeed if we turn and look
back at ourselves after long, active, chatty careers and
can only see ... well-established, upwardly mobile, end-
lessly aspirant dullards ... [who put] our dignity before
our conscience or our desire to be accepted before our
desire to tell the truth."

The American gentleman-lawyer's ethic as it survived
in northeastern cities in the early twentieth century
would, I think, be part of what Viscusi warned his fellow
"Italian Americans of professional rank" against—and he
warned them against it for good reason. In warning them
as he did, Viscusi pointed to a preference for the moral
aspiration of his Italian heritage, and away from the cul-

tural traps laid for upwardly mobile immigrants by Protestant Americans. Mary and I propose, in chapters five,
six, and seven, the possibility of an American lawyer's ex-
plaining herself as belonging to one of those "communities of memory" the late immigrants brought to America.

Walter Brueggemann, theologian and scripture scholar,
once wrote of teaching children in the Sunday schools of
the Hebraic communities that religious formation is a
matter of learning that people of faith are separate. He
said that education in the religious tradition is "education in passion ... nurture into a distinct community that
knows itself to be at odds with dominant assumptions ...
an insistence on being ... chosen, summoned, com-
manded, and promised." He said such an education—
such a belonging and sense of belonging—is "concrete
and specific ... nurture in particularity ... that produces
adults who know so well who they are and what is com-
manded that they value and celebrate their oddity in the
face of every seductive and powerful imperial alternative." In the final chapter I propose to consider this oddity and particularity as a legal ethic that rests in the
paradox and contradiction that is the story of Israel and
of the Cross.

CHAPTER TWO

The Gentleman's Community

Only when he has linked the parts together in
well-tempered harmony and has made himself
one man instead of many, will he be able to go
about whatever he may have to do.

Plato

Television in America has never been without a prime-
time series about lawyers. People my age remember
"The Defenders," with E. G. Marshall as the stalwart
Lawrence Preston in practice with his son. Virtually all
popular entertainment that deals with associations of
people in a profession put an elder practitioner together
with an energetic youngster; "The Defenders" put them
in the same family. Today, my students watch "L.A. Law,"
about a law firm that is like a family, or about "Matlock,"
who practices law with his daughter.

Such stories are about morals as much as they are
about law. They speak about legal ethics and to the popular interest in how a good person goes about being a
lawyer. They do this as stories, not through lessons but
through persons, and each series of stories about American lawyers has a culturally particular ethics person—
the lawyer E. G. Marshall played, Burl Ives's character in
one of the series, Andy Griffith when he got old enough,
and Leland McKenzie of "L.A. Law." All of these lawyer-
story ethics persons are older, male, white, sententious,

and honorable. Raymond Burr, who plays Perry Mason, and Richard Dysart, who plays Mr. McKenzie, have spoken to A.B.A. meetings, about legal ethics. Neither is a lawyer.

When the plot in one of our lawyer stories requires that moral issues be resolved, or at least demonstrated, the facts are filtered through the experience and judgment of this older, male person, as the wise elder who is skilled in professional craftsmanship. The stories say that formation in the craft of the profession and formation in its practice as a moral endeavor are related. The ethics person in a popular lawyer story is in both ways a source of example and of wisdom to those who are young in the profession.

The original producers of "L.A. Law" were Steven Bochco and Terry Louise Fisher. Miss Fisher is a lawyer; Mr. Bochco is a veteran creator of television entertainment. He produced "St. Elsewhere" and "Hill Street Blues." In his lawyer series he repeated what he had done successfully in his physician and police-officer projects: Leland McKenzie is the law-office version of the testy heart surgeon, Mark Craig, M.D., and of Captain Francis Furillo. In each of the three series, television drama faces its issues through the person of an elder white (and, in two out of three cases, Protestant) male exemplar and teacher.

Dr. Craig's position in "St. Elsewhere" was a focus for moral difficulties in the practice of medicine, between patient and doctor, among doctors, and in the operation of an institution committed to caring for sick people. Dr. Craig met moral difficulties with bombast and arrogance—but he ended up being right, or being sorry when he wasn't, almost every week. He was truculent with his juniors (like a forebear in American doctor stories, Dr. Gillespie of the Dr. Kildare stories). He indulged his inherited racism and sexism more than is fashionable; he was a snob; he did not always manage to separate moral issues in treating patients and teaching young doctors from the sexual practices of the next generation; and he was truthful in his medical judgments.

When I say "truthful in his medical judgments," I do not mean to argue about whether Dr. Craig was an honest man; he was about as honest and dishonest as anybody else in the stories—and he was probably more self-deceived than most of the other physicians at St. Eligius Hospital. When I speak of medical judgments, I mean that he demonstrated to his junior colleagues that a truthful account of what is going on when a doctor deals with disease and death, and a truthful memory of what went on, after a medical case ends in failure, is essential in the practice of medicine. (Charles Bosk memorialized the idea when he called his book on teaching hospitals *Forgive and Remember: Managing Medical Failure.*) Truthfulness is prominent in medicine because medicine claims to be scientific; because of this claim, truthfulness is a medical super-virtue—as justice is a super-virtue among lawyers, who claim to administer and dispense justice.

An example in the "St. Elsewhere" stories was the slip of Dr. Craig's scalpel as he performed open-heart surgery on Mrs. Hufnagel; Mrs. Hufnagel died as a result. One of the surgical residents did an autopsy and reported that there was a surgical nick in one of Mrs. Hufnagel's coronary arteries. Dr. Craig exploded at the suggestion that his surgery had been faulty; residents, interns, nurses, and orderlies (maybe even an inconspicuous teacher of medical ethics) trembled at his wrath. He stormed into his office and played back the tape recording of the Hufnagel surgery—and listened to himself make the mistake. ("Oops," he said to himself from the tape recorder.) He threw the tape into the wastebasket. But, before the end of the program, he had gone to the morbidity conference and admitted to his young colleagues that the autopsy report was accurate, that his mistake caused Mrs. Hufnagel's death.

The profession, to Dr. Craig, was appropriately dominated by older, white males. *Protestant* white males, in
fact: His contemporaries, Dr. Westfall, a Catholic, and Dr.
Auschlander, a Jew, shared his power, but Dr. Craig considered his own background more appropriate for professional leadership. He was first among equals. He
respected physicians who were not older or white or
male or Protestant, but only after they demonstrated
their competence to him. Many of the plots in the series
were devoted to young doctors of all colors and both
sexes going through rituals of competence under his sar-
castic, demanding scrutiny.

Half of the point of his being in the series was that he
was a model of medical competence. He claimed a certain natural, cultural superiority, but he got his power
over other doctors because he was a good doctor. The
other half of his being in the series was that he understood and worked at the essential morality of being a
doctor and a good person. He was always, finally, before
the credits came on the screen at the end of the hour,
and according to the demands of the story for that week,
truthful, fair, or compassionate—and sometimes all
three.

Our forebears in the law or in medicine would not
have taken this many words to describe the importance
of older white males in popular stories about doctors and
lawyers; our forebears would have said that Lawrence
Preston, Leland McKenzie, and Drs. Gillespie and Craig
were *gentlemen.* The "St. Elsewhere" stories are, by and
large, positive examples of the gentleman's ethic in the
practice of medicine. Something C. G. Jung once wrote to
Sigmund Freud, about their colleague, Karl Abraham, is a
negative example (and also shows how the old shorthand
made the point): "I have an undisguised contempt for
some of A's idiosyncracies. In spite of his estimable qualities and sundry virtues, he is simply not a gentleman. In
my eyes, just about the worst thing that can happen to

anyone." Jung meant the worst thing that could happen to anyone—professionally.

We have retained the stories and the "role models" in the stories, but we have stopped using the word our forebears used to describe the ethic. If we put the two back together again—for purposes of analysis—we will describe a powerful, traditional, and still implicit ethical argument: The morals of the gentleman are an ethic for the professions. Television preserves for us an old and still prevalent way to be a lawyer (or a physician) and a good person: Be a gentleman. The gentleman's ethic is described in our stories, even our most popular and most trendy stories, which is to say that, whatever the gentleman's ethic is, we have not managed to get rid of it. For that reason, if for no other, it is useful to attempt to describe it.

The first step is to swallow immediate misgivings and restore the word—for purposes of analysis. Then it may help to notice more carefully where it has not died out. "Gentleman" is still used in the old-fashioned way as praise for the morals of individuals. Newspaper obituaries are an example: Richard Coe's 1984 obituary for Brooks Atkinson said that what made Mr. Atkinson a gentleman was that he was truthful. James Reston said that Averell Harriman was "a gentleman who did not apologize for his old-fashioned concept of *noblesse oblige*." Charles Trueheart said (not in an obituary) that what makes Anthony Powell a gentleman is that he is formal as well as kind. And, lest *noblesse oblige* be thought essential to being a gentleman, Tom Shales said Cary Grant was "an egalitarian gentleman," and Katharine Graham said of Carroll Kilpatrick that what made him a gentleman and a journalist was that he was modest, gentle, and considerate, as well as skeptical.

When this sort of moral assessment is applied to a lawyer, the speaker (or writer) will usually add something about the gentleman's use of power. William Harbaugh, in his 1955 obituary for John W. Davis, said: "He was a gentleman in the sense that Confucius used that much abused word—a superior man, with a courtliness that came from a fine intellect and a warm heart and a gentle manner. In whatever circle he moved, there was none other who seemed fitted to be at the head of the table." Mr. Harbaugh alluded to our southern-gentleman-lawyer stories. (His was an ethical *argument* really, but one feels uncomfortable identifying a line in an obituary as an argument.) Leadership, he implied, when genuine, when it rings true, depends on character.

Southern-gentleman-lawyer stories also say that character depends on background. A southern gentleman, as Atticus Finch's sister said, is a person of background. The *American Bar Association Journal* got this wrong when it saluted Justice Lewis F. Powell as he retired from the federal supreme court. An editorial entitled "The Southern Gentleman" spoke of Justice Powell's qualities of character as including the ability to disassociate himself from "what he might consider undue influence," including "from his own background." It was as if Justice Powell's good character had come to him out of the air (of Washington, D.C., not of Richmond), rather than from his family, his town, his religious congregation, and his education at Washington and Lee, an old college named for two Southern gentlemen who did not disassociate themselves from their background.

If disassociation from background is how a gentleman who is also a judge goes about being fair, how does he know what fairness is? The essence of the gentleman in our stories (including television stories) is that he is all together, of a piece, and consistent—background and all. He is not divided, and so, as Plato said, he is able to do what he has to do. "The mark of a gentleman is ... an ability to work conscientiously without losing himself," as Shirley Letwin put it. If service on the federal supreme court requires a gentleman to leave his background at home, then, our republican forebears in the nineteenth century would have said, it is not fit work for a gentleman.

Many political Liberals[1] in legal education, including me, supported the nomination of Justice Powell. The country had gone through two divisive Senate battles on nominations of southern judges. The common understanding was that President Nixon still meant to appoint a southerner. He would keep nominating southerners until one of them got through. Our point in urging him to nominate Lewis Powell was that Mr. Powell's southern background was relevant to his service as a judge, as it had been relevant to his service as president of the American Bar Association and his conspicuous support of legal services for poor people. If he had been a merely nominal southerner, or a southerner who could put aside where he came from and who he was, the President would not have wanted to nominate him. A gentleman belongs to where he came from.

* * * * *

A few scholars in literature and in ethics provide more general and abstract material for the description of gentleman's ethics, and both kinds of scholarly literature seem for some reason to be increasing. Shirley Letwin, for example, in her careful study of gentlemen in the novels of Anthony Trollope, argues that the ethics of the Victorian English gentleman transcended sex, wealth, and class. Hers is an argument for the return of the gentleman to serious ethical discussion. To make her claim work she has to eliminate the possibility that a person is *born* a gentleman. She can then claim, as she does, that

---

1. I am using "Liberal" to mean a modern American whose political positions are left of center, and "liberal" to mean one whose philosophical views derive from the Enlightenment and tend to emphasize autonomy as a fundamental value. And I use "republican" (but not "Republican") to refer to the Jeffersonian political vision that appears to have governed gentleman's ethics in America before the Civil War. Maxwell Bloomfield's essay on Hoffman's ethics is helpful on this use of "republican."

the morals of the gentleman are interesting, that those of us who teach ethics in the university would profit intellectually from taking the gentleman more seriously.[2]

Glenn Tinder's study of the virtue of tolerance is an account of the way gentlemen listen, learn, and argue in a democracy. Tinder's claim is that learning, self-awareness, and civility in communal life turn on a sound perception of human personality, rather than on the "marketplace of ideas" that lawyers and political thinkers have first fashioned from the Scots Enlightenment, and then read into the first amendment to the federal constitution. Tinder claims tolerance as the virtue that makes communities possible, and that makes it possible for them to survive contention, and he claims that the gentleman learns to be tolerant in his community. Justice Powell learned gentle tolerance in his community in the Old Dominion part of Virginia; the A.B.A. *Journal* noticed the tolerance and mistook it for absence of character.

Tinder's description contemplates the ethical substance of Dr. Craig's medical world and Leland McKenzie's legal world. It is a world where being able to see what is going on is a moral process, a process of listening and learning, with skills the gentleman brings to the profession from his culture. It is not that the gentleman does the right thing from the beginning; in the useful stories he never does. Mr. McKenzie often makes a wrong-headed start, and Dr. Craig almost always did. (Lord Peter Wimsey's "man" Bunter said the mark of a true gentleman is that he is slightly flawed.) Moral excellence in these cases is an ability to perceive the situation differently as it goes along—to learn from it by seeing and

---

2. "Interesting" is the adjective that qualifies an idea or an argument for ethics. Ethics is not the same thing as morals; ethics is description and discussion of morals. Something is worthwhile ethically when it is worth describing and discussing.

saying truthfully. Seeing is a moral art; each of us, as Tinder says it, is bound by his institutions and beliefs, but none of us is bound absolutely. Seeing is a moral art.

I think of the episode in "St. Elsewhere" in which Dr. Craig decided that the hospital needed publicity. He arranged for a television crew to film a documentary on medicine at St. Eligius, and especially, of course, on Dr. Craig's practice in heart surgery. He even tolerated television people in his operating room. He changed his mind during the filming of a conversation he had with a patient who was being rejected as a candidate for a heart-transplant: His physician's task was to tell the patient she could not be treated. He had permitted the television crew to film even that. When Dr. Craig had finished the conversation, the director of the crew said he had failed to get it on film the way he wanted it and asked Dr. Craig to do it over. Finally, then, ten minutes after the point had occurred to the rest of us, Dr. Craig understood that the filmmaker valued his film more than he valued this suffering person—and that the surgeon had been valuing his eminence more than he valued his patient—and Dr. Craig asked the film crew to leave the hospital.

Scholars in moral philosophy and theology have, I think, too quickly come to ignore or reject the notion that the gentleman *is* an ethical argument. They may still—even now—need to see what makes the gentleman tick or risk being out of touch with the professions they propose to instruct. Alasdair MacIntyre's influential *After Virtue* provides an example of how that might be done (although MacIntyre is one of the philosophers who denies any interest in the gentleman as a cultural focus for his work). *After Virtue* is in large part a brief for Aristotle's ethics of virtue. Those of us who seek to understand gentleman's ethics (not including MacIntyre) would say that the virtues are the moral qualities of a gentleman; the virtues in Aristotle are the moral qualities of "the man of practical wisdom," that is, the Athenian gentleman, as the qualities of a good Boy Scout (as I learned them in the *Scout Handbook*) are the qualities of a young gentleman in America: A Scout is trustworthy, loyal, helpful, friendly, courteous, kind, obedient, cheerful, thrifty, brave, clean, and reverent. Those are virtues, gentleman's virtues.

There is now a formidable school of moral theology among Jews and Christians which argues that character is the fundamental category for defining the Hebraic way of life. Character as a focus for ethics turns on personal qualities or dispositions, on what the medieval writers translated as good habits, on what some of the modern students of character would call skills. We learn about character by observing people who have it, and we "do" ethics when we attempt to describe what makes such people admirable. What we describe are virtues.

When we decide to have good qualities, we do not decide in the abstract. Usually we do not decide to *acquire* a virtue; we decide to keep on having it. We learn the virtues at home, as Aristotle said. We learn them, at home, before we learn that they are good qualities. Justice is an example: Justice is not something lawyers get from the government, as if the courts were a system of wholesale distributors and law offices the retail segment in a market. (We lawyers speak of ourselves as if we were *dispensers* of justice, but we know better.) Justice is something we have learned to give to one another—and our learning was for the most part complete before we began to study "the administration of justice."

Dr. Craig understands and practices justice in this way—as a virtue. He made a speech in the operating room after he completed his first heart-transplant operation, in November 1983. He spoke on the job, not at a press conference, and he spoke not of his skill, nor of the hospital's technology, nor of the patient's prognosis, but of the generosity of the young woman who had donated her heart for transplant. He praised her for her practice of the virtue of *justice*. Then he went to his private office

and shut the door and refused to talk to the press. The
lesson he wanted to teach about justice was a lesson for
his colleagues, not for reporters. Dr. Craig is a professional gentleman—and by that I mean that he *wants* to
be a gentleman in his profession. He joins the literary
critic, the political scientist, the philosophers and the
theologians, in inviting those who are interested in legal
ethics, in the 1990s, to think again about the gentleman.

*　*　*　*　*

Gentleman's ethics are descriptions of what gentlemen
do in their communities. The ethic is a cultural ethic. Describing it is a process of inductive reasoning; the raw
materials for induction are what gentlemen do. Gentleman's ethics do not rest on principles (although they often make use of principles). Letwin takes up Kant's
quandary about the murderer who pursues his next victim and asks the bystander which way the victim went.
She says, "A gentleman will lie to a murderer in order to
save his friend, but his honesty will keep him from pretending . . . he has not lied"—an exercise not of principle
about telling the truth but of the habit of truthfulness.
(The titular crisis in *To Kill a Mockingbird* rests on the
same distinction.) Nor does this gentleman's ethic depend on quandaries and choices: Letwin's gentleman lies
to the murderer without pausing to think about it. This is
an ethic that considers persons rather than choices—
which is to say that it explains choices by describing
persons who choose. Gentleman's ethics depend on sto-
rytellers and anthropologists, historians and biographers.
Ethical discussion starts with the storyteller—with locating some gentlemen to talk about.

The old-fashioned way of saying we knew who was a
gentleman and who was not was that we just did: General Robert E. Lee was a gentleman; my grandmother always said that General Ulysses S. Grant was not, but I
think she was probably wrong (and I think General Lee
would have agreed with me, not Grandma). When I first

aired the ideas in this chapter at Queen's University in Ontario, my genial hosts tuned in to my game and said Chief Justice Bora Laskin was a gentleman, as was Prime Minister Lester Pearson. Trollope's Dr. Thorne was a gentleman (and a physician), as was his Phineas Finn (a lawyer). So was Plantagenet Palliser, the young Duke of Omnium, although his uncle, the old duke, was not.

The photo-album method of getting started in a discussion of gentleman's ethics works because we know before we start what a gentleman is. Our lives and our stories—before we start to describe—have gentlemen in them; we have come to know who the gentlemen are. I once asked a class of students in legal ethics how a gentleman knows the right thing to do; the answer Dr. Craig or Gavin Stevens, Faulkner's lawyer, would have liked best is that a gentleman has confidence in the hope that what he will end up doing is the right thing to do. Thus, Jem Finch, Atticus Finch's twelve-year-old son, enters upon his rite of passage to adult responsibility when he says, "Atticus is a gentleman, and so am I." Jem has come to understand who the gentlemen in Maycomb are, and to understand also that he can safely let himself be influenced by gentlemen.

Samuel Butler described the sort of discovery Jem made: "We are not won by arguments that we can analyse but by tone and temper, by the manner which is the man himself." The mystery writer, Dick Francis, quotes a British horseman on the gentleman's ethic in British horse racing: "When I look back on my life on the Turf, I am astonished at how many men I have known that you could bet your life on their doing the right thing."

Jem's experience is a literary way to get at the substance of the gentleman's ethic, but it is still not the clear road sign ethics ought to be able to provide; if experience were enough we would be well advised to leave ethics to the poets. Ethics needs to get to what we already know and describe it for us, so that we can know that we know it. Philosophers and theologians are more difficult for lawyers to read, but reading them seems to have become necessary for legal ethics. (That, by the way, is a lesson we teachers of legal ethics have learned only lately. We used to think we could do it with judicial opinions and bar-association committee reports.)

Aristotle got into ethical descriptions, of the sort I am after, through teleology, through a consideration, first, of the goal of the moral life, and then of the personal qualities or dispositions (virtues) that move a person toward or away from the goal. H. Richard Niebuhr used an engineer's metaphor for it; he called it "man the maker" ethics. Alasdair MacIntyre uses a pilgrim metaphor:

> If a human life is understood as a progress through harms and dangers, moral and physical, which someone may encounter and overcome in better and worse ways and with a greater or lesser measure of success, the virtues will find their place as those qualities the possession and exercise of which generally tend to success in this enterprise and the vices as qualities which ... tend to failure.

With either metaphor, and with MacIntyre's more than Niebuhr's, we have to know, or be able to find out, where we want our lives to be headed, and—an even harder task (as Dr. Craig would tell us)—we have to be able to see and to say where our lives are in fact headed. (Niebuhr said the two relevant questions were: [i] To whom am I responsible? And [ii] in what community?) MacIntyre and Aristotle speak of the good life, of flourishing (which I understand to mean using well—perfecting— one's human capacities, *and* enjoying them).

The point can be taken back to lawyer and doctor stories where the best people in the stories are those who strive to be good people, who do that in their professional lives and *through* them. For example, the best of the lawyers, bureaucrats, nurses, physicians, teachers, scientists, and governors that C. P. Snow wrote about say that the hardest job, and the job they most want to do well, is to become good people in their work.

Some of them redefine—and, in some cases, sacrifice—conventional professional success in journeys that are practical examples of MacIntyre's metaphor. And some of them choose poorly because their vices keep them from seeing the road ahead.

The usual way to describe the gentleman's ethic with the methods of philosophy and theology, then, is to catalogue the qualities we admire in the gentlemen we know. That fits into MacIntyre's metaphor; it is the way Aristotle's *Nichomachean Ethics* described virtues. It is also what Shirley Letwin does in her brief for the gentlemen in Trollope's novels:

Civility. Letwin says that a gentleman is civil; Tinder would say tolerant. Cardinal Newman said a gentleman avoids the infliction of pain. Scout Finch said her father Atticus was so civil that he could make the trial of someone accused of rape as dry as a sermon. Trollope's Dr. Thorne was discharged as physician for the children of Squire Gresham and his wife, Lady Arabella, because he was not fashionable. But he was called in again when two children died at the hands of Dr. Thorne's rival, Dr. Fillgrave. Lady Arabella asked Dr. Thorne to come back and "humbled herself, or would have done so, had the doctor permitted her. But he, with his eyes full of tears, stopped the utterance of her apology, took her two hands in his, pressed them warmly, and assured her that his joy in returning would be great."

General Lee said that a gentleman cannot help being humbled when he has to humble others. He left an important legacy to the post-bellum South when he welcomed federal officers and their families back to the Virginia mountain resorts, and let it be known that he disapproved of criticism of his late enemy, General Grant. The lesson for the South was a lesson in civics as well as personal morals: Gentlemen in the post-war union had to learn to listen to, or, as Tinder put it, "wait on" other persons, especially those in the North. Communal life depended on it.

Self-possession. Letwin says that the sexual morality of Trollope's gentlemen is a matter, not of suppressing urges, but of thinking straight. A fancier of Trollope's stories may think here of some of Trollope's purposeful women, or of John Gray, Alice Vavasour's lover (lover in the Victorian sense), sometime fiancé, and finally husband, in *Can You Forgive Her?* John is passionately in love with Alice, but he keeps his composure. Others do not—notably Alice's other lover, her cousin George, who is no gentleman. Thinking straight is essential to the practice of all of the virtues; it is what Aristotelians mean when they use the English phrase, "practical wisdom," that is, prudence: the ability to deliberate well. Practical wisdom is the coordinator of the virtues. Much of Trollope's tongue-in-cheek doubt about whether Phineas Finn, his volatile Irish lawyer-politician, is a gentleman turns on Phineas's recurrent failure to think straight. Virtue finally leads Phineas to a blissful marriage with Madame Max, but only after an unfortunate first marriage back in Ireland, and early widowhood. Virtue finally leads him to effective leadership in Parliament, but only after he fights a duel and is tried for murder.

Trollope's gentlemen are (or finally become) steady in social and political leadership. The gentlemen who wield power in the parliamentary novels dream (in Letwin's phrase) of something better, and fear something worse. Power is not a matter of merit; it is a matter of circumstance. The gentleman-lawyer's use of power is not the same as *noblesse oblige*, which regards power as appropriate and seeks to justify having it. The thought of Trollope's ideal aristocrat, the self-possessed young duke, Plantagenet Palliser (and of General Lee), is that power, whether appropriate or not, is a fact; the moral way to cope with the fact of power is to regard it as an opportunity for service.[3]

---

3. Mary points out that *noblesse oblige* may retain this meaning in France: Nobility (as a situation) creates the obligation.

The virtue of self-possession in the use of power is worth following for a while, mostly because this is a discussion of lawyers' ethics. Lawyers use power professionally; they use power they do not have, which means they are accountable not only to those on whom power is brought to bear but also to those whose power they appropriate. Legitimacy in the use of power depends not on the circumstance of having power, but on what one does with power: "Just because the command of God can... put me in a privileged place, the question is always acute whether I am in fact privileged... or whether... my legitimately occupied and defended place of privilege... is an insolent usurpation," Karl Barth said in his *Ethics*. "If within the civil order... I occupy a position in which... I stand in the sun... I cannot excuse myself... that in virtue of my calling I have claim that this should be so."

Discrimination. "When faced with transgressors," Letwin says, the gentleman "will consider whether he is faced with an eccentric, a ruffian, or a villain." Depending on what he decides, he may smile, go get his horsewhip, or call the police. Lewis Thomas's father, an old-fashioned family doctor, showed how discrimination works when he parked his car around the corner from the home of his Christian Science patient. Atticus Finch described discrimination humbly when he told his children that before one acts with (or acts upon) the other fellow, he has to get inside his skin, a particularly poignant metaphor when one theme in the story is racism. Atticus demonstrated what he meant when he turned away after Bob Ewell spat in his face. That silent moment in the movie was Gregory Peck's greatest success at showing what moral strength is like. The scene also illustrated the virtue of discrimination: If Atticus ever had had a physical fight with anyone, it would not have been with Bob Ewell.

Diffidence. Gentlemen are firm in their morals, but they are not without doubt about them; their doubt keeps them curious, and it keeps them from becoming

oppressive. A southern gentleman's version of Kant's dilemma is the main plot line in *To Kill a Mockingbird*, a
novel that, according to its author, is the story of a conscience. Atticus did not duck complicity in the lie of
Sheriff Tate, that in the scuffle with Scout and Jem, at the
end of the story, Bob Ewell fell on his own knife and
died. In fact, Atticus's neighbor Boo Radley killed Bob
Ewell. Sheriff Tate lied to save Radley from public scrutiny. Atticus lied to save his neighbor, but he did not pretend that he had not lied.

The moral person described in the gentleman's ethic
seems in his diffidence to be aware of things he cannot
know; there is a consciousness of self and other in his
dealings that can operate on possibilities, without objective knowledge, and that is therefore able to welcome op-
portunities for association with other persons—and,
ultimately, for community. From this consciousness
comes what Martin Buber called the heavenly bread of
self-being. Awareness of the other, and the moral person's
awareness of himself, are reciprocal: One is possible because of the other. Letwin's word, diffidence, is, I suppose, a stuffy word for it, but the word is a bit surprising
in this context, and that makes it useful. Iris Murdoch
uses the word "humility." What she and Letwin and I are
trying to describe is the way a gentleman goes about being firm in his morals but also open to other people, as
Atticus Finch was open both to black people and to big-
ots in his Alabama town in 1935, and as General Lee was
open both to his students at Washington College and to
officers from the North, after the war. We are trying to
describe the gentleman's way to self-realization in his
community.

* * * * *

I need now to turn to the difficulties in this gentleman's ethic:
(1) Can the gentleman's ethic survive delusions of class
     (especially gender), and professionalism?

(2) Can it provide the moral skills a lawyer needs for dealing with power?

(3) Does it take into account the tragic nature of moral life?

(4) Does it give adequate consideration to the significance of suffering?

CHAPTER THREE

Class and Professionalism in the Gentleman's Community

> More: Norfolk, you're a fool.... You
> and your class have "given in"....
> Norfolk: Well, that's a foolish saying for
> a start; the nobility of England has
> always been—
> More: The nobility of England, my lord,
> would have snored through the Sermon
> on the Mount. But you'll labor like
> Thomas Aquinas over a rat-dog's pedigree.

A Man for All Seasons

The first two objections to the gentleman's ethic for lawyers are that it is an ethic based on delusions (i) of class and (ii) of professionalism. These are not the same. One continues an old argument; the other has become so pervasive among lawyers as to offer a sort of idolatry. The two arguments come together only because modern lawyer professionalism attempts to appropriate the ethic of gentlemen.

The cultural and moral ancestors of the gentleman understood that they were an aristocracy, and did not see that fact as a valid objection to their ethic; they justified their ethic, in that regard, with the understanding that status was necessary to service. Class becomes an objection to the gentleman's ethic when, in a society such as ours, equality becomes a dominant value. I argue in this chapter that the gentleman's ethic is capable of meeting this egalitarian challenge; it can overcome its attachment to class. The old (and new) argument is whether it should.

The ethics of *professionalism* is as modern as the egalitarianism that challenges the gentleman's ethic. The egalitarian objection to gentleman's ethics is a principal source of the ethics of professionalism: The principal ethical enterprise in the American professions—notably the principal effort of the organized bar—is a campaign to appropriate the gentleman's ethic in a new democratic ethic of professionalism. This project teems with moral problems, only one of which is its failure to solve the problem of equality. The premise of the current enterprise is that there is no egalitarian objection to professionalism, but I suggest that there is as much objection based on equality to the one ethic as to the other.

Professionalism is as elitist as class is, although modern democratic lawyers, in their esteem for expertise, seem not to notice. Professionalism is also open to far more serious moral objection: Its claim to objectivity is a way for it to avoid relationships with clients and deny ordinary notions of responsibility; its esteem for professional fraternity is an ethic of honor rather than of virtue; the hubris of its rhetoric is so arrogant as to begin to sound like worship. I argue in this chapter, first, that the ethic of professionalism does not overcome these objections; and, second, that the gentleman's ethic is not where legal professionalism comes from: Professionalism is not consistent with the ethics of the gentleman.[1]

---

1. Both class-based ethics and professionalism also invite Robert E. Rodes's objection that they involve domination, and the oppression of powerless people, without accountability to the wider community. That objection has to do with the gentleman's use of power, which is the subject of the next chapter.

Class and the Gentleman-Lawyer

The nineteenth-century gentleman in North America gave us slavery, Manifest Destiny, the theft of half of Mexico, gunboat diplomacy, the subjugation of women, the exploitation of immigrant children, Pinkerton detectives, yellow-dog contracts, and the genocide of American Indians. One could make a case—Lawrence Preston, Dr. Craig, and Leland McKenzie to the contrary notwithstanding—that the gentleman's ethic is not to be taken seriously in a modern profession. If the gentleman has left the professions (and I don't think he has), the best thing for us would be to bar the door lest he get back in. William Dean Howells's Silas Lapham said, at the end of the last century, "Gentlemaning as a profession has got to play out in a generation or two." Maybe we should hope that he was right, or soon will be, and that his prediction included professionalizing as a gentleman.[2]

When I proposed this topic for a lecture at Queen's University, my kind Canadian host wrote me: "There are those who see appeals to gentlemen's ethics as anachronistic and unsuited to contemporary Canadian conditions in the professions. They may see appeals to preserve such a system as attempts to perpetuate the unethical."

And, above all else in the mind of a teacher who has worked in two law schools that were until recently all male, who joined in the decision at one of them to admit women, and who saw the feminine presence in both

---

2. The reader may have nodded agreement to this paragraph. If so, I must ask her to forgive me for seeming credulous in the affection with which I introduced the subject in the last chapter, and with which I will proceed to account for it in this chapter and the next. Credulity is the way my poor mind works: Liberal education is said to create skepticism, and I occasionally notice that effect in my children and my students, but forty years of it have not made my mind work that way. I need to buy whatever is being sold before I can begin to think critically about it—and I *will* get around to criticism. Besides that, I suspect that most readers who agree with this paragraph also remember their grandfathers: They are probably ambivalent about gentleman's ethics. So am I.

grow from one or two brave pioneers to student popula-
tions that are nearly half women, the gentleman's ethic is
patriarchical. It is not only sexist (in that gentlemen are
men) but also oppressive (in that it seems to imply that
it is appropriate that gentlemen be in charge). The most
piercing comments I got from women who heard me
give this material in lectures at Queen's, and later at
Vanderbilt, was that the ethic I was talking about had
nothing to do with them.[3]

The gentleman's ethic is either inherently useless or it
has been damaged on the way to us. Gentlemen in the
professions have, at best, deceived themselves, often and
thoroughly: The gentlemen who dominate all of our legal
institutions enjoy a comfort they do not deserve; they
are like the nobles of sixteenth-century England. If they
have not snored through the Sermon on the Mount, they
have snored through something almost as important. The
history of professional institutions controlled by gentlemen—schools, hospitals, law firms, clinics—is so devas-
tating and so pervasively bad that the only sensible
approach is description, rather than defense. The reason
for description is that the gentleman's ethic in the American professions, in the 1990s, is still a *fact*. I deal with it
as a fact; it is the ethical situation of the North American
legal profession, or a big part of it, and I am trying to see
if we can make something out of our ethical situation.

As I endeavored to show in the last chapter, the gentleman is the most vivid and the most enduring figure in
American professional ethics. He is everywhere, and

---

3. I am afraid that most of the nouns and pronouns in this chapter
and the next are going to attract the same reaction. I must again ask
the reader to be patient. I agree that the gentleman's ethic is male; I
do not want to evade the point by pretending it is not (through the
use of "inclusive" language, for example). I need to describe the
ethic, and when I do that I seem to overlook women: If I am true to
my argument about the ethic being male, though, and if I also describe the ethic adequately, it may begin to become clearer why it
overlooked women; then the issue will be whether it can stop over-
looking them.

when he seems to be gone he keeps coming back; he is
on television; his silhouette shows through statements of
moral standards for physicians and lawyers; his ethic is
the moral background in our codes—medical codes
from the late eighteenth century on, statements from the
earliest days of American law schools, in the 1820s;
through the first American lawyers' code, in the 1880s in
Alabama; through three generations of consensus codal
projects of the American Bar Association. The word remains for us a word of praise for introductions, eloquent
salutations, and obituaries.

The morals of the gentleman are the American lawyer's unavoidable ethical inheritance. The gentleman
looks down on us from the walls of courthouses, hospitals, and schools. His is the statue in the village square,
the enduring image in our hero stories; his name is on
the cornerstones and over the main doors of our university buildings. We cannot abolish the gentleman's ethic
from the professions; we could more easily abolish our
grandparents. We cannot even choose against it; as Gavin
Stevens said, "The past is not dead; it is not even past."
The least we can do with the gentleman in our ethic is to
treat him as we would a charming black-sheep uncle: We
can try to be truthful to him and truthful about him.

That is the least; but perhaps we can do more. Perhaps
we can approach the gentleman's ethic with another metaphor: Think of it as if it were old family silver—
tarnished but not spoiled underneath. That, I suppose, is
the affection hidden in More's tirade against the nobility
of England. (He was picking a quarrel with Norfolk to
protect Norfolk from Thomas Cromwell's conspiracy
against the nobility of England.) In the curious dynamics
of self-deception, the nobler the morality the more likely
it is that it will deceive itself. There is a difference between a corrupt morality and a tarnished morality—between, say, the racism of Hitler and the racism of Rudyard
Kipling. It may be that the gentleman's morality, with its
elitism a thing as old as Aristotle's ethics, can be de-

scribed carefully enough so that its persistence in the legal profession will be useful and not merely inevitable.

The first issue for this chapter is this issue about class:[4] Can the gentleman's ethic survive our tendency to lord it over one another? That may turn out to be a stern test. No less an admirer of gentlemen than John Henry Newman applied the test and voted against the gentleman. Although Newman admired the modest righteousness of the best of nineteenth-century English gentlemen, those whom Disraeli called "muscular Christians," Newman did not think their ethic was sufficient to explain their modesty, let alone to sustain it. Newman admired the qualities of the gentlemen he knew, but, he said, those qualities were too fragile to be adequate as an ethic. Gentlemen's morals are neither evidence of virtue nor dependable tests for what virtue is; they "are no guarantee for sanctity or even for conscientiousness; they may attach to the man of the world, the profligate, the heartless," as much as to the virtuous, he said.

The noble qualities of gentlemen, even if it were possible to protect them from the vicious, would not be equal to the self-deception and hubris of *good* people: "Quarry the granite rock with razors, or moor the vessel with a thread of silk: then may you hope with such keen and delicate instruments to contend against those giants, the passion and the pride of man."

Newman's argument is broad and deep, and this chapter is considering only one narrow set of objections to the gentleman's ethic in the American legal profession; we will have to return to Newman when we talk about power, tragedy, and suffering in subsequent chapters. On the single question of elitism, what Newman said, in my

----

4. "Class" as a point of reference here is more descriptive than "aristocracy," in that the latter word is best limited to the exercise of power—to a *ruling* class. Letwin, Mason, Judith Martin (Miss Manners), and the writers of obituaries, in their use of "class," make a broader cultural reference than that. I will look more specifically in the next chapter at the gentleman-lawyer's *aristocracy.*

reading, is that the gentleman is subject to the self-deception and hubris of good people, that his attachment to a gentlemanly class is the expectable corruption of a noble ethic. Shirley Letwin's argument, that the Victorian gentlemen in Trollope's stories had an admirable ethic, also depends on her success in showing that the attachment of these gentlemen to their class was tarnish.[5]

Can the ethic of the American gentleman-lawyer get along without its attachment to economic and social privilege? I think so. I suggest that it can be done through tradition, craftsmanship, and the subversion of patriarchy. (But note again, please, that all I claim to do here is to remove this one objection to the gentleman's ethic in the legal profession. There are other and more difficult objections ahead.)

Tradition. The gentleman has usually, but not always, been "a person of background," which means that there has been distinction in his ancestry and that he owns something. The ethical argument in Letwin's study of Trollope's gentlemen was that background, breeding, and ownership were not essential. Dr. Thorne had an adequate ancestry but not ownership. Phineas Finn, the son of an Irish physician, had neither. Both were gentlemen. Lizzie Eustace (Letwin's example), who had both ancestry and ownership, was not a gentleman; neither was the old Duke of Omnium, who had both; but Lord Chiltern, who had both, and whose manners were crude, was a gentleman. (Chiltern shows that being a gentleman is not a matter of manners either.) What kept Lizzie and the old duke from being gentlemen, and showed that Dr. Thorne,

---

5. Philip Mason, interpreting Newman, characterizes this as the argument that the gentleman's ethic in Victorian England was a "subcult" of Christianity that was not really interested in the Cross. Letwin underestimates this problem, but Newman, in my reading, was not as hard on gentlemen as Mason is; Newman was speaking to them as Christians, and saying that the moral theology of Israel and of the church provided a corrective to their hubris—that their ethic was Christian. It was tarnished but not spoiled underneath.

Phineas, Madame Max Goessler, and Lord Chiltern were gentlemen, was not origin or status but character.

Still, the gentleman is *concerned* about breeding, and that, as my host at Queen's suggested, tells against his ethic. The way I would make something interesting out of concern for breeding is to say that the moral meaning of it (using a distinction suggested by Letwin) is a concern for tradition: The gentleman acknowledges what he has inherited. He does not regard himself as either an autonomous moral agent or a self-made person. He represents, preserves, and honors the values of his culture.

He honors his culture. Thus, when he stands against his community—and American gentleman-lawyer stories often pit the gentleman against his community—he stands there, as the Hebrew prophets did, in fear and trembling. The image in southern gentleman-lawyer stories is the defense lawyer who waits through the night outside the jail where his black client is held, ready to face the lynch mob: Gregory Peck reading the newspaper, his floor lamp and chair on the sidewalk, as if he were in his living room. The gentleman-lawyer, pitted against his neighbors, proclaims the terrible truth. He is an Isaiah: "I am a man of unclean lips, and I dwell in the midst of a people of unclean lips. . . . Here I am; send me." But the prophet tells his people a truth they *know*—a truth they have *preserved* and *taught to him*. That is the truth they cannot bear to hear.

The prophet Isaiah's proclamation is in this way like the argument of lawyers who invoke "due process of law" against those who want to root out their country's enemies. Due process is a lot more than procedure. It is a value America has taught to its children, and committed its lawyers to, for more than two centuries. But applications of due process (the privilege against self-incrimination, for example) would not have survived a popular referendum at any point in that history. Isaiah's is an argument in ancient Israel, like the argument, in modern Israel, of those who speak out against the excesses of

Israeli nationalism: Martin Buber said, to the leaders of his country, "You... would readily approve any idol-worship if only the idols bear Jewish names."

The gentleman-lawyer acknowledges his heritage, which is also the heritage of his community (no more, no less), and reminds his community of what its values are. His argument to his community is, as he sees it, not destructive; it is a memory that is, as he sees it, essential to survival[6]—the side of the raft he stands on while he repairs the other side. He says that those in institutions ought to look at what they are doing (that is the meaning of white-southern-lawyer stories such as *To Kill a Mockingbird* and *Intruder in the Dust*). He refuses to behave as if events were too big or too complicated for him: "Experience is not what happens to a man," Letwin says; "it is what he does with what happens to him."[7]

Craftsmanship. Alasdair MacIntyre fashioned from Aristotle's ethics the notion of the practice. The notion depends on a distinction between the two kinds of benefits we gain from the pursuit of our callings—one external (*e.g.*, money) and the other internal; internal benefits relate to the joy of doing what we do, of sharing that joy with our colleagues, and of subjecting what we do to standards of performance we inherit from masters, preserve among colleagues, and pass on to apprentices and students. It is what causes us to do good work and to share in the benefits of being among those who do good work.

---

6. Witness William Faulkner's views about racism in the South—views that were scorned on both sides of the civil-rights struggle.

7. It is important to notice, though, that this ethic does not bind a person to any *particular* description of the tradition. The real trick in deriving this ethical point from stories—a method that seems to have a built-in bias for turning history into command—is to ask whether the tradition is described so that it includes the means to correct its errors. The southern-white-lawyer heroes in the civil-rights stories were confident that it did; so was Isaiah. The point is also relevant with respect to patriarchy in the gentleman's ethic.

For example, science, including medical science, and law have practice-oriented ways of dealing with what in other callings would be trade secrets. If one of us discovers something, or thinks she has discovered something, she turns it over to the profession—for use, for evaluation, and for improvement. If one of us were to fail to do that, she would corrupt an internal good. We would say to her—in our "professional" arrogance—that she might as well have been in a *trade*, that she is turning our craft into a trade. On the other hand, in our collective self-deception we may withhold the discovery, or the ability to use the discovery, from those *outside* the profession and tell ourselves that our doing so is for the protection of the ignorant. That does not prove that professions cannot be practices. It is an instance of self-deception as the occupational disease of the well-intentioned. (Stanley Hauerwas, who also makes extensive use of the notion of practice in his Christian ethics, is more attentive to self-deception than MacIntyre is.)

When our activity in locating, testing, and promulgating our knowledge is done with honesty and civility, the practice is a school for virtue. It preserves itself as it honors professional ancestors and teachers and celebrates the present generation's debt to them. It might even reach beyond professional fashion and fad and give each of us a way to learn who he is, since the ability of a practice to preserve craftsmanship depends on truthfulness in accounting for what those in the practice are doing and have done.

If we keep our metaphors straight, the practice is a way to avoid the delusions of professionalism: For example, craftsmanship is not *art*. When we call what we do art, we withdraw it from the honesty and civility of evaluation and use by our colleagues; we begin to think that what we do is too special for them. What we do can be called *work*, rather than art, but only if we understand work as the Hasidic Rabbis did, as participation in Cre-

ation; or, as John Calvin understood it, as a theatre for
the glory of God. A diminished view of what work is, a
consumer's view that takes the dignity out of work, that
sees it as a means to the means for leisure, is what leads
us to the claim that we are not responsible for what our
institutions do: "I don't make the rules, I just do my
job.... I would like to help you, but it's not part of my
job description."

The Subversion of Patriarchy.[8] "Gentleman" is a masculine word; the English culture that produced and esteemed the gentleman, as well as the American culture
that esteems and imitates the English gentleman, is both
masculine and patriarchical. Nineteenth-century England
developed, and America imitated, an ethic for the professions that was centered in the lives and values of older,
white men, as it endeavored to make its established patriarchical church resolutely Protestant.

If the gentleman's ethic in the legal profession is inherently patriarchical, it can no longer be defended. The injustice of domination and oppression would condemn it,
even if equality did not. If a patriarchical ethic survives
into the next century (whether or not it is defended),
when half or more of American lawyers will be women,
it will become an object of revolution. If the gentleman
does not acknowledge the immorality of the patriarchy in
his ethic, he could end up without his head. (The inco-
herence and ineptitude of the American Bar Association,
on professionalism and on social issues such as abortion,
are, I think, early evidence of the revolution.)

---

8. I mean by "patriarchy" an ethic or in this case part of an ethic
that preserves and defends a preference for men in positions of power.
Overt discrimination against women in law firms is evidence of it; so
are employment arrangements, in law firms, universities, and companies, that make it sacrificial for young professionals to care for their
children. Patriarchs have other adults to care for their children. When
the young parent is a mother, the implication is that she should not be
working in the profession; when the young parent is a father, the implication is that he should have a wife at home to take care of his
children.

One way to approach this issue is with the claim—my claim—that any professional ethic is cultural: What keeps the culture's ethic from being evil? The answer is that it keeps itself from being evil, which means that the more exact ethical question is whether it can locate the tools necessary to identify and correct its mistakes. When I suggest that the ethic of the American gentleman-lawyer can subvert patriarchy, the task I set myself is to locate some tools: We look to the gentleman's legal ethic itself for values that condemn its patriarchy. The method here is what, in the Bible, is called prophetic; the prophet condemns what his leaders are doing by reminding them of their culture, of its values, and of what its values cost.

The other way to do something about patriarchy is an alternative biblical category, the apocalyptic. It may be that neither the feminist influence on the profession and in it, nor the liberal egalitarian influence (to mention two possibilities), will be able to find values in the gentleman's ethic that can overcome its patriarchy; the gentleman may have to be persuaded to turn around. My guess is that the American gentleman-lawyer will finally either remember or be converted or both; the prophetic and the apocalyptic in his ethic will save his head for him.

(a) *The Prophetic.* It is possible to describe the gentleman's legal ethic in such a way that it includes, underneath and most deeply, a feminine ethic. The "different voice" that Carol Gilligan identified is, she says, not necessarily a woman's voice. Her *In a Different Voice* reminded me that the analytical psychology of Carl G. Jung used the word *anima* (a feminine word) to describe the psyche of a man (and *animus* to describe a woman's psyche). It is possible to locate feminine meaning in the gentleman's ethic, as in our southern gentleman-lawyer stories we understand the hero (Atticus, Gavin Stevens) through the relationships he has with women in the story (Scout, Calpurnia, Miss Maudie, Margaret Stevens Mallison, and even Eula Varner Snopes and Linda Snopes Cole). From being put in touch with its feminine spirit, as feminist scholarship is beginning to influence virtually every academic discipline, the gentleman's ethic might begin to come to terms with its other dissonances—its racism, for example; or its paternalism (parentalism), which is its prejudice against the young.

The best in stories about the gentleman's ethic is prophetic: These are stories about virtuous women. Letwin's work on Trollope even identifies virtuous women *as* gentlemen. (This was a bold thing for Letwin to do, certainly, but it is not useful because it avoids differences that have to be described before patriarchy even becomes evident.) The part of Letwin's territory that shows us the English gentleman's legal ethic is mostly in the six parliamentary novels. The cast of women in those stories ranges from bright, often irreverent, unmarried women (Alice Vavasour, Violet Effingham), to wily widows (Madame Max, Lizzie Eustace), to compassionate, perceptive, but not always clever victims of arranged marriages among the wealthy (Lucy Morris; Lady Glencora Palliser, later the Duchess of Omnium; and Arabella Trefoil of *The American Senator*). These able women—some of them courageous, some pitiable, a few mildly victorious—are disabled by their patriarchical society.

Trollope, a gentleman and a perceptive exponent of the gentleman's ethic, knew those women were disabled. Most of the women in his parliamentary stories are informed about and interested in politics, for example, but their political action has to be indirect and tentative. Everything a woman wants done in the public life of imperial Victorian England—even what the Queen herself wants done—has to be approved by men. Unmarried women have to be calculating in their plans for marriage because a married woman (the Queen excepted) loses control of her life, her property, even her ideals: Lady Laura Standish, later Kennedy, is a study in how that happens, as is Mrs. Trevelyan in *He Knew He Was Right*. Alice Vavasour and Madame Max are studies in how and why intelligent unmarried women are not anxious to marry. Women who are without wealth of their own cannot even afford to be calculating about power, though: Lucy Morris has all of the moral qualities of the impecunious and ambitious men in her story (the lawyers Phineas Finn and Frank Greystock), but Lucy's choice is to marry or to be a governess.

Trollope shows how women in a culture of patriarchy were virtuous—how they went about it, how their way of being virtuous fit their disabilities. Their achievement of virtue was an achievement built on disability, rather than on the wealth, power, status, and security of being among the ruling class in an imperial nation-state. There are two prophetic lessons in these stories: One is that the unjust situation of these women is a product of the gentleman's ethic. (Letwin and I would say: a corruption of it—tarnish). The other is that these women were virtuous against conventional odds, and that is not only instructive for a modern gentleman's legal ethic; it is *part of it*.

Here is a story about a prophet:

The American gentleman-lawyer took on cultural identity during the two generations after our revolution. This was the generation Willard Hurst called the golden era of American lawyers. The first law schools and the first statement of legal ethics (both were American inventions) came out of this time. Women were ignored in the statements and excluded from the schools. Some women prepared for the profession in apprenticeships, only to find that they were excluded from bar examinations or, if they took and passed the examinations, from admission to the Bar.

There was litigation in several states to force admission of women, as a matter of common-law or constitutional right; the usual result was denial, often with descriptions of the fragile nature of women and of the destructive vulgarity of law practice; these opinions were full of the rhetoric of gentleman's legal ethics. The federal supreme court used such rhetoric to hold that qualification for the legal profession was a matter for state law: There was no federal constitutional right to be a lawyer.

Myra Bradwell (1831–1894) was one of the unsuccessful petitioners. She belonged to the generation of Illinois lawyers just after Abraham Lincoln's. She and her husband James raised a family in Chicago; James became a prominent lawyer, then a judge, and then a member of the legislature. When her children were out of diapers, Mrs. Bradwell served an apprenticeship in a law office, and took and passed the Illinois bar examination, but she was denied admission to practice and her appeal to the federal supreme court was unsuccessful. She never practiced law. (She was finally admitted to the Bar in 1890, at the age of fifty-nine, four years before she died.)

Mrs. Bradwell turned to professional activities that did not require a license to practice law. She founded and managed a lawyers' newspaper in Chicago. She led campaigns for law reform and civic improvement, most of which had to do with making the legal profession more accountable. She was responsible for codified professional standards for lawyers in Illinois; for pleading rules that improved fairness to litigants; for rules requiring civil treatment of witnesses in trials; for a judicial retirement system; and for the requirement that all lawyers have a legal education. A paragraph in Caroline Bird's bicentennial book on American women, published in 1976, implied that Mrs. Bradwell had done more for the legal profession in Illinois than she would have done if she had been licensed to practice law, "in part, perhaps, because as a woman she was an outsider."

Myra Bradwell was a prophetic figure among Illinois lawyers. She was *among* them, as Jeremiah was in Judea. She was able to perceive the truth about conditions in the profession and to describe them truthfully because she could see around and behind the privileges enjoyed by gentleman-lawyers such as her husband—and that implies, as the stories of the prophets of Israel do, that prophetic witness is more likely in the absence of the power and status both of the gentleman and of the modern professional person.

But a prophet is also, always and undeniably, within her culture. Bird is not quite right when she says that Myra Bradwell was an outsider; the point is more subtle than that. Trollope's heroines, married and unmarried, like the Hebrew prophets and the black preachers of the civil-rights revolution, were within and present to the culture. They were finally able to demand that the culture listen to them—as Nathan could demand that King David hear the truth. The demand depends on membership. It has to be made inside; its message has to be spoken within the practice and its effect has to become, as psychology says it these days, internalized. It works from the inside out.

Larry Churchill, writing about medicine, said that professional ethics becomes accountable when it develops a prophetic capacity (or at least the capacity to listen to prophets), within the profession and within the professional person. "The capacity for self-restriction and self-criticism" is what the prophet aims for in those who hear him. Otherwise, when outsiders speak to the practice, or when the prophet within the practice speaks to the person, "all questions raised seem to be an attack and . . . the healer's mantle [becomes] an aegis from the variety of values held by . . . patients." And not only held by patients and clients, but held *within* the practice—the gentleman's values that the prophet invokes and relies on as she talks to gentlemen.

(b) *The Apocalyptic.* The prominent theologian Rosemary Radford Ruether took up the argument that feminist ethics will not only speak to patriarchy, in contexts such as the legal profession, but will, through challenge to the dominance of white, Protestant men, also cause patriarchy to turn from other injustice: "Woman becomes the symbol of the unknown possibility of a humanity beyond and outside the entire system of such a world... the 'new thing' which God has created on earth." That is eloquent but not prophetic; it is apocalyptic. It is not an utterance that depends on values in the system it calls into question; it depends on new values. To argue as Ruether does in feminist theology is to argue for a radical transformation of the present order.[9]

Sally Purvis argues that feminist theology should build on the construed experience of women, which requires, first, a reliable account of experience and then reasoned reflection on experience. The stories of gentlemen (such as the stories I use here and have used in my other work) are not reliable for feminist theology, Purvis says, because they do not describe (or are not accurate in describing) the experience of women. She implies that movement toward a feminist ethic for and in the legal profession will require a *reconstrual* of experience— new stories about lawyers, women's stories. The prophetic will not be enough. Purvis relates reconstrual to Jesus's parables; the new feminine narratives will, like the parables, break down conventional meanings, look at reality upside down, challenge notions of what is important, and undermine arrangements of power.[10] They will, when played out as ethics, reorient reality, invite (mascu-

---

9. By "system" here I mean something less than, and within, a moral culture. A profession is a system in that sense. The sort of reform I am calling apocalyptic is a "new thing" so far as the profession is concerned. The apocalyptic is not outside the moral culture; if it were it would not be heeded because no one could understand it. The Book of Daniel and the New Testament Apocalypse (Book of Revelation) were not written for strangers.

10. The tradition in Israel, building from the description of imperial power in Exodus, contained the means for such an apocalyptic change. Much of Walter Brueggemann's biblical scholarship develops this theme. Purvis and Brueggemann do not argue from outside the tradition; neither did Jesus.

line ethics to) assent, and, finally, advocate ethics and politics that are radically communal.[11]

Purvis's conclusion, this last point, is a guess on her part. She admits that feminist theology is not able to say what a non-patriarchical order will be like; but she thinks it will be more relational and communal than the patriarchical (hierarchical) orders we have now, especially in universities, in the church, and in the professions. I hope she is right. I yearn for the coming of that kingdom. The question for my work will be whether the gentleman's ethic for lawyers can also be reconstrued—and I think it can. Which is to say, as to the first issue raised in this chapter, that elitism is not essential to the gentleman's legal ethic.

Professionalism and the Gentleman-Lawyer

In 1984, Chief Justice Warren Burger said he thought American lawyers were "moving away from the principles of professionalism." He asked the American Bar Association to study the matter. Two years later a commission of eminent lawyers, chaired by Justin Stanley, a former president of the Association, presented its report, called "In the Spirit of Public Service: A Blueprint for the Rekindling of Lawyer Professionalism." The report was so important that it was published in the *Federal Rules Decisions*, in pages more often reserved for the opinions of federal judges. Since then, professionalism has become the A.B.A. party line; lawyer professionalism has a national office, a logo, a motto, its own journal (called *The Professional Lawyer*), and a budget.

---

11. Some feminist theologians are not so willing to accept reorientation. Jean Myers argues, for example, that radical theories of feminist liberation (such as the claim that feminist theology cannot be Jewish or Christian) would deprive women of their heritage, including the understanding they have from their mothers and grandmothers of what suffering by women means. Jesus, Myers says, was killed because he refused to give up his relationships.

From the mixed metaphor of its title through a series of reforms that lawyers are admonished to undertake, individually and collectively, the Stanley Report compounds etiquette with homilies on obedience to law, complaints about judicial decisions that keep lawyers from fixing prices, and parental advice to law schools. All of this is related to what the Report calls professionalism. It is all related to a set of propositions that say:

—to individual lawyers, that the way to be a good person and a lawyer is (i) to be professional and (ii) to be *in* the profession, to be *of* it; and

—to associations of lawyers (local bar associations, law firms, legal departments in companies, law faculties) that the way to be schools of virtue for their members is to strive to be a profession.

The Stanley Report and the judicial address that provoked it also seem to be tacit appeals for the resuscitation of the American lawyer-gentleman. I infer those appeals from the perception that the Stanley Report, like any set of moral admonitions—from Socrates to John Rawls—rests on a culture and a story. The appeal to "principles of professionalism" that have been moved away from, made first by the Chief Justice, then by members of the Commission, and finally in the bureaucratic apparatus maintained by the A.B.A., is not an exception and, because it invokes a culture and a story, its argument is more specific than it appears to be.

The inference I propose here is that the appeal in this case (and in contemporary and similar admonitions in medicine, dentistry, journalism, advertising, and business management) gets its plausibility from a particular, remembered vision of community; from a particular, remembered moral order; from a particular, remembered (and unidentified) moral leadership; and from a particular (and unidentified) personal prominence and power. It depends on an image the Chief Justice, the Commission, and the Association have of the lawyer titans who have ruled America since the Revolution and whose power has seemed, beginning with Watergate, to slip away. It depends on the gentleman, on keeping him around or, if he is gone (and I don't think he is), on getting him back again.

The A.B.A. campaign would be useful for discussions of legal ethics, and more persuasive as public relations, if it acknowledged the dependence. The reason it does not is that no one in the A.B.A. seems to know how to fit the gentleman into our notions about equality. The gentleman's ethic, in and out of the legal profession, has always implied and often said that gentlemen are superior people. If the A.B.A. were to admit that what it is appropriating is the gentleman's ethic, it would find itself involved in a latter-day defense of elitism—of a superiority the American lawyer-gentleman has always taken for granted —and that does not seem just now to be a promising posture for maintaining or regaining the prominence of lawyers in American society.

The difficulty is deeper than a problem with *theories* of equality and of virtue, because the gentleman-lawyer is not a theory; he is a substantive figure, and he really is an aristocrat. The A.B.A. can attempt to use him to sell its (new) ethic of professionalism—and, in my reading of the Stanley Report, that is what it does—but it cannot fashion him to its own purposes; it cannot deny him the reasons behind his assumption of superiority, or (as it tries to do) hide his assumption of superiority behind the claim that its new professionalism does not offend egalitarian values as much as the old aristocracy does.

The moral worthy whom the Stanley Report claims it wants to place before American lawyers is not a superior person; he is merely an expert. The A.B.A wants to appropriate our deep cultural affection for the gentleman-lawyer and apply it to "the professional," who is not the same sort of moral figure at all. More exactly, the Commission's tactic is to move the moral issue from superiority to expertise and then claim that it has avoided the problem of elitism. Its ideal lawyer is not a gentleman; he or she is a *specialist* in the administration of justice. One problem with this move is that it does not resolve the issue of elitism; its system of specialists is a hierarchy, as much as the gentleman's system was. A second problem with the A.B.A.'s move from the ethics of the gentleman-lawyer to what it calls the ethics of professionalism is its false claim that professionalism has the gentleman's pedigree. But professionalism is not in continuity with the gentleman's ethic; professionalism as an ethical argument is novel—and it is a sort of idolatry:

(a) *The New Class.* Lionel Trilling noticed what others call the new hierarchy more than a generation ago, in C. P. Snow's description of Snow's "new men" of post-war British technology—academic scientists who had worked for the government during World War II, "men who, by their talents, have risen from the lower classes." In the world of the new men, "differences of social origin are modified by the attitudes of the scientific group," Trilling said. Class was replaced by hierarchies of expertise. "Thus, all the physicists, no matter what their social origin, are at one in their alienation from the engineers, whom they regard as of a lower social order." Trilling's perception was that the new system replaced the old: The government's need for the valuable knowledge of the new men brought a different class structure.

The new hierarchy of expertise has, since Snow's post-war novel was published, become familiar if not obvious in professional life. All of us who are paid to work on questions that we think cannot be understood by those who pay us know about it. We have hierarchies of experts in our institutions that are like the physicists and engineers Trilling noticed: lawyers, paralegals, and secretaries; attending physicians, residents, nurses, orderlies; the tenured, the untenured, the adjunct, the instructors and teaching assistants.

When Trilling's observation is moved to a profession (that is, to experts who serve clients), there appears another hierarchy, within (or under) the hierarchy of the "new men"—the hierarchy of professional over client. That hierarchy depends on access to power. Those who practice in both hierarchies are not only the "new men" of Snow's description; they are also the "new class" that Robert E. Rodes, Jr. (following Milovan Djilas) fits into the Marxist theory of class struggle.

But the morals of professionalism that are used both to justify and to explain these hierarchies are not, as Trilling might have expected, the morals of the displaced class system. The morals of expertise are different; they are not continuous with the class-based morals of the gentleman. And they were in place, in Britain and North America, well before World War II. Durkheim described this new thing in morals as a "market morality" and located it in the Industrial Revolution. Michael Schudson, following Durkheim, located the lawyers' part of it in legal service to the post-Civil-War robber barons and the journalists' part to the late nineteenth-century newspaper barons. The new class is not the moral equivalent of the old class. The morals of professionalism have been around a long time, and the gentleman has fought them all the way.

The gentleman admitted his class-based status and sought to justify it either with *noblesse oblige* (care for others as the price of status) or opportunity for service (status as a circumstance that indicated service and made service possible). Professionalism does not admit that its excuse for holding power is as much a claim of superiority as the gentleman's was. If it notices that professional systems are hierarchies, it claims that professional hierarchies depend on expertise rather than on status, and are therefore not systems of privilege. It claims instead to be objective. Objectivity is the definitive virtue for the ethics of professionalism; it is, for example, the way the Stanley Report can distinguish the acquisitive American business person from the lawyer who is paid, out of what the business person acquires, to preserve and protect the enterprise that does the acquiring. The claim is not that the lawyer is a morally superior person; it is that the lawyer is a professional who is objective and the business person is neither a professional nor objective. (The Report in this way visits its moral disapproval on lawyers who behave as if they were in business.)

Objectivity is the "virtue" that keeps professionalism from admitting its elitism. Objectivity as a principle teaches professionals to disengage themselves from their clients. The professional gentleman always resisted such disengagement. As I endeavored to show in the last chapter, he dealt with people in a hierarchy through his practice of the virtue of discrimination. He took account of each person, and he treated each person in a way that was personal and appropriate to who that person was. The practice of the virtue of discrimination needed to be tempered by the practice of virtues such as prudence (practical wisdom) and humility; otherwise discrimination led to hubris. But, when discrimination was tempered by the other virtues, its practice occurred in and seemed to depend on a class structure.

The gentleman would say that objectivity is a false virtue because it teaches a lawyer to treat *no one* personally; it denies the significance of the personal in the world of work. It supports the tendency in all professions in the West to separate those toward the top of the hierarchy from their clients (patients), and to train those toward the bottom of the hierarchy to treat clients in an impersonal way. The false virtue of objectivity divides people according to categories defined by expertise, and then bids the experts to treat not people or communities of people but parts of people: throats, hearts, and psyches; investments, businesses, and—not families or marriages, but—contracts.

In one of his "psychological reflections," Jung said, of a similar tendency in medicine, that we must see "whether we cannot learn something from the medical philosophers of a remote past when body and soul had not yet been torn asunder and handed over to separate faculties." Lewis Thomas, reflecting on his father's generation of family doctors, said that the essence of medicine then was a "uniquely subtle, personal relationship" between doctor and patient that "has roots that go back to the beginnings of medicine's history." He said it requires "the best of doctors, the best of friends," that the word "medicine" and the word "modesty" have the same root. The management of specialization, the understanding that it is as much a way to divide and conquer clients as it is a shelter for the power experts have over us, seems to have come to the medical profession rather sooner than it has come to the legal—but it is clear enough, in both places, to have become an issue for professional ethics. The movement for professionalization is one side of that issue.

It is important that ethics in general not surrender to that side. It is important that the new hierarchies of professional practice, and the dismemberment of people and communities to fit categories of expertise, remain subject to general moral analysis. The obstacle to general moral analysis is the claim that only those who are admitted to the profession's mysteries can judge those who practice them, and therefore the ethics of professionalism is, as the ethics of honor once was, not subject to standards either of culture or of reason: Professionals operate outside the boundaries of ordinary morality. That claim of immunity is the other problem with professionalism. It is . . .

(b) *A Sort of Idolatry*. The ethic of professionalism divides the client and in that way attempts to evade ordinary moral responsibility. It also divides the professional person, and that becomes a sort of idolatry.

Judge Sharswood said, in 1854, "The good opinion and confidence of the members of the same profession, like the King's name or the field of battle, is . . . the title of legitimacy." Several years later, Silas Lapham's wife Persis told him, "You have made paint your god." Silas, who was only a businessman (Lapham Paint Company) and who did not claim to be a professional, had the good sense to worry about what Persis said. I cannot tell that Judge Sharswood, who was a clubbable chief justice and law dean, worried about making professional honor his god. I suppose not; he and his generation of lawyers felt more firmly than ours does that only God is god. Even so, our ethical inheritance would have been richer if the judge had given as much consideration to the warning as Silas Lapham did.

If the suggestion of idolatry seems ridiculous to lawyers, we ought to reflect on how deeply the claim that we create our own legitimacy has affected our rules for practice. It may be that professionalism is not so much idolatry as just an instance of the false virtue of honor, an ethical mistake of more modest depth, but, if that is so, the mistake has nonetheless been serious, maybe even as serious as idolatry would have been. Consider, for example, what we American lawyers have done with our version of what Durkheim called market morality, our adversary ethic—how we have proclaimed it, for a century, as an ethic that allows lawyers to refuse to be accountable to those they harm, to the community, and to their clients. Reflect on how our consensus statements on the moral practice of law purport to give us a license to lie, to cheat, and to abuse, if only we are *professional* when we do it.[12]

* * * * *

Finally, there is no connection between the gentleman-lawyer's ethic and the new ethic of professionalism. The

12. Those are complaints about our ethics, our official or collective moral reasoning: I have never seen persuasive evidence that American lawyers are faithful to the adversary ethic. My argument on professionalism is also an argument about ethics: I don't expect to see persuasive evidence that American lawyers make professionalism their god as much as their ethic invites them to.

Stanley Report seems to me to argue that the gentleman's ethic can be an ethic of professionalism. It wants, I think, to keep the gentleman, give him a new name, and identify him as a democratic professional. But professionalism has no such pedigree. The gentleman lawyer is not responsible for professionalism. He did not cause it, except in the sense that the A.B.A.'s neglect of the gentleman's ethic, as it prepared and promulgated its codes in the 1960s and 1970s, and the Stanley Commission's attempting to keep the word gentleman out of sight, probably, in some way, led to a current, popular focus on the professional expertise as an ethical category. The American gentleman-lawyer of our stories—Auchincloss's Henry Knox, say, or Faulkner's Gavin Stevens, or Howells's Eustace Atherton—would be the first to object to the morals of professionalism. He would say that professionalism does not promote integrity—it prevents it. Professionalism as manifested in the adversary ethic of the American legal profession requires a setting aside of the lawyer's self, as much as the false virtue of objectivity requires a setting aside of the client's self.

Professionalism, the old-fashioned doctor or lawyer would say, cannot truthfully be justified in terms of service; it is at war with the sort of service that gives us the wise counselors of our stories: "The personality of the patient demands the personality of the doctor," Jung said. Professionalism will not survive the gentleman's insistence that he has to be (as Atticus Finch put it) the same person in town and at home. The gentleman-lawyer, if we manage to keep him in view truthfully, will not buy into professionalism. The source of the professional idol, if it is an idol, has not been the gentleman's ethic, but neglect of the gentleman's ethic.

We turn now to charges against the gentleman's ethic that are as grave as these and harder to meet: its abuse of power, its distorted view of tragedy, and its inability to endure suffering.

CHAPTER FOUR

Power, Tragedy, and Suffering in the Gentleman's Community

> A gentleman accepts the responsibility of his actions and bears the burden of their consequences, even when he did not himself instigate them but only acquiesced to them, didn't say No though he knew he should.
>
> William Faulkner

Power: "Dont Stop"

William Faulkner's "civil rights" novel, *Intruder in the Dust*, is a deep, complex mystery story about a gentleman-lawyer's use of power. Gavin Stevens is Faulkner's lawyer in this story and several others. Gavin's client in *Intruder* is Lucas Beauchamp, a black man held in the county jail, accused of murdering a white man. Lucas in his trouble sends for Gavin; Lucas's defense is that he did not do the deed. Gavin does not believe the denial and does not listen to Lucas. Gavin is wrong not to listen, wrong not to hope that the community will listen. He does not live up to what being a gentleman requires of a lawyer. He does not give the other his due (which is what the virtue of justice would require); he does not wait for the other (which is what the virtue of civility

would require); he does not, with the other, seek to col-
laborate for good (which is what the virtue of friendship
would require).

Gavin is nonetheless a gentleman. The reason for his
lapse in this case is that the other is a powerless black
person and Gavin is a white person whose first reaction
is not to wait for his black client but instead to use the
power he has as a gentleman and a lawyer. The power
Gavin has is white, racist power. Gavin does not, of
course, think of himself as an oppressive racist: He tells
himself that he is protecting the weak. He said later that
he tended to protect the weak who weren't even weak.

What marks Gavin as a gentleman in his use of such
power in such a community is that complicity became
and remained an issue for him. The story Faulkner tells is
the story of what Gavin does about his complicity—what
he thinks he is able to do, which is finally to help Lucas
be heard; and what he accepts responsibility for not doing, which is to help his community listen to the truth.
Telling the truth in the community is the direction of his
action; his method, as he points himself in that direction,
is his integrity. His integrity lies in his ability to be of a
piece, to be who he is, and in his practice of what Stanley
Hauerwas has called the virtue of constancy, the virtue
of being able to be who he is.

Gavin is also, finally, able to practice the virtue of tolerance (waiting for the other). Tolerance points him in
the right direction; being pointed in the right direction
is the meaning of the word "repentance." His tolerance
and his repentance are the products of his listening—
not, at first, to his client, but to a boy, Chick Mallison, his
nephew, and a brave old woman, Miss Habersham. Miss
Habersham makes Faulkner's argument that the culture of
the South would teach its children, black and white, the
courage and truthfulness needed to overcome racism.
Southern gentleman-lawyer stories demonstrate moral
substance and bravery through women, sometimes old

women such as Miss Habersham, or Mrs. Dubose, who teaches courage to the children of Atticus Finch.

Gavin, at the beginning, ignored Lucas's denial and planned to use a plea of guilty and then to invoke aristocratic white patronage available from Lucas's mother's associations as a servant for white families. Lucas would have gone to jail but he would have been saved from the electric chair. Chick and Miss Habersham changed Gavin's mind about Lucas's innocence when they took Gavin through a harrowing and suspenseful adventure. The three of them dug up graves and raced down country roads at night; they faced the lynch mob at the jail; they explained the evidence that had seemed to point to Lucas Beauchamp's guilt. Gavin not only changed his mind, but he came to understand that complicity in his community's evil is what gave him a mind that had to be changed.

The story shows how a gentleman learns to notice his participation in oppressive uses of power and then to repent, and that he knows how to repent because his culture knows how and has taught him what it knows. Because he can repent—can turn and then go on in the right direction—the gentleman can tell the truth and, when the gentleman is a lawyer, can get out of his client's way, so that his client can tell the truth. When, in such a story, the gentleman is a lawyer, he has a license to use power he has not been given; he has the opportunity to be a prophet—to remind his community of what it already knows about repentance.

However, American gentleman-lawyer stories do not often end in the repentance of the community. Neither do the stories of the Hebrew prophets. The use of power in the community remains oppressive, and the community's explanation for its evil remains self-deceptive. The theme of the southern gentleman-lawyer stories on this point is that, when the lawyer is not able to bring his community to repentance, he retains optimism that other gentlemen may be able to do it. The theme is an attempt at hope.[1] Faulkner provided it with clipped, man-to-boy, patriarchical indirection:

> "It's all right to be righteous," his uncle said. "Maybe you were right and they were wrong. Just dont stop."
>
> "Dont stop what?" he said.
>
> "Even bragging and boasting is all right too," his uncle said. "Just dont stop."
>
> "Dont stop what?" he said again. But he knew what now; he said:
>
> "Aint it about time you stopped being a Tenderfoot scout too?"
>
> "This is not Tenderfoot," his uncle said. "This is the third degree. What do you call it?—"
>
> "Eagle scout," he said.
>
> "Eagle Scout," his uncle said. "Tenderfoot is, Dont accept. Eagle scout is, Dont stop. You see? No, that's wrong. Dont bother to see. Dont even bother not to forget it. Just dont stop."

What Gavin finally does, and teaches Chick to do, both because Gavin is a gentleman and because he is a lawyer and has a license to use power he has not been given, is to tell the truth, and help his client tell the truth in his community. That does not mean the community will listen; it is persistently able to be indifferent, especially to what it already knows and values.

Gavin, the gentleman, does not claim to know anything the community does not already know. The gentleman stands out among others only because he is not able to be indifferent: He does not let himself stop. If he is less self-deceived than his neighbors, it is only by a little. He is distinctive only because he is not as able as they are to be irresponsible. He is able—a bit more than they are—to respond. That means two things: First, he has been

---

1. It is not hope, though—but only an attempt, as I try to show in the third part of this chapter: Faulkner was optimistic; Dr. King was hopeful. The difference has to do with suffering.

trained, in the community, in virtues of truthfulness and
tolerance; he has the good habits that let him listen even
to a black man, a boy, and an old woman. Second, once
he has listened, he can risk telling the truth because the
community has trained him in the virtues of courage and
constancy. Gavin repents and finally listens to and tells
the truth; he affirms the values his community taught
him. He reminds his community of those values and
teaches them to his nephew.

Intruder in the Dust is at first a story more of repentance than of witness. It shows how a gentleman comes
to see that his community's manner, its customs, and its
delusions protect it from seeing the truth of its evil, and
have protected him in the same way. The intellectual maturity that Gavin shows to Chick, after the mystery is
solved and the gentleman-lawyer is pointed in the right
direction by the boy and the old woman, is that learning
in repentance is a matter of looking at the community
from a point of view provided by describing the values
the community believes, teaches, and hides from.

To this point, the boy has been the teacher. After this
point, the boy's time as a student begins. The lesson the
boy learns from his uncle is that integrity means a gentleman knows where his morals come from. The morals
he argues for (and that make it possible for him to argue)
come from his community. He cannot avoid the community's evil use of power by fleeing from the community,
because flight will take him away from the resources he
has to have to cope with evil uses of power. Chick needs
to learn the virtue of constancy. He has to repent for his
failure to understand, first, that formation in the virtues
necessary for uses of power is something that happens at
home, in his town; and then that it is a painful lesson for
those who are willing to learn it.[2] Chick, who tried to

---

2. My friend Stanley Hauerwas has noticed that this way of describing the gentleman's ethic seems to leave no possibility of exit—

run away, to leave his neighbors and their evil behind, has failed to be constant, and because of that he has failed to be tolerant.

"They were his own and he wanted no more save to stand with them unalterable and impregnable: one shame if shame must be, one expiation since expiation must surely be but above all one unalterable durable impregnable one: one people one heart one land." Complicity remains the issue, even if (as Faulkner thought) complicity is unavoidable. It remains the issue for Chick the gentleman-in-training as much as for Gavin the gentleman-lawyer. The gentleman copes with his use of institutional power by keeping alive the issue of complicity.[3]

I think this ethical position can be expanded from its narrative setting in the South to a more general description of the gentleman-lawyer's ethic, and that it can be related to theology, to the memory of the church. The dichotomies of moral life, the biblical (and Augustinian and Lutheran) distinction between the world and the Kingdom of God, do not separate forces in a Manichean cosmos. The dichotomies are within; they are in each of us. There are not here, in this corner of the cosmological struggle, the righteous; and there, in that corner, the

---

of flight from complicity in evil. I think Hauerwas is right about that; but I also think that I am right about Faulkner's and Harper Lee's understanding of the gentleman's ethic: There *is* no exit. Even when gentlemen leave they take the community's moral culture with them, complicity and all. If that is so, of course, the corrupted culture either has to have a way to overcome its evil or the gentleman, in staying put, will be corrupted by it. If the latter alternative is correct, Hauerwas's question leads to an objection to the lawyer-gentleman's ethic: It is a prison. If the former alternative is correct, my argument on power assumes either that *any* culture can save itself or that there is a reliable way—a reliable epistemology, as the philosophers say—to keep the culture on course: "Expiation must surely be." This issue is the subject of the last chapter in this book.

3. There remains here a question about whether the gentleman will be able to countenance the harm that will result to the community if the gentleman is effective as a practitioner and an agent of repentance. That is a question I take up in the last part of this chapter.

practitioners of coercive power. The community's moral culture is not a limit on the self; it is *inside* the self.[4]

The gentleman's ethic of power and complicity has a law-office dimension. Lawyers have oppressive power over their clients. If we narrow the complicity-in-oppression argument I mean to make here to a more specifically professional context—a lawyer-client context—the test may be what the lawyer sees when she looks across the desk at her client: Is that other person a threat or a gift? An occasion for learning, the "other" whom one is to wait for, or an intrusive bundle of movements and words? A subject or an aggregation of interests? The specifically professional context for the issue of law-office power is whether a lawyer's work for clients is an occasion for telling the truth or an occasion for the demonstration of power: Gavin Stevens had the power to bargain a plea for Lucas Beauchamp; he set out to do that at first because, in his complicity, he did not see how he could serve a black man by telling the truth. As Gavin saw it, then, Lucas was weak, and Gavin did not value telling the truth enough to risk *not* protecting the weak.

At the end of the story, Lucas Beauchamp comes to Gavin's law office to forgive him for not believing his client; Gavin and Chick see Lucas coming across the street, on his way to the office. Gavin tells his nephew that, because Lucas Beauchamp is a gentleman, he will be able to forgive without mentioning what is forgiven. Gavin knows then, I think, that his client has been a gift; for both of these gentlemen—maybe for all three—as another southern writer (Robert Penn Warren) saw it, "The recognition of complicity is the beginning of innocence."

Tragedy

A Bible story: Saul, King of Israel, was ordered by God to make war on the Amalekites and to put them all to

---

4. This is also a political theology: The gentleman's ethic honors tradition and constancy by arguing that integrity is important not only for virtue's sake but also for the community's sake.

death. Saul made war, and killed as ordered, but he made an exception: He spared Agag, King of the Amalekites. The Lord was displeased; He took the kingdom away from Saul. "Saul was wrong in sparing King Agag," Elie Weisel says in *A Jew Today*. "The Talmud spells it out: whoever shows mercy for the merciless will end up by becoming merciless toward men committed to mercy.... Saul was wrong, but we love him for it, and so does our tradition. We love him because he did not kill, because he dared transgress the command and let the Amalekite king live. Saul fell victim to his own humanism and thus became a tragic hero."

In what sense is Saul a tragic hero? Is it helpful in legal ethics to talk about tragic heroes? Occasions such as the story of Saul and Agag are episodic evidence of how a moral tradition is formed—in this case a moral tradition that values life. (Compare the rabbinical tradition on commands in the Torah that disobedient children and adulterers be stoned to death.) The story shows how a moral tradition is formed, as the story of Abraham and Isaac shows how the Hebrew people, alone among their contemporaries, rejected the practice of human sacrifice. Any culture's morality is worked out in the face of inducements against the direction it is taking. We often refer to an occasion for noticing this as tragic, or we refer to it as presenting a hard case (a case that tests the soundness of the moral direction), but what is really happening is that a morality is being formed, and what we have done, in retelling the story as Elie Weisel does, is to notice an occasion of that development as we might notice one of the rings in a stump. Such occasions do not mean that the moral direction is mistaken, or even that it is being tested; what they mean is that the moral life involves suffering.

The question for the gentleman is whether his ethic equips him to deal in a truthful and courageous way with such occasions—often spoken of as Weisel spoke of Saul's story, as stories of "tragic choice." The story of Saul and the story of Abraham and Isaac are examples from the religious tradition; the stories of Antigone and of Socrates staying in Athens to be killed by the state, when he could have escaped, are examples from the philosophical tradition. *Intruder in the Dust* is a southern-gentleman-lawyer story in which the gentleman learns, when he is young, that gentlemen don't leave home because home is evil: Chick Mallison turned around at the edge of town, when he was on his way to somewhere else, and came back to join his uncle. He was like Saul and Antigone and Socrates. But when a commentator pulls such occasions out of a story and identifies them as choices, and when he then identifies the choices as tragic, he is making two ethical arguments which I propose to be skeptical about.

I prefer to use the word "tragedy," as Hauerwas does, in a more eccentric and tendentious way: Tragedy (not tragic *choice*) is the triumph of meaning over power. The meaning of Saul's story is the saving of life; the power is nothing less than the Ruler of the Universe.[5] The meaning of Chick Mallison's story (and of Socrates's) is constancy; the power is rectitude. The stories are not stories of choice so much as they are stories of formation. They don't so much test the validity of the ethic as they demonstrate how much it costs to be faithful to the ethic. Contemplation of the cost of faithfulness is a way to form the learner in the virtues of truthfulness and courage. Such stories in the gentleman's ethic are not so much about moral principles as they are about how to live with moral principles. The same can be said of Weisel's reading of the story of Saul and Agag.

The gentleman passes through and takes moral direction from episodes of tragedy (in my tendentious use of the word). In his integrity, and rooted in his culture, he

---

5. Jewish theology is an argument with God. Weisel's explanation of the story of Saul is safe in the tradition. Perhaps it is theologically sounder to say that the power that kills the Amalekites is the power that drove Cain to kill Abel, etc., but that would rob Weisel's point of the ironic power that is in an argument with God.

deals with tragedy. That means that he is often not sure that he is right; he practices what Letwin calls the virtue of diffidence. His not being sure is not a failing, though; it is a strength. It comes about because he is virtuous in a world in which the interesting moral lessons are like those in the stories of Saul and Antigone. Sir Thomas More's refusal to take the Oath of Supremacy, when the nobles and bishops of England had taken it, is personal in this way: A gentleman-lawyer displays the moral formation he has taken from his culture. More finally says that what others have taken for eccentricity is the integrity he learned from his persecutors—and from the common law itself. He also says that his culture's ability to teach integrity depends on the exercise of integrity by individuals such as himself, that the statesman who betrays conscience leads his country by a short route to chaos. More's direction was political as well as professional, and professional—legal—as well as personal. He was *not* an autonomous moral hero making lonely choices; the "adamantine sense of self" that Robert Bolt celebrated in his play about More was cultural before it was personal. More, like everybody else, had to learn how to be good.

Learning how to be good is also the center of narratives where the tragedies and crises are intimate and minor and the gentleman is apparently fixed in his habits and attitudes. Tragedy has a domestic dimension. My favorite examples are the young Duke of Omnium, Plantagenet Palliser, in Trollope's story, *The Duke's Children*; and Arthur Brown, the courtly, clubbable academic in two of C. P. Snow's novels, *The Masters* and *The Affair*. The hardest thing for laconic "realist" novelists, such as Trollope, Snow, and William Dean Howells, is to show how a good person changes his mind. The Duke comes, despite his rectitude, to apologize to Madame Max for accusing her of being involved in his daughter's plan to marry unsuitably; and then he comes to accept the unsuitable marriage itself. Arthur Brown comes, despite patriotism and gratitude to the heroes of the war, to see that justice requires support for a cowardly and subversive person who has been wronged. These stories say that the gentleman's moral life is a life of learning (of formation rather than lonely choice), and particularly of learning how to pay the cost that being good exacts. They refute in the clearest way the trite falsehood that a twenty-two-year-old in a university law school is too old to learn morals. The Duke and Professor Brown would say that the law student's problem is that he is still too young.[6]

As Hauerwas puts it: I try, in such learning, to explicate a history "sufficient to give me a sense of self, one which looks not only to my past but points to the future, thereby giving my life a telos and a direction.... My act is not something I cause, as though it were external to me, but is mine because I am able to 'fit' it into my ... story." He would say that of Saul and Socrates and the Duke and Chick Mallison. If the Duke were to notice an ethical lesson in the stressful months of his daughter's courtship and marriage, or if he had to locate a lesson from the story of King Saul, he would say, as Hauerwas does: "Ethics is not primarily about rules and principles, rather it is about how the self must be transformed to see the world truthfully."

But this formation is not radically individual; that is what was behind More's point about the statesman's conscience: No one becomes virtuous alone. We learn in the community what virtue is and how to practice it: We learn as we are part of the community. The Jews do not love life because of Saul's decision to spare the king; they love Saul because he shows them how much Jews love life. If such stories were stories of individualism they would not, as they do, show how these moral heroes re-

---

6. Mary urges here a distinction between the morality in which one is formed and occasions in which a person, already formed, wakes up to his morals. The waking up, she says, is what the Duke and Professor Brown would say the 22-year-old is still too young to do. Maybe he needs his sleep.

spect the direction they seem not to take. Why respect it when its only value would have come from choosing it? *Antigone* is a story of how a Greek family honored its dead, but the Greeks also honored the gods. Saul's story is a story of how much the Jews love life, but the story of the Jews is the story of a love affair with God.[7] These are stories of love of God, rather than (or as well as) stories of refusal to obey. An ethical theory that focuses on tragedy as choice can account for power but it cannot account for love.

It is important, then, not to rest ethical weight on what are called tragic choices or hard cases. The gentleman's ethic tells us that we understand what a good person is because we see that what the good person does fits. We understand what she does in great matters because we have seen or heard about what she does in small matters. Miss Habersham, Atticus, and Gavin are able to be heroic in telling the truth because they have been ordinary in telling the truth. Formation in a community rests on small matters, not great ones. We do not talk about the tragic nature of the moral life when the matter is small; we talk then in trite phrases. We law teachers talk, for example, about how we teach tolerance for ambiguity, which really means tolerance for the way people are, for the reality that people are not interchangeable. People who have learned to wait for each other teach us teachers that the other is different: We say no two *cases* are alike; we mean no two *people* are alike.

Tragedy defined as choice is, then, not a helpful word for looking at the price we pay for our morals. In the tendentious meaning I have borrowed from Hauerwas, tragedy is a useful word because it saves us from having to talk about necessary evil: Evil is not necessary. The

---

7. The stories of Israel and of the Cross are not stories that say everything is going to be all right. They are stories about faithfulness, and faithfulness may require what is sometimes thought of as tragic choice. I pass by that possibility here, but take it up in the final chapter.

question is not whether we have to bear the evil, but whether we can bear the pain that living morally causes—pain to ourselves and pain to others. The first part of that has not been a difficult question for the gentleman-lawyer, who suffers for righteousness's sake and who esteems bravery and endurance. But the second part is different.

Suffering

> Remove from Christianity its ability to shock... and it is altogether destroyed. It then becomes a tiny, superficial thing, capable neither of inflicting deep wounds nor of healing them.
>
> Soren Kierkegaard

The gentleman knows that he must suffer for his principles. Our gentleman-lawyer stories are stories of heroes suffering as the price of virtue, from wounds in battle to being spat upon, to endurance of the privations of hunger and cold as an expression of love, to suffering fools gladly. Some of this is conventional patience, like standing on the bus so that someone else may sit down; some of it is the unselfishness of good manners; some of it is extraordinary courage. Here, too, though, the extraordinary builds on the conventional; both come about because they are expected. The gentleman understands his suffering as a matter of duty and kindness, a consequence of his situation. He has learned, in family, town, and religious congregation, how to live with suffering.

Much of the understanding of suffering in the gentleman-lawyer's ethic is Stoic, but there is a strain in it that is more purely Hebraic, that comes to the gentleman through the religious tradition. That strain looks beyond suffering as the consequence of leading a good life to the religious notion that suffering is a way to overcome evil.

Jews understand the suffering of Israel, for example, as pain endured so that God's kingdom may come, for the sake of all humanity. That is the tradition's understanding of the suffering servant described in the Book of Daniel and in the prophets. Israel is the suffering servant; Jews are the suffering servant: "A thing despised and rejected of men, a man of sorrows and familiar with suffering, a man to make people screen their faces ... like a lamb that is led to the slaughterhouse ... through him what the Lord wishes will be done" (Isaiah 53:3, 9–10). Christians appropriated the poetry and the image of the prophet and applied them to Jesus, the Lamb of God, whose way of dealing with evil was to tell the truth and to suffer violence rather than to be violent. Jesus even said the suffering servant was subordinate: "For who is greater: the one at table or the one who serves? The one at table, surely? Yet here am I among you as one who serves" (Luke 22:27).

Which brings me to the last and most intractable objection to the gentleman's legal ethic: It does not know how to account for the suffering of others. If suffering is understood as suffering *by* the gentleman-lawyer, either as the conventional price of the virtuous life or as the means of overcoming evil, the gentleman's ethic takes suffering into account and makes sense of it. Its grandest moments have to do with gentlemen who suffer: Andrew Hamilton, John Adams, and James Edwin Horton are examples of American lawyer-heroes whose stories teach the lesson, as Atticus Finch and Gavin Stevens teach it in American lawyer fiction. Hamilton came out of comfortable retirement to the risk of defending Peter Zenger's defiance of colonial government. Adams endured Boston's violent, popular disapproval in order to provide legal counsel to the British soldiers who fired on the crowd in the Boston Massacre. Horton, the "good judge" of the Scottsboro cases, risked his judicial career—and lost it, as he knew he would—when he granted a motion for a new trial in the prosecution of Haywood Patterson.

Fiat justicia ruat coelum,[8] he said. Atticus and Miss
Habersham and Gavin Stevens stood outside the jail and
held off the lynch mobs. Our stories tell us that the
gentleman-lawyer repents for injustice (the argument of
the first part of this chapter), and that he suffers for
justice.

The gentleman-lawyer's ethic fails, though, when the
consequence of sound morals is that *others* suffer. Consider Thomas Furnival, barrister, defense counsel in *R.* v.
Mason, in Trollope's *Orley Farm*, and compare him with
Lady Mason's neighbor and friend Mrs. Orme, who was
neither a gentleman nor a lawyer. Lady Mason was accused of perjury. She was guilty and Furnival knew she
was guilty; she had forged her husband's signature on a
will so that her son (her husband's second son) would
inherit some of his father's wealth. Furnival found a way
to defend her, as lawyers do; and he won—she was
acquitted.[9]

Furnival, as we say, got Lady Mason off; but he could
not find a way to help Lady Mason to peace in her guilt
or to reconciliation with her family and her community.
She was finally rejected even by the son she sought to
protect; he could not bear that his mother was a forger,
even an acquitted forger, even a forger who got his
wealth for him, even a woman who did for her child
what the biblical matriarch Rebecca did for hers. The
reason Furnival could not serve his client *in* her community, rather than *against* it, was that he could not bear
the suffering she would invite when she told the truth.
She did not need to tell the truth in court; he could manage her silence there: He abused truthful witnesses, scandalized a young colleague, and contributed to cynicism

---

8. Let justice be done though the heavens fall.

9. The way his gentleman-lawyer's ethic allowed him to serve the
guilty and to frustrate British justice scandalized Trollope, who compared the gentleman-lawyer's ethic to that of an Irish bandit. Henry
Drinker (see chapter one), in a preface to the 1950s edition of *Orley
Farm*, said Trollope did not understand lawyers.

in and about his profession; he pretended he thought
Lady Mason innocent when he knew that she was guilty.
Lady Mason was acquitted because Furnival was, in those
ways, an effective advocate, but the meaning of the story
is that her lawyer did her no good at all.

Lady Mason's comforter was Mrs. Orme, whose skills
were the skills of a truthful friend. Mrs. Orme was not
clever; her advice to Lady Mason was to tell the truth.
Lady Mason finally did tell the truth, after her lawyers
had left the scene, and, of course, she suffered. At the
end of the story she left England, alone, acquitted at law
but rejected in the community. England's lawyers were
adept at deliverance but they had no skills for reconciliation. British justice could find Lady Mason not guilty
when she was guilty, but it could not restore Lady Mason
to her family and her neighbors.

It is a fair reading of the story that Lady Mason wanted
to tell the truth all along, but that she had no counselor
or advocate who knew how to help her do it. She needed
a brother or sister who would wait for her, but her lawyers treated her less as a person to be waited for than as
a set of interests. By their lights they protected her, but
only as much as their professional job descriptions provided for. They had to pretend to themselves that that
sort of professional protection was what their client
wanted and needed. Furnival finally supposed his licensed function was the most important thing he could
do, the most important thing to be done in the case, not
because he thought of his function narrowly but because
he thought his function was the way to save his client
from suffering.

Part of that mistake was hubris. Furnival at first
thought he had the power to restore his client to her
community: "Mr. Furnival did think that he might induce
a jury to acquit her. . . . [He] seemed to feel that it would
suffice for him if he could so bring it about that her
other friends should think her innocent." He was so
wrong about that as to have been out of touch with real-

ity—not a good situation for a lawyer, but a situation one expects to find, sooner or later, among those who wield power and seek, in wielding power, to protect the weak. (It is, I think, the delusion that Dr. Martin Luther King, in his ministry to virtuous southern white gentlemen, straightened out. In protecting black people, white gentlemen were protecting the weak who were not weak.)

Another part of Furnival's mistake in the *Mason* case was that his gentleman-lawyer's ethic sought to make things come out right, without suffering. Trollope's contemporary, John Henry Newman, warned gentlemen that their gentlemanly optimism was too fragile to be useful in a moral life. He warned them about "the greatness and littleness of man, his far-reaching aims, his short duration, the curtain hung over his futurity, the disappointments of life, the defeat of good, the success of evil, physical pain, mental anguish, the prevalence and intensity of sin, the pervading idolatries, the corruptions, the dreary hopeless irreligion, that condition of the whole race, so fearfully yet exactly described in the Apostle's words, 'having no hope and without God in the world'—all this is a vision to dizzy and appall; and inflicts upon the mind the sense of a profound mystery, which is absolutely beyond human solution."

To rely on the gentleman's ethic, in such a world, was, Newman said, to moor your vessel with a silken thread and to quarry your granite with a razor. The English gentleman's ethic was connected to his Christianity, but, Newman said, the gentleman had become merely optimistic ("muscular," Disraeli said) where the faithful Jew or Christian was hopeful: Hope is optimism that is truthful. It rejoices in the truth. When it comes to the gentleman's ethic, the virtue of hope can come to terms with and deal truthfully with the certainty that the moral life will cause others to suffer. Hope, which says that the Ruler of the Universe is in charge, that fate is finally benign, also says that the harm that may come to others is not an argument against taking a moral direction. It was hope that caused Mrs. Orme to advise Lady Mason to tell the truth, as it was mere optimism that led Thomas Furnival to use his lawyer's skill to keep her from telling the truth. That is where the gentleman's sense of responsibility for what happens—confidence in his own ability, optimism born of his view that a person chooses what happens to him—works against his ethic: He wants too much for things to come out right.

Gentlemen-lawyers come to think of themselves as specialists in the prevention of pain and to define what they do for their clients in those terms. That subverts the substance and the purpose of the virtues in the practice of law. Furnival subverted the substance and the purpose of the virtues in the life of Lady Mason. The Attorney General, Sir Abraham, in another of Trollope's novels, *The Warden*, attempted to subvert the purposes of his virtuous client, Septimus Harding, because Sir Abraham, like Furnival, thought he could protect his client from the truth:

Mr. Harding was a clergyman and the manager of an endowed rest home for poor old men. The rest home got more money than it needed; clerical trade unionism had for generations used professional power to create and preserve legal rules under which the surplus was paid to the clergyman in charge. The surplus could have been paid to the residents of the home, who had nothing. It took time and a bit of prodding, but Mr. Harding, a truthful man and a Christian professional who did not suppose that he could make things come out right, came to believe that he was receiving money that should have been given to the poor, and to see as well that he had to say so. He decided that he would do what he could to get the income for the poor, and, if he could not get the income paid to the poor, he would resign.

The immediate price of Mr. Harding's rectitude was suffering by the person Mr. Harding loved most. He was a widower, the sole support of an adult daughter, and most of his income was from his position at the rest home:

"God bless me!" Sir Abraham said to him. "Why, Mr. Harding, how do you mean to live? . . . Have you not a daughter,—an unmarried daughter? . . . Surely . . . you should be prudent on her behalf. She is young, and does not know the meaning of living on an income of a hundred and fifty pounds a year. On her account give up this idea. Believe me, it is sheer Quixotism." Mr. Harding said that it would be better for him and his daughter to beg than to take money from the poor.

There was another price, a price Mr. Harding's colleagues in the clergy would have to pay. The church's abuse of endowments was, just then, a popular political issue, one that received attention in the press and in Parliament. Mr. Harding was a communal man; his community was in the cathedral close in Barchester; he was a precentor in the cathedral; the bishop was his closest friend; the archdeacon was another of his sons-in-law. The consequences to his friends and, as the archdeacon put it, his "order," were the first thing Mr. Harding thought of: "He knew well how strongly he would be supported . . . if he could bring himself to put his cause into the archdeacon's hands and to allow him to fight the battle; but he knew also that he would find no sympathy there for his doubts, no friendly feeling, no inward comfort. [The archdeacon] would be ready enough to take up his cudgel against all comers on behalf of the church militant, but he would do so on the distasteful ground of the church's infallibility. Such a contest would give no comfort to Mr. Harding's doubts. He was not so anxious to prove himself right, as to be so."

The Attorney General, a gentleman-lawyer like Thomas Furnival, saw interests where an ordinary English Christian would have seen a person—an unusual person in this case (but, then, the point of mentioning the person is that every person is unusual). Sir Abraham had determined and arranged things so that Mr. Harding's income would be upheld; the payment of the income to Mr. Harding was, through the lawyer's efforts, now legally safe. A good lawyer had seen well to his client's interests. When the client nonetheless proposed to surrender what the lawyer had made safe for him, the lawyer thought the client was addled: "There is no further ground for any question ... nobody now questions its justness. ... A man is never the best judge of his own position." None of that legal advice had any effect; Sir Abraham referred his client to the ministry of non-lawyer relatives.

The gentleman-lawyer comes to think that he is able to control even such ultimate events as the discovery of his own identity in his community, and the identity, in the community, of those he serves. Thus Gavin Stevens centered his professionalism in the Beauchamp case in the benevolent racism of patronage; he thought he could use white gentlemen's power to save his black client's life. He was not even interested in finding out who his black client *was*. Thus Atticus Finch lied to protect the reclusive Boo Radley from facing the community, and left him to hide and to be hidden from it. Thus Dr. Thorne, in another of Trollope's novels, protected the orphaned Mary Thorne from meeting the drunken Sir Roger Scatcherd, and from learning the painful fact that Sir Roger was her uncle. Thus Thomas Furnival, barrister, saved Lady Mason from the pain and the promise of being reconciled to her neighbors. Thus the Attorney General of England thought it was insane for a Christian gentleman to risk his daughter's welfare and his colleagues' prosperity by refusing to take money from the poor.

This view of the suffering of others is in all of the gentleman-lawyer stories. Protection of the weak who are not weak turns out to be near the heart of the gentleman-lawyer's ethic. Newman's observation that the gentleman cannot bear to *inflict* pain becomes an ethic that says the gentleman-lawyer has to *prevent* pain. He cannot do that, of course, and so he hides from what he cannot do in the delusions of his optimism. These delusions corrupt his ethic by turning it from an ethic of the virtues to an ethic of honor and shame. His dependence on the approval of other gentlemen obscures the *telos*, the goal and purpose of the good life, on which an ethic of virtue rests. The goal and purpose of a virtuous life is to become a good person; the goal and purpose of a virtuous life in a profession is to help others become good persons—friendship, collaboration in the good.

Shirley Letwin's celebration of the Victorian gentleman does not take seriously enough this flaw in the gentleman's understanding of his own integrity. I suspect that is because she does not relate the gentleman's rendition of his religion to his esteem for honor and his horror of shame. She does not seem to see that the ethic of Trollope's gentlemen could not come to terms with the fact that the moral life brings harm to other people. Religion would have taught the gentleman that as it could have taught him not to depend in his ethic on the approval of other gentlemen.

Ancient Judaism thus faithfully preserved the stories of the suffering children of Israel in Egypt. Christians who reflect on their crucified Lord must know that much of his suffering was in the knowledge that his followers would suffer because of what he had done. There is no honor in Gethsemane, as C. S. Lewis put it. But biblical suffering is not prominent in the Christian gentleman's religion. "Most of our caste in this country, if they only knew it," said Galsworthy's English gentleman, Winifred Desert, "are Confucian rather than Christian. Belief in ancestors, and tradition, respect for parents, honesty, moderation of conduct, kind treatment of animals and dependents, absence of self-obtrusion, and stoicism in face of pain and death" are their ethic.

I have argued, so far in this book, that the gentleman's ethic is the ethic that modern American lawyers have not to choose. They have it as their anthropology. But I have also argued that it contains within itself both the cultural endurance and the coherence to come to terms with the objections that it is elitist, racist, and sexist; that it is in complicity with abuses of power; that it is unable to endure tragedy; and that it is not able to understand that the gentleman must suffer for his goodness. But I cannot locate a way to say that the ethic of the gentleman-lawyer comes to terms with the suffering that the moral life brings to others.

The gentleman's ethic is remarkably healthy, though— as a matter of anthropology. It turns up in television programs—one mostly about young lawyers in Los Angeles; one mostly about young physicians in inner-city Boston; one mostly about police officers. It turns up in our cowboy stories, our sailor stories, our soldier stories, and our feminist stories. (I think, on this last example, of Jane Austen and George Eliot.) It looks down on us from the portraits on the walls of our schools, our hospitals, and our courthouses. It turns up in law-school classrooms; my students, by and large, love the gentleman and seek to imitate him. I try, in the interest of ethical analysis, and almost always fail, to persuade them that Atticus Finch made moral mistakes. The students will not stand for it. They confront the fact that Atticus is a man with a patriarchical ethic by saying that ladies can be gentlemen too.

We probe the fibers of the gentleman-lawyer's ethic and find Aristotle—not a bad mentor. We test the ethic and find that it is not essentially dependent on class or status or wealth or breeding, and that its *noblesse oblige* is not of the usual sort. The ethic of the gentleman-lawyer withstands tragedy and the pain that personal courage necessarily demands. But, finally, the gentleman cannot account for the pain that is beyond the reach of his integrity: Suffering is an acceptable price when it is paid for his own physical courage and for his confronting of evil, but it is too great a price when the gentleman must endure or even require it of those he proposes to protect.

I bring myself to this point and find that I lament the fact that we cannot invent an ethic, or fashion one from an inventory of useful ideas. If this issue were an issue for the shop, I would find somebody to make me a gentleman's ethic that would survive this last difficulty. But we do not choose our morals; the best we can hope to do is to describe them, as we describe ourselves. Approaching the gentleman-lawyer's ethic in this cultural way, I think we could say that the gentleman's ethic, like his English culture, went wrong when it turned its religious inheritance into what Dietrich Bonhoeffer called crossless Christianity.[10] Once that happened, the English Christian community that had produced saints and martyrs was remembered untruthfully. It became an elite community that preserved itself in the false virtue of honor as it dissipated the teleological nature of its virtues. In England, and then in North America, it began by protecting the weak who were not weak and it ended with apologies for racism and economic injustice, for (in Miss Manners's phrase) exploiting the serfs and marrying for money.

You cannot select a professional ethic as you would decide on a husband or a place to live or a church to go to. A professional ethic is mostly something you have, something that you can choose only in a sense, and not even then unless you describe it carefully before you choose or seem to choose. We North American professionals cannot excise Robert E. Lee or Lewis Thomas's father or Leland McKenzie from our lives; they are what we have been and what we are. We can be false to them, as we are often, in our professionalism, false to ourselves and to our clients. We can pretend to forget the gentleman, but he will not go away.

* * * * *

The gentleman-lawyer's ethic is a communal ethic. It is an ethic for a lawyer in her community. It is the dominant ethic in the legal profession in North America,

---

10. This passes by, for the present, the deeper question of how a person in the religious tradition looks at the life of being a lawyer. I take that up in the final chapter.

as durable at least as our enduring affection for British lawyers, for turning moral questions into legal questions, or for turning legal questions into questions about autonomy.

But the ethic of the gentleman is not the only communal ethic at work in the lives and practices of lawyers. Many lawyers in North America met the gentleman (or at any rate met the possibility that he had an ethic) as they came into the profession, when they were carrying another communal ethic with them. Mary and I turn now to those lawyers, in two ways: First as users of power who stood (and who stand) at the line that divides one moral culture from another; and then as members of a different moral culture.

CHAPTER FIVE

Between the Gentleman's Community and the Other Community*

In one sense he is the salt of humanity with his tremendous energy and ambition. But being salt, he gives humanity high blood pressure. He's neither a real Jew nor a real Gentile. He has no roots in any group. He digs all the time in other people's soil, but he never reaches any roots. He tries consciously and subconsciously to wipe out the individuality of nations and cultures. Like those who built the Tower of Babel, he often tries to transmute the whole world into one style. He often preaches a sort of liberalism which is false and is the opposite of liberal. The worst thing about the assimilationist is that he has no pride.... He always wants to be where he is not wanted.

The idea of roots is not to deny anything. You have to make the best of your origin and your upbringing. You did not grow up in a vacuum.... there isn't such a thing as 'just a human being.'

Isaac Bashevis Singer

* Chapters Five, Six, and Seven are written in collaboration with my daughter, Mary M. Shaffer. She holds degrees from the University of Virginia and the Johns Hopkins University: she studied and taught in Italy for three years before her graduate studies and now lives in Paris with her husband Bernard Seytre.

The United States, more than most nation-states, has a history of confrontations between one culture and another, and of law as a means of ending cultural confrontations. Again and again in America, the gentleman-lawyer's Anglo-Saxon Protestant culture has dealt with an alien culture and, as the story is usually told, overcome it. The gentleman-lawyer has used the law to bring the vulnerable culture into conformity to what we have referred to as "the American way."

This has been true where the vulnerable culture came here—as was the case of the African slaves and of the European immigrants who came to farm the Midwest and to tend the machinery of the industrial Northeast. It has been true when the dominant culture was the invader, as was the case all over the continent when our European ancestors settled in territories populated by native Americans—from the commercial adventurers of the Southeast, to the Pilgrims in Massachusetts Bay, to the Conquistadores among the Navajo, to Father Junipero Serra among the Indians of California, to my pioneer ancestors among the Arapaho of central Wyoming.

Coercion administered by white Protestant gentlemen-lawyers is the usual means of domination, more than overt force, in all of these cases; American cultural domination has been turned over to lawyers more often than it has been turned over to soldiers. In most cases lawyers have served the function soldiers would have: The professional mission was conquest; law was force used by the gentleman's culture, and lawyers were the legions of the law. If the dominant society has sometimes shown mercy to the conquered, the result in the American case—unlike that of the Romans in Palestine or Joshua in Canaan—is that the law has dealt with the individual, not with the conquered culture. Our jurisprudence became "liberal"; it came to speak in terms of individual rights—rights not of a culture or a people, but rights of individuals who are considered one at a time, and dealt with in terms defined by the individualistic law and morals of democratic liberal political theory. That was true of the nation-state's treatment of the Mormon culture that found biblical warrant for the practice of polygamy in the nineteenth century; it has been true, so far, of Indian tribes that use hallucinogens in religious ritual; it was true a few years ago of a Jewish military chaplain who wanted to wear a yarmulke under his military hat.

American law thus deals with vulnerable cultures in terms of the rights of individuals. It ignores or at least bypasses cultures by focusing on the individual as if he were the cause of his own culture. But the law's narrow focus on rights does not dispose of cultures. As Colonel Purdy learned in *Teahouse of the August Moon*, the law's pretending that cultures are absent does not make them absent. Judge Learned Hand, for example, wrote some of the opinions for the federal court of appeals in a series of cases involving a clause in the immigration statute that says an immigrant applying for citizenship is required to demonstrate that he has "good moral character." Such cases raise the cultural question of what character means and often involve a confrontation between two cultures. They have involved evidence of mercy killing, of living with a person of the opposite sex without benefit of marriage, of visits to prostitutes, and, in one case, an applicant who had married his niece—a practice that was not considered immoral in his immigrant culture but was immoral so far as the gentlemen-lawyers in the federal justice department were concerned.

These situations were typically situations in which law expressed the gentleman's moral judgment: Marriage to a niece, for example, was illegal and invalid, as much as a polygamous Mormon marriage would have been. The issue was not whether the law allowed what the immigrant had done; it was what good moral character means. The federal judges in those cases were not willing to ignore the law; but they were not always willing to reason that violation of the law demonstrated bad moral character. There were at least three other ways available. One was to consult public opinion. Judge Hand declined to do that; he thought it wasn't judicial. A second method, one suggested to him by a law-review editor, would have been to claim universal validity, "immutable objective morality," for the judgment of American culture (expressed, e.g., in the law of marriage); Hand did not discuss that, but there was warrant for it in the precedents. The third method would have spoken of an individual's "right" to his cultural view of marriage—saying, in effect, that such a marriage is not allowed but a person has a "right" to believe privately that it should be. Character requirements cannot intrude into that privacy, as, in a recent decision of the Supreme Court of Virginia, character requirements for admission to the Bar could not intrude into the privacy of an applicant who was living with her boyfriend.

Judge Hand can be read to have taken the third alternative. Gentlemen-lawyers who were persuaded by theories of liberal individualism agreed with him. He can also be read to have taken the vulnerable immigrant *culture* into account in deciding what good moral character meant. (That is, a person who acts within the morals of his culture has good moral character.) Hand was relatively calm in such cases—he usually ordered the government to grant citizenship—perhaps because he saw himself, a lawyer and a judge, standing between two cultures and having to deal with the morals of each, rather than as a dispenser of rights to individuals. The possibility suggests a notion of the lawyer, not as an agent of conquest, nor as a guardian of security from the vulnerable culture, but as a legal professional who uses power to reconcile cultures.

A rather different example here is the group of black civil-rights lawyers who gathered in the 1930s and 1940s around Dean Charles Hamilton Houston: Thurgood Marshall, Spottswood Robinson, William Hastie, James W. Nabrit, Jr., Robert L. Carter, Oliver W. Hill. They were the architects of a stunning change in American constitu-

tional law. It took years of wary, wily, patient lawyers'
work, in scores of cases. It was an argument over three
decades, and it was an argument between the gentleman-
lawyer's culture and African-American culture. We law
teachers talk of it as a matter of rights, but it was at its
deepest not that at all. It was argued in terms of rights
because that was the category laid down by the liberal
gentlemen-lawyers on the federal supreme court.

But this movement, from the *Gaines* case in 1938[1]
through the last of the education cases in the 1970s, was
an argument not for individual rights but for participation in America by a culture of oppressed American people. That is why integrated education was critical in
Dean Houston's view. The law's task, as he saw it, was to
reconcile two cultures: It would not have been enough to
confer rights on the individual black person. Neither
Houston nor the great prophet of the movement, Dr. Martin Luther King, Jr., argued from Hobbes and Rousseau;
Dr. King argued from the Bible and from the music of the
black church; black people in America are, like biblical
Israel, a people, he said.[2]

* * * * *

Let me see if I can pose my proposition with a couple
of anecdotes. I am a descendant of pioneer women and
cowboys. I am the only male in three generations in my
family who is not a cowboy (and my wife sometimes

---

1. *Gaines* involved racial segregation in the law school at the University of Missouri. The state of Missouri proposed to pay Mr. Gaines's
expenses at a school outside Missouri.

2. Like Moses, Dr. King said to the gentleman's culture: "Let my
people go." One of Dean Houston's black lawyers, who went on to
become a federal judge, said, "The purpose was to bend the law to
the needs of blacks." Richard Kluger says that Dean Houston believed
that "a law case was a splendid opportunity to lead and teach the
black population in whatever community the case arose." Houston
was so earnest in this that he had at first preferred to avoid the federal courts and argue his cases before local judges and juries—*i.e.,* to
argue them as confrontations between cultures rather than as matters
of federal constitutional right.

wonders about me); all four of my grandparents and six of my great-grandparents homesteaded in Montana, Wyoming, and Colorado. My maternal grandfather was one of the first sheriffs of Hot Springs County, Wyoming. As far as I can tell, he was the first who was earnest about bringing law and order to Thermopolis, a little cow town that, in those days, had more saloons than it had churches. Both sides of my family were Baptist settlers; they went to churches, not to saloons; they sank roots and tried to make a living from raising the gentle, durable little Hereford cattle that British investors imported into the Mountain West at about the time my ancestors settled there.

The Herefords shared the mountains and prairies with native wild life; the cows and the settlers learned to adapt their immigrant culture to the creatures who were there first. Jim Burden's grandmother, in Willa Cather's *My Antonia*, decided to put up with the badger in her garden in Nebraska, even though, as she put it, "He takes a chicken once in a while, but I won't let the men harm him. In a new country a body feels friendly to the animals. I like to have him come out and watch me when I'm at work." But the settlers also took what God had provided for them in nature: They killed the animals they needed for food, when they needed food. I can remember going for two weeks with our neighbor, who had a summer pasture high in the mountains: We took some flour, sugar, baking powder, and bags of potatoes and apples, but no meat. The first thing we did when we got to the summer camp with our pack horses was to kill a deer—out of season.

We had, even as late as my childhood in Western Colorado, a settled, white-man's, frontier culture. The gentleman's culture came to it, though, much as the Pilgrims had come to Massachusetts, and there were confrontations. Game and fish laws are an example. With those laws came peace officers who had the power to arrest a cowboy who killed a deer for his summer food—out of season, or without a license, or when he was not wearing the prescribed clothing, or all three.

In his autobiography, Farrington R. Carpenter tells of coming in 1912 from the Harvard Law School to practice law in the town of Hayden, in Routt County, Colorado. Hayden is a cow town, still under 2,000 in population, on the road from Steamboat Springs to Craig, not far from where I grew up. The first thing Carpenter says he noticed in Hayden, an event that had a lot to do with his learning to practice law there, was a confrontation between the gentleman's culture and the frontier culture. The gentleman who came to town was a game warden named Hobson. He came from Eastern Colorado, settled in a bit, and obtained from Denver official credentials that empowered him to enforce the game and fish laws. Officer Hobson arrested a rancher named Matt Gates, at Gates's ranch, on the charge of having there killed three sage chickens, out of season.

"News of this arrest spread like wildfire and aroused great indignation all over the county," Mr. Carpenter said. "Many of the inhabitants felt they had a constitutional right[3] to shoot sage chickens any time they wanted to on their own land, for their needs. A committee of the most prominent citizens... tried to persuade James C. Gentry, the District Attorney, to dismiss the case. When Mr. Gentry refused, they came back predicting that he would be overwhelmingly defeated at the next election.

"On the day the case was called in the... log cabin courthouse, the room was crowded with concerned spectators.... Officer Hobson took the stand, and Mr. Gentry had him tell what he had seen the accused do. Finally, Gentry asked him, 'Are you sure it was sage chickens that were killed?'

"'Yes,' answered the witness, 'I took possession of them as evidence, and placed them in a gunny sack

---

3. I doubt that they put it that way. Mr. Carpenter had been to law school in New England.

in the vault of the Courthouse. They are here with me today.'

" 'Show them to the jury,' demanded Mr. Gentry in a stentorian voice. The witness carefully emptied the sack in front of the jury.

"Three dead owls fell out.

"Hobson turned plaintively to the Judge and said, 'Your Honor, someone has played a joke on me'.... Against a background of feet shuffling on the floor, the Judge beckoned the Sheriff and ordered him to escort the witness out of the courtroom.

"The Sheriff took Hobson out the back door and he was never seen again in Routt County."

Mr. Carpenter leaves us to our own conclusions as to how the dead owls got into the gunny sack. I think we are free to guess that the District Attorney knew the answer. He was a lawyer standing between cultures. Maybe he manipulated the evidence a bit, as Faulkner's Gavin Stevens, Mississippi county attorney, did in a similar case.[4]

The other anecdote comes from Utica, New York. In the first few years of this century—a decade before Farrington Carpenter went from Cambridge to Hayden to practice law—there was in Utica, as in many American cities, a community of immigrants from Southern Italy. There were a couple of Italian-language newspapers published there, both of which carried items of local interest for those who could read Italian or knew someone who would read it to them. One was called *L'Avvenire*; the other was *La Luce*. There is a series of stories in those papers about an immigrant who stood between the two cultures in Utica—a man named Nick Camelo.

Nick Camelo was, functionally, as much a lawyer as Mr. Gentry in Hayden or Mr. Stevens in Jefferson, Mississippi—although he was not educated or licensed to be

---

4. I have in mind the episode in *The Town,* in which bootleg whiskey is found in Montgomery Ward Snopes's back-alley picture room, with the consequence that M. W. is sent to the state penitentiary instead of federal prison.

a lawyer. He first appears in the news in 1900, when he was elected secretary of a company that manufactured liqueurs. He appears again in 1902 when he was nominated by both police and fire commissioners to be *speciale polisie [poliziotto] della città Utica*, a representative to these agencies, apparently, from the Italian community. The writer for *L'Avvenire* said the commissioners could not have chosen a better person "than this fine young man who willingly lends himself for the good of all."

The same paper reported the next year that Camelo had managed to get one Michele Lombardi out of prison. Lombardi was unjustly sentenced, *L'Avvenire* said, by a judge in Greene, New York, on a charge of third-degree assault. He was accused, as the newspaper reported it, of *aggressione*. "Young and valiant Nick Camelo," the newspaper said, was able to obtain an annulment of the sentence and Lombardi's liberation from prison. *La Luce* reported the same story and added the fact that it had cost Mr. Camelo two hundred dollars—the paper did not say to whom the money was paid or where Mr. Camelo got it. He was functioning as a lawyer, in the gentleman-lawyer's system, but possibly with the methods and values of the other culture.

In 1904, *L'Avvenire* reported that Mr. Camelo had defended an Italian immigrant who was stopped on the street, taken to prison, and fined fifty dollars. This person was unable to pay the fine and had been in prison fifty-nine days before Mr. Camelo learned about him. Mr. Camelo had, by this time, apparently left the liqueur business and was operating as a notary public and banking and steamship agent for families who sought to bring relatives to this country from Italy. He was also working as an interpreter in the city court, the paper said.

Mr. Camelo was asked to run for alderman in Utica in 1905; he declined, but he said he would continue to listen to his people.

* * * * *

We want now to look more closely at the situation displayed in these stories from Hayden and from Utica, to look at the lawyer as he stood in these stories between the gentleman's culture and the other, vulnerable culture. We suggest that such a figure has two ways of using legal power to deal between cultures—ways that are different in their effect on both cultures. One way is to conform the other culture to the gentleman's culture: That is the way of *assimilation.*[5] The other way is to protect the other culture and, as the lawyer manages to locate openings in the law and politics of the time, to manipulate the gentleman's culture into coming to terms with it. That is the way of *preservation.*

In America, both methods have resulted in substantial freedom for the individual in the other culture, but the freedom that has resulted from assimilation has been a freedom expressed in theories of rights, and therefore a freedom that belongs to the individual without regard to her culture. She is, in one way of putting it, free to notice and adhere to her culture or to abandon it. If her culture is in some way preserved in her, or through her, it is not because the culture has value but because she has rights.

The freedom that results from the preservation of culture is different ethically and politically: If the other culture is preserved rather than assimilated, it is usually because the gentleman's culture accords it value and—to use a word the Italian immigrants used—respect. That means the gentleman's culture has rendered itself vulner-

---

5. The *Oxford English Dictionary* gives five definitions of assimilation: (1) the state of being like, of similarity, resemblance; (2) the action of becoming conformed; (3) the acknowledgment of likening; (4) "conversion into a similar substance," which is physiological but also metaphorical, as in Burke's reference to "the sentiments which beautify and soften private society"; and (5) the change of bodily fluids after death, into "the nature of morbific matter" (pathology), another usage that has metaphorical promise for our argument.

able: It has put itself in a position to learn from the other culture. It is in danger of change as a result of what it learns.[6]

Two Models: Cotillo

About a decade after Nick Camelo told the gentlemen of Utica that he would prefer not to be an alderman, but would continue to listen to his people, Salvatore A. Cotillo functioned as a licensed lawyer in Little Italy, in Harlem. Justice Cotillo's family emigrated from Naples in 1892, when Salvatore was six years old. He went to school in New York. He earned a law degree from Fordham in 1911 and was admitted to the New York Bar in 1912. He would later be the first Italian American to serve in either house of the New York legislature (he served in both), and the first to sit on the bench of the New York Supreme Court. But in the days when he was acting as Nick Camelo had in Utica, he was a lawyer practicing in the street in front of his father's gelato and pastry shop on East 116th Street.

He was a scrivener for his clients, most of whom could not read or write in either language. "He was ... required to translate intimately personal letters, business papers and legal documents," Nat Joseph Ferber, his biographer, says. "Neighbors and friends sought his aid in the preparation of applications for various licenses, or petitions on behalf of their relatives who wished to emigrate to the United States. Justice Cotillo served an apprenticeship in human problems. ... " He was the only lawyer in the neighborhood; Ferber says there were forty or fifty Italian-American lawyers working there thirty years later.

Justice Cotillo, like Nick Camelo, advised and represented his clients as they faced the world outside their Italian neighborhood. "Many problems were personal; but some had a community aspect and Cotillo was exhil-

---

6. The civil rights movement's partial success is the most prominent modern American example.

arated by the challenge they offered to find a solution. . . .
An earnest group of the more frequent callers regarded
him as their leader in planning for the realization of a
better life for their immigrant neighbors."

One way to put the comparison of assimilation and
preservation is to ask a question about this "better life," a
question also about what *L'Avvenire* meant when it said
Nick Camelo, although he had been *speciale polisie*, declined nomination for alderman and said he would continue to listen to his people. These lawyers interpreted
one community to the other. When they were willing to
mute or even renounce the power they had to serve the
conquerors, they interpreted the other community of
Italians to the culture of gentlemen-lawyers. Camelo and
Cotillo in this way interpreted the Protestant and Irish-
Catholic, English-speaking communities of Utica and New
York City to the vulnerable Calabrian and Sicilian communities Southern Italians formed in the United States
when they came here, ninety years ago, looking for work.
And they interpreted the Calabrians and Sicilians to the
gentlemen-lawyers of New York.

There is probably a hope, when lawyers interpret as
these lawyers did, that they or their descendants can
achieve a cultural synthesis, that they can *mix* the cultures, rather than help them work together. There is a
hope that the need for interpretation will disappear, because the differences between the cultures will disappear. That was the hope of Dean Houston in the
integration cases; when the focus was immigration rather
than the badges of slavery, it was the romantic American
dream of the melting pot. American lawyers who dealt
with the immigrants no doubt often did what they did
because they thought of themselves as guardians of the
melting pot. Arthur Miller's Italian-American lawyer, Mr.
Alfieri, in *A View from the Bridge*, was a guardian of the
melting pot. Marco, the illegal Italian immigrant who
had, as we say, taken the law into his own hands, said to
Mr. Alfieri, "All the law is not in a book." "Yes," Mr. Alfi-

eri said. "In a book. There is no other law." Mr. Alfieri
was an assimilator, and it was important to him that
Marco know who wrote the assimilator's book. Marco
had to be conquered; his Italian culture had to become
irrelevant. Mr. Alfieri was the servant, not of Marco's culture, but of Marco's rights.

I pass by this melting-pot possibility for moral reasons.
The melting pot is an assimilationist prospect; it means
what Officer Hobson meant when he arrested Matt Gates
at the Gates ranch near Hayden—not that the game laws
would adjust to ranchers (they never have) but that
ranchers would stop shooting sage chickens out of season. The melting pot is not a desirable possibility; it
never was. It was a comfort to Anglo-Saxon conscience,
but it did not honestly hope for a synthesis of cultures in
America.

"Melting pot" meant, to Italians who came here at the
time Nick Camelo and Justice Cotillo did, that they
would melt into the republican society Thomas Jefferson
and Benjamin Franklin described: God's New Israel. President Reagan invoked the melting pot when he said, as he
left office, that America is the keeper of the miracle.
There is no trace of Italy in such a miracle—no trace of
Latin America or Africa or China, either. The first Italian
immigrants to America compared what they found here
with what they brought with them; from that point of
view, the melting pot that had evolved here in 1900,
from this Jeffersonian vision, was dishonest, crude, materialistic, and frantic. Most of the Italians, and the lawyers
who sought to preserve Italian culture in America, were
not interested in being melted into that pot.

Two Models: Mariano

The principal example we will use of the lawyer as *assimilator* is John Horace Mariano,[7] an Italian immigrant,

---

7. Dr. Mariano was a psychologist, sociologist, divorce lawyer, and
a sometime academic. He died in 1959, at the age of 81, after a long

American lawyer, and sociologist, who published, in 1925, a book called *The Italian Immigrant and Our Courts*. He was somewhat more successful in his work— or at any rate somewhat more persuasive—than Game Warden Hobson was in Routt County. The example we are using of the lawyer as *preserver* is Salvatore Cotillo, immigrant lawyer, Tammany Hall politician, and Italian-American leader.

The Mariano and Cotillo vantage points on Italian immigrants confronting American law were substantially identical: They were contemporaries; both were in New York City. The immigrant families they addressed were in cohesive Italian-American communities; the families they spoke of were families of Italian-speaking immigrant parents and American-born children who reached adulthood as World War I ended. Both Cotillo and Mariano lived and wrote in contemplation of extensive, pervasive prejudice against Italians, and in the last years of open immigration, just before Congress closed the door on Italians in 1924. Ferber describes the prejudice: "The . . . olive-skinned, dark-eyed children of Europe's southland were a markedly alien breed. . . . Their hands were generally gnarled and stained by grime and soil, hands which fashioned objects, large and small. They performed the heaviest work, burrowing underground in tunnels, erecting sky-piercing, ornate structures, providing healthful sanitation for the many while themselves living under conditions too 'reprehensible' for their so-called betters to contemplate."

(a) *Assimilation.* Dr. Mariano generalized the legal situation of these families as one in which (1) American-

---

and eminent career in all four disciplines. Two of his books were on psychological problems in marriage; he was counsel for the New York State Psychological Association, for the United Transit Association, and for unions in cases involving the Busch Jewelry Company and its affiliates. He had his education (B.A., LL.B., and Ph.D.) from Columbia, and was a member of the New York Bar. His books, for present purposes, include *The Italian Immigrant and Our Courts* (1925) and *The Italian Contribution to American Democracy* (1921, 1975).

born Italian children met the law as delinquents, despite the fact that their parents were law-abiding people; and (2) Italian families did not turn to the law for protection, for planning, or for rights. In one direction, the social problem Dr. Mariano sought to describe was deviance— too much involvement with the law. In the other direction the problem as he saw it was too little involvement: Individual Italians failed to use American law when they might have used it to ease their adjustment to their new country. His cure, for both problems, was assimilation.

He said the first generation of Italian Americans born here were afflicted with a disease. The disease was that they were neither Italians nor Americans. He called them "Americans of Italian extraction." Evidence of the disease was that too many members of this generation were defendants in criminal and juvenile courts. Dr. Mariano's cure was not to form children in the law-abiding culture of their parents, but to keep them from being Italians.

He demonstrated that Italian immigrants were law-abiding people. For example, they were rarely in trouble because of alcohol. Alcohol (wine and cordials) is, to Italians, food, he said, "Abuses of it are rarely encountered." He was vociferous in defense of Italian immigrants who were said to be unreliable witnesses (and parties) in court. He reacted with umbrage to suggestions by leaders of the American and New York bar associations that Italian-American lawyers and law students would lack the sophistication to carry on the institutions and traditions of American law.

But, he argued, the children of these people should not be taught to be Italians. "The American of Italian extraction has been born here, passed through our schools and knows little, and appreciates less, of whatever is Italian or pertains to Italian culture." This child of immigrants was not an American, either, but he should have been. The schools through which he passed had not done for him what school did for Americans whose families had been in this country longer. The schools failed, but, still, the solution was assimilation, and that meant it was the *families*, not the schools, that had to be reformed.

"A corps of trained and experienced investigators ought to be kept constantly at work on this problem, seeking the causes in the different [Italian] homes," he said. For example, it may be that Italian children did not realize the importance of curbing self-expression when it is "tabooed by our man-made [read made by gentlemen-lawyers] laws." Therefore, the cure was to "Americanize" the homes in which the children were growing up; they would learn appropriate reticence from reformed Italian mothers who, he seemed to think, would be like those in Louisa May Alcott stories.

Deeper evidence from the lives of those Dr. Mariano was talking about is quizzical—representing, more than anything else, the fact that Italian Americans of the first generation born in America were ambivalent about being Italians. It was not so much (as Dr. Mariano thought) that these children were in neither culture as it was that they were in both. Helen Barolini's novel *Umbertina* (1979) describes this painful, hybrid identity through three generations of Italian-American women. Miss Barolini also edited an anthology of memoirs of Italian-American women, *The Dream Book*, which gives biographical accounts of the situation of Italian-American women. One of these women, Fran Claro, says that the troubles she felt as an Italian American were the troubles of her mother (a first-generation-born Italian American). Miss Claro's mother was a person who tried too hard to make herself into an American. She created frustration for her children and for herself. Fran Claro's story indicates that Dr. Mariano was wrong about reforming Italian homes in America, or, at any rate, that he failed to count the cost.

Miss Claro's mother cherished stories of Anglo-Saxon American girls, as the teenagers in *Umbertina* learned about America at the Saturday matinees: She escaped from her Italian world by reading. *Rebecca of Sunnybrook Farm* became her favorite book. For long hours—

after she finished helping her mother with the younger
children and the sewing homework—she would sit and
read. Her heroines were fair-skinned, blonde, blue-eyed.
She could not identify with them, but their world in-
trigued her. She wanted to absorb the culture of these
American heroines. Because her parents were not educated (in American culture), she grew up listening to
Italian soap operas and being entertained at street festivals. She rebelled against this gaudy, flashy brand of entertainment. As she grew into adulthood, her childhood
dreams of American respectability grew into a determination to separate her children from a culture she had
learned to despise. She would not allow her children to
get involved with any of the activities which were dear
to her parents' hearts. Their culture, she believed, was
not one to pass on to a new generation.

(b) *Preservation.* Similar evidence, as to both generations, is available in the lives of other early Italian-
American lawyers. But there is more evidence in those
lives of opposite convictions, of the desire to be Italian in
America, rather than Americans of Italian extraction. Ferber's biography of Justice Cotillo paints the picture of a
young lawyer, legislator, and judge attached to and representative of American-born Italians, and much more at
one with them in a cohesive Italian culture in Harlem's
Little Italy than Dr. Mariano allowed or hoped for.

The immigrants and young Italian-Americans of Justice
Cotillo's early practice were more often victims of American society (and sometimes of their Italian neighbors)
than rebels against it. Ferber says,

> Cotillo's activities in the courts [in his first year as a law-
> yer] more than ever convinced him that the body politic
> was too often responsible for the ills of his neighbors.
> Italian Americans intent on honest employment, even if
> only at the pushcarts, were told they must pay illicit trib-
> ute to get permits. Others seeking berths in the munici-
> pal street-cleaning department were asked to pledge

themselves to pay weeks and months of their earnings when appointed. Recreation pier concessions were paid for. So, too, were even permits for bootblacks and newsstands. Each had its price. The exploiters, in the main, came from among their own. This racket system preyed on the fears and ignorance of the poor. The victims poured their troubles into the ears of Frank Cotillo.

"Certainly," Frank Cotillo said to his son, "these people ask little enough. They are eager to do the humblest work, by no means in competition with *your Americans* [emphasis added], and they are asked to pay bribes. Is it any wonder that they resist Americanization?" His biographer says: "Young Cotillo set aside several hours of each day and almost all of the evenings to take up the problems of his father's friends. Above all, he learned, they were puzzled. They could not understand why in this land, where freedom was presumed to await them, they should be denied the right to work. Some were subdued, broken by this interference with their making a livelihood. Others, recalcitrant, called down anathema on the heads of the politicians, officeholders and the commonwealth itself." A few no doubt dealt with their persecutors as Miller's Marco dealt with his: All the law is not in a book.

(c) *The Law*. Dr. Mariano's view of the immigrant generation was that they could not be Americanized, and therefore had to be endured. Meanwhile Italians had to learn to trust the gentleman-lawyer's legal institutions. Dr. Mariano recognized that these immigrants saved from their meager wages toward ownership of their homes and small businesses; he saw that they needed legal services to protect them as they did so. (He said the *contadini* were mistaken in their preference for urban life. More of them should be, as they had been in the Mezzogiorno and in Sicily, farmers.) He argued that the Italian immigrants needed to be taught to trust other American institutions as well —courts, banks, land brokers. They would

have to turn to these institutions, he thought, if they
were to own farms, businesses, and homes.

The older generation of Italians in America, Dr. Mariano said, suffered from "indifference to our method of
righting wrongs." The immigrant's thoughts about American law "need guidance or they will soon lapse from
mere indifference into contempt and disdain." The Italian
immigrant "needs to be shown that the measure of justice [is] ... what the public opinion of the community demands.... He should not be allowed to drift into racial
communities, forming habits of thot [sic] and ways of
thinking that are limited and warped." The fact that the
immigrants were law-abiding and respected legal authority should have made it easy for assimilators "to help
them adopt an attitude of mind toward our courts, both
proper and sane." That this did not work out to be so
easy after all was, he said, due to Italian habits of secre-
tiveness in business and family matters; but that, too,
would yield to reform. Of course, he said, "the training
period for the Italian... should be longer than it prop-
erly is for others who have no such traditional background to overcome."

Dr. Mariano's argument for reforming Italian families
resembled Leonard Covello's more famous 1967 study of
Italian-American school children, those in the first generation born in America. "It is necessary to take into account the adverse influence of the Italian family mores
upon the process of formal school education. The problem... would seem to suggest a need to modify Italian
family mores—an undertaking which is tantamount to
cultural modification... a substitution of American patterns for old-world patterns."

Italian-Americans, when they did get into criminal
trouble, Dr. Mariano said, tended to commit crimes of violence rather than crimes of stealth. Often, he said, as
Miller's Mr. Alfieri would have, such incidents occurred
because Italians had an emotional and pressing sense of
injustice and applied the law that was not written in

books. For such cases, they had to be taught restraint, and patience for the bureaucratic, mundane operation of American law enforcement and American courts. "It may be said without fear of contradiction that the Italian is a peaceful, law-abiding, thrifty and home-loving citizen," he said (speaking of the immigrants, again, not of their American-born children). Italians had only to learn that justice can still be justice without "long and impassioned oration" and the absence of uniforms, and can be justice despite the presence of protracted laconic arguments over the admission of evidence, "great importance ... attributed to the taking of the oath ... the brusqueness of the court attendants ... but little show and no seeming authority ... [and] an entire absence of atmosphere befitting a place where judgments deciding rights, duties, and obligations ... are permanently passed upon."

The lawyers who would preside over the change in these immigrant Italian attitudes would not be Italians. The lawyers Dr. Mariano talked about were Anglo-Saxon gentlemen. Italians who were qualified as lawyers in Italy, before emigration, could not function in this country as lawyers, and few Italian immigrants were able to undertake and complete law study here. Dr. Mariano mentioned this obstacle to the preparation of Italian-American lawyers; he also mentioned "cultural difficulties," but he did not mention money, although money was undoubtedly a factor, along with the fact that most of the immigrants he referred to were Southern Italian peasants—illiterate, wary of institutions, often without training in useful trades, and pervasively discriminated against in America. In any case, there were virtually no Italian-speaking lawyers in the immigrant generation.

(d) *Power.* Salvatore A. Cotillo saw the confrontation of immigrant and American law more in terms of power and less in terms of the excellence of American institutions—and he spoke far less of the Italians coming to terms with (as Dr. Mariano put it) "our" courts and much more in the language of Southern Italian peasant

wisdom: The barrier was language, Justice Cotillo said—
language not as a carrier of culture but as a handle on
power. Once that handle was seized, Italians would be
capable of seeing to their own social welfare. The per-
centage of illiteracy, he said, was about the same on the
Mayflower as it was in Harlem's Little Italy when he went
to law school, but the Pilgrims were illiterate in English:
As far as power in America was concerned, even literacy
in Italian was illiteracy. Beyond language, Justice Cotillo
appears to have had in mind, as relevant to Italian-
American politics, the bitter history of the peasant village
in Southern Italy and the fact that the political power of
the village and of its old way, *la via vecchia*, in the extended family, was its ability to draw into itself and survive—literally and culturally—the corrupting force of
powerful outsiders.

Justice Cotillo did not emphasize being American. He
emphasized voting:

> Become citizens. You will then have the right to take part
> in the government. This is a system of self-government.
> You Italians, more than others, should understand...
> [that] so long as you leave it to others you will be op-
> pressed by these others.... The longer you remain inar-
> ticulate and inactive, by so much longer will you be
> looked upon as not merely alien in blood and tempera-
> ment, but in thought and moral philosophy. You will be
> looked upon as outlaws. Do not delay, for the longer you
> are held in low esteem, so much the longer will it require
> to establish yourselves as worthy citizens in the eyes of
> those who today look down on you.

(e) *Italian-American Lawyers.* Whether the American
legal system was as benign and nurturing as Dr. Mariano
said, or as power-driven as Justice Cotillo expected it to
be, the first generation of American-born Italian-American
lawyers should have been in a position to mediate between the gentleman's legal culture they learned about

in law school and the other culture that was their own.[8] Dr. Mariano thought Italian distrust of American law got in the way of what Italian-American lawyers were able to do. Italians often let their legal rights go unvindicated "for fear of falling into the hands of unscrupulous attorneys," he said, because "in the past . . . the illiterate were easy prey for the unscrupulous fellow Italians." He does not mention—as other descriptions of this immigrant society often do—the possibility that the Italian-American lawyer, who had gone out from the community to study English common law, in English, with Anglo-Saxon, Protestant Americans, was seen as a threat to the old way, *la via vecchia*, and distrusted for that reason—not because he was either simple-minded or a swindler, but because he proposed the corruption of Italian family culture, *l'ordine della famiglia*.

Fiorello LaGuardia is an example. Many—in some elections more than half—of the Italian Americans in New York City voted for LaGuardia's opponents. His personal life (he had married a non-Italian who was not a Catholic) and his political program threatened *la via vecchia*; it did not matter enough that he was an Italian American. Ethnic loyalty was not what was at stake; the preservation of culture was at stake. The possibilities Dr. Mariano neglected were that Americanizers were distrusted and lawyers, Italian or not, were seen as Americanizers.

Dr. Mariano says another reason Southern Italians and their children did not go to Italian-American lawyers was that they did not like to give personal information to any-

---

8. There were Italian-American lawyers in the generation that grew up in America in the 1920s. In his 1925 book, Dr. Mariano counted 300 Italian-American law students in New York City and estimated that ten years earlier there had been as few as 50. The Italian population of New York City was 750,000 when he wrote and there were not "even one thousand lawyers of Italian parentage" in the city. One of our helpers said that when he grew up in an Italian neighborhood in Brooklyn in the 1950s, Italian Americans went to Jewish lawyers.

body they knew, and did not trust professional assur-
ances of confidentiality. He may have been closer to the
real reason when he hinted that the immigrants and their
children did not believe, as he did, that the Italian-
speaking lawyer was "a power for untold good among his
people ... the one person who by training and by experience is best fitted to interpret his people to others ...
their best *public* interpreter." Our suggestion is that an
Italian-American lawyer had to demonstrate that he was
not an assimilator. (In a cultural sense, maybe he had to
demonstrate that he was a *paesano*[9] and not a gentleman.) He had the burden of proof, and he sometimes
failed to meet it to the satisfaction of the wary Southern
Italians Dr. Mariano wanted him to assimilate.

Dr. Mariano had hope for the future, hope for Italian-
American lawyers as they became more numerous and
experienced. But the hope he had was for an assimilated
Italian citizenry—assimilated in significant part by the
efforts of gentlemen-lawyers (who by then would include
lawyers "of Italian extraction"). These lawyers would
themselves come from assimilated Italian families, he
said, "along the same lines as ... among the members of
other racial groups ... who are older here in point of
time." They would teach their Italian neighbor that "the
laws of this land are made for his good ... and that there
is usually sound reason for many of the laws and prohibi-
tions that face the bewildered newcomer." Dr. Mariano
said the task of the Italian-American lawyer was the task
"of Americanizing the Italian," teaching him to esteem
the Stars and Stripes rather than "the Flag of the House of
Savoy" (as if the Calabrian *contadini* cared a fig for the
flag of the House of Savoy). This change in flags would
give Italian Americans an understanding of spiritual and
economic opportunity in America, and a common lan-

---

9. A person from the same place (*paese*). This is an Italian-
American word; we discuss it and its cultural setting in the next
chapter.

guage, Mariano said, developing among Italians "American nationalism in times of peace as well as in times of war... patriotism and loyalty to American tradition... the elimination of race hatreds... an American standard of living... [and] the full and free emancipation of the Italian woman."

Justice Cotillo as a Preserver

Salvatore A. Cotillo's life as a young lawyer in Harlem's Little Italy was more clearly an Italian experience than the life of the Americanized Italian gentleman-lawyer as Dr. Mariano visualized it. In many ways what Justice Cotillo did for his clients in Little Italy was what their parish priests would have done for them, had their parish priests been Italians. He was a legal counselor and much more in his neighborhood, but he was also, in those years, attorney for the Bank of Naples and Consul General in New York City for the government of Italy. During World War I, when he was within the first five years of his practice, he lived in Italy and there represented the American Bureau of Public Information.

He was not Americanized, but Justice Cotillo exhibited the professional rectitude Dr. Mariano hoped for in the new generation of American-born lawyers "of Italian extraction." For example, there were unscrupulous Italians in the Cotillos' neighborhood—notably bankers, steamshipticket sellers, and thugs. One of these, Giosue Gallucci, met American law with bribery and violence. He boasted that he could "fix" things with the police and gain advantage through force and intimidation where Cotillo sought advantage, then and later, through compromise and political competence. Ferber says,

> Gallucci boasted that murder could be bought and paid
> for. Stories were circulated that he caused witnesses to
> disappear, that an unwanted wife could be loaded upon a
> boat, given some money, and shanghaied back to "the old

country." Gallucci was arrested for carrying concealed weapons, and Cotillo was asked to testify on his behalf as a character witness. He refused, making palpable the breach between himself and the district's underworld. After Cotillo was admitted to the Bar, he refused, despite the tender of attractive fees, to help men of Gallucci's character secure pistol permits and the break flared into open hostility.

Justice Cotillo dealt with employment and family situations, with swindlers, and with the bias and weakness of the law. He functioned as listener and guide in a way that was more like the lives of nineteenth-century American "republican" lawyers than the lives of lawyers in Southern Italy:

> Coming home at night Cotillo often found groups of young people on the front stoop. They had gathered for what they knew would prove an interesting and inspiring talk. Before he went in for dinner, Sal spoke to them. There were discussions about every conceivable topic, but dominating everything that Cotillo had to say was his conviction that the new Italian element in American life ought to command an important role in the process and drama of government. This role, he told his listeners, could begin in their own neighborhood.

Ferber's biography also describes from Justice Cotillo's early law practice a lot of uncompensated charity for neighbors. But it is evident in Ferber's description that Justice Cotillo was building alliances, from his earliest days as a lawyer, that would make it possible for him to use un-Americanized, Italian-voter power as his Irish elders in New York and Boston were using the power of other immigrant groups.

His opinion of American jurisprudence was different from Dr. Mariano's. He saw that American law was flawed, and particularly so as it was imposed on and used to exploit immigrants and their children. His early career went well beyond what Dr. Mariano described as the practice of Italian-American lawyers in New York City. He used political means to preserve Italian culture where Dr. Mariano would have used professional influence to turn the immigrants into melting-pot Americans. He went from his law practice to become the first Italian-American assemblyman, thence to become the first Italian-American senator in the New York legislature— and in both houses his principal activity was the development and passage of social-welfare legislation that would benefit immigrant families. He was later the first Italian-American appointed to the Supreme Court (trial) bench in New York.

Ferber, who, I think, missed the point, celebrated Justice Cotillo's judicial qualities with a quotation from Shakespeare. He might better have used Dante—or even Machiavelli or Castiglione. Justice Cotillo's position within Little Italy was an Italian position, particularly in his insistence that Italians in America would not be able to take advantage of American opportunity unless they did so with political power, and in his courageous resistance to the darker elements in Little Italy's culture. An example on both points involves his early encounter, as a beginning lawyer, with a gangster:

> He was retained to defend a man involved in a sex crime. The next day he was waited upon by the local Camorra leader—son of a Camorraist notorious in the old country. This fellow blandly announced that he would arrange Counsellor Cotillo's fee in the case; that henceforth all defense arrangements for persons arrested for crime would be handled by the Camorra leader or his lieutenants, and that the young attorney must govern his conduct and regulate his fees by his dictation. By way of mitigating his effrontery, the Camorraist assured Cotillo that if he fell in with this plan, his speedy financial independence was assured; but that, on the other hand, if he did not, great harm would come not only to him but to his family as well.

In response, Cotillo, young, idealistic and with his recent quaffing at the cup of legal ethics pounding righteously in his bosom, rose to daring and dramatic heights. He replied that his law practice was his own; that he would look for guidance only to the courts and the tenets of the Bar Association; that the Camorra might know once and for all that he did not intend to be coerced or intimidated. He ordered the man from his office. The enraged Camorraist lifted his cane and this struck Sal as funny. Though the moment had been tense, he smiled. The mobster was puzzled by the smile. It unnerved him. He hesitated. Men threatened by him did not smile.

In that fleeting moment Cotillo recalled that a useless antique gun lay in his desk. It had been given to him as a harmless toy... by his grandfather. Cotillo reached into a drawer, withdrew the pistol and leveled it at the bandit.... The terror-dealing Camorraist lost his nerve... shrieked in fear.... Cotillo booted him out of his office....

News of how young Cotillo had dealt with the much-feared bad man spread rapidly among the Italians of the city. The better element, enormously in the majority, applauded his courage. He became their champion; and was from that day feared and avoided by the underworld.

* * * * *

The significant contrast between the gentleman-lawyer of Italian extraction whom Dr. Mariano envisioned and hoped for and the Italian-American lawyer Justice Cotillo exemplified is an earthy appreciation for the uses of power. It was, as the biographer says, a matter of ethics— but the ethic has more of Italy in it than of the vaporous and contemporary rhetoric of the Bar Association of the City of New York. The antique pistol Cotillo kept in his law office was not, after all, a toy; it was the effective device of a wily, resourceful young lawyer, who—as is often the case with lawyers—found out how to use power he did not have.

Justice Cotillo knew that the legal institutions maintained by the gentlemen-lawyers of New York were *not* excellent and that native Italians' disgust for all institutions, as well as their specific disgust at the hypocrisy of American legal institutions, would make it impossible for Italians to trust American law. But, whether the institutions remained as they were or became—not excellent, but useful—the key to justice for Italians was to *use* these institutions and with them gain political power.

Justice Cotillo's entry into New York politics is an example. He was a co-founder, with his father, of an Italian-American political club called the Tomahawk Democratic Club. The Cotillos and their club took on the Hayes machine in 1911. The club lost the electoral contest, but Cotillo made a deal with Hayes that gave Little Italy a political foothold in the city. The Italian community later brought as much pressure as it had to bear on Hayes, and Hayes and his machine put Cotillo in the legislature.

"I want to help my people," Salvatore A. Cotillo said, "and can do so only with the backing of those in power." It is indicative of the arguments he made when he spoke in Little Italy that he, alone among the speakers who attacked Hayes in 1911, was left alone by Hayes's goons. He was as bold with his voice and (very local) influence as he had been with his grandfather's antique pistol:

> [I]t was on the stump that [the club] encountered all their difficulties. For no sooner did they mount the tailboard of a truck at some street corner than they were stoned and thrown off. The only one immune from such treatment was the popular young Cotillo. Throwing stones or offering violence to one of their own—an Italian—particularly this popular son of a popular father, was taboo. Even the fiery Hayes took heed of this viewpoint of his Italian constituents and ordered that young Cotillo should not be molested when making a speech, regardless how bitter his attack, even on Hayes himself. Cotillo thus became the lone champion of his group,

fighting single-handed against an array of Tammany orators long schooled in their work.

Italian culture in America has survived longer than Dr. Mariano thought it would. It has survived long enough to be valued by the dominant culture, even to be learned from. We think Italian culture in America will survive as a permanent influence on the practice of law in America, as well as on American politics. There is evidence of influence in the daily newspapers: One of the country's most prominent and popular governors; its first female candidate for national office; many judges, mayors, legislators, and presidential advisors; and the first Italian-American on the bench of the federal supreme court. All of these national leaders are lawyers and all are visible and openly within their Italian culture. They are Italian Americans. In some ways, they are, as their immigrant ancestors were, Italians in America.

This other culture is now a culture of lawyers in America. We now need to turn our attention from the border between the two cultures, to the substance of the moral culture Italian Americans brought into the legal profession.

CHAPTER SIX

Virtue in the Other Community

Chi lascia la via vecchia per la nuova, sa quel
che perde e non sa quel che trova.[1]

No one is born a lawyer. Those who come to American law schools come with a moral order that is ignored or explicated, challenged or supported, as part of their legal education and of their apprenticeship in the American legal profession. Their moral order affects the way they look at the law; it determines their jurisprudence. It determines as well the way they look at their clients, their colleagues in the practice, and the opponents of their clients. The moral order a person brings to the profession determines whether she even thinks about the question of how to be a good person and a lawyer.

I suggest (as Thomas Aquinas did) that there are two kinds of moral order people bring to their work in the world. The *first moral order* is the one Alexis de Tocqueville called "habits of the heart";[2] Michael Joseph Oakeshott extended the notion to "habits of affection *and conduct.*" Salvatore Cotillo's Italian moral order, which Mary and I will describe at length in this chapter and the next, is an example of it.

---

1. "Whoever forsakes the old way for the new knows what he is losing, but not what he will find," a proverb quoted by Richard Gambino.

2. Robert Bellah and his colleagues borrowed Tocqueville's phrase for their recent book on communities in America.

127

The moral order of the American gentleman-lawyer is another example of the first moral order. It, like Cotillo's moral order, is communitarian and cultural. For people in the first moral order, Oakeshott says, "most of the current situations of life do not appear as occasions calling for judgment, or as problems requiring solutions." In most situations, "there is no weighing up of alternatives or reflection on consequences, no uncertainty, no battle of scruples." Moral behavior is a matter of "following... a tradition of conduct in which we have been brought up." Tocqueville observed this sort of morality among American lawyers in the 1820s, before the immigration of Jews and Roman Catholics from Eastern and Southern Europe. A century later, Salvatore Cotillo built a career on the protection of such a moral order in the Italian immigrant community in Harlem.

The *second moral order* is characterized by reflection, decision, and defense. "It requires of us," Gilbert C. Meilaender says, "a kind of critical, self-reflective ability to defend our moral ideals or rules against all challenges." It is what I have referred to, in chapter one, as a moral order of choosers. "From this perspective," Meilaender says, "the moral life requires that we set out its proper form in systematic, connected fashion and then seek to practice it.... There must be constant criticism and analysis to determine whether our practice adequately reflects the principles and ideals we have adopted."

The two kinds of moral order differ in their development and in their demise. A person who grows up in the first moral order learns his morals as he learns his language. "We learn from those around us," Meilaender says, "from living with people who habitually behave in certain ways, and from being thereby initiated into a tradition of conduct." Like our language, our morality is "the form of life in which we [are] immersed.... It is the sea in which we float and then, perhaps, swim." Change occurs in a first-order moral world; it deals, constantly, with change, and it changes constantly. It is a stable moral world, not because it resists change, but because it adjusts to what is new from the standpoint of what is old; it never collapses all at once. The demise of such a moral world is neither destruction nor transformation, but decadence. It knows how to adapt, but it does not know how to question itself. Thus, much of the problem Newman had with the gentleman's ethic was its lack of insight about itself.

"Precisely because it offers the ability to act without hesitation or doubt," Meilaender says of the first moral order, "it does not offer the critical ability to analyze and evaluate the shape of the society's moral life." It lacks the self-critical powers that a more analytical moral system has. It can therefore "degenerate into mere superstition (may be unable to distinguish its moral code from a collection of taboos) and may be unable to deal with external challenge based on critical principles." Meilaender shows here how the gentleman's ethic becomes an ethic of honor and shame rather than an ethic of character.[3]

Growing up in the *second* moral order (if it is possible to imagine a child in such a world) is less cultural than conceptual. It is less formative than the first moral order is, but more instructive. In it, "we will need an intellectual training in the rules or ideals themselves: training in how to apply and defend them." Its disadvantage, when compared to the first moral order, is that it is not as confident of itself. People who live in it will understand moral principles as they understand mathematical principles; they will have a firm idea of the criteria they have learned, thought about, and chosen for moral decision; but they will not be as confident as people in the first moral order are, not as sure of themselves, not as resolute. They will be able to think pretty well; but they will be less able to do things than people in the first moral

---

3. This, on Wyatt-Brown's account, is what happened to the gentleman's ethic in the American South in the nineteenth century.

order. "The constant encouragement of self-reflection un-
dermines the ability to act habitually and confidently,"
Meilaender says. "The pause for reflection that is always
needed before one acts can paralyze."

The second moral order adapts to change through the
intellectual tools we value in the "science" of ethics—
through argument, insight, and persuasion. When it collapses it collapses suddenly. "For although its adherents
may have acquired considerable ability to resist external,
critical challenge, should that resistance be broken, little
is left (since their moral life is not undergirded by habit
and custom). It is likely to change suddenly and rapidly."
One of the reasons for this, I think, is that the second
moral order has tended—perhaps not logically, but historically—to teach that what validates behavior is that
the person who has considered it has chosen it. Choice is
more flexible than habit.

Both the gentleman's legal ethic and the other, late-
immigrant legal ethic were formed in the first kind of
moral world.[4] The ethic of the gentleman-lawyer comes
from the American republican and biblical order Tocqueville characterized as habits of the heart. The ethics of
the late immigrants who became American lawyers after
Salvatore Cotillo's day were ethics formed in cohesive

---

4. It seems that any ethic, except, perhaps, one invented by a
scholar, is formed in the first moral world. An ethic is something one
finds in a community. An ethic that is not found in a community is not
an ethic; it is only somebody's idea. Notice, for example, that the description Oakeshott and Meilaender provide of the second moral
world does not account for moral formation earlier than the age when
a child is interested in formulating and arguing about concepts. Children in communities don't appear as educable adults, and they do not
appear for adolescence as blank slates. When they enroll in school
they have already been formed morally in families, neighborhoods,
towns, and religious congregations. Descriptions of the second moral
order do a poor job of accounting for the associations we do not
choose. The notion of moral autonomy is useful only in describing a
moral world we can grow into (i) out of the first moral world, and
(ii) when we are old enough.

moral cultures that were religious, ethnic, and even tribal. The difference between the gentleman's legal ethic and the other legal ethic was not that one was a cultural moral order and the other was a moral order of principle and choice. They were both cultural. The difference between them was historical: The dominant force in the profession as Salvatore Cotillo met it in New York was a gentleman-lawyer's culture three generations removed from its birthplace. It functioned, or it had begun to pretend that it functioned, in the second moral order; but it had not grown up there.

It is clear enough—from, say, the text of David Hoffman's "Fifty Resolutions" of 1836, and from the reception they received in the America Tocqueville observed—that the ethics described for the American legal profession Tocqueville saw were communitarian ethics. This was a cultural world of Protestant, republican, white, Jeffersonian gentlemen who were well off and who committed themselves to the maintenance of substantive justice in the United States. They did not learn their morals as they learned their law; their law teachers assumed they were gentlemen when they came to study law. "Our student (now about to commence the practice)," Hoffman said, was "a young man of the soundest morals, and of the most urbane, and honourable deportment." The purpose of Hoffman's "Resolutions" was "that he should be fortified with a few rules for his future government" as a lawyer.

This republican and biblical moral order had decayed by 1890, in fact if not always in rhetoric, into (i) the market morality of the Industrial Revolution, and (ii) the division of moral formation between home and commercial world. In the market morality, the best lawyers accepted the robber barons as clients, translated ethical statements such as Hoffman's into codes, and invented bar associations, including the American Bar Association. They, not incidentally, also invented the adversary ethic, which teaches that lawyers are not responsible for what their clients do and is a second-order morality if ever there was one.

The separation of moral education between mothers and male professional mentors such as Hoffman meant that formation in the virtues was the province of women in the home and Sunday school, and education for morals in business and the professions was the separate province of elders in business and professional practice. The gentleman-law teacher of Hoffman's day depended on his students' being formed and conscious of the virtues, a dependence that did not separate the morals of home life from the morals of professional life. Professional ethics were continuous with the virtues; concern for substantive justice, for example, was an explication of the virtue of justice that the young lawyer had learned at home.

In nineteenth-century industrial America, men went out to work for wages, commissions, fees, and profits. Women mostly stayed home with children. (Some few devoted themselves to Sunday school, teaching in schools for girls, and the primitive beginnings of organized political consciousness.) What Hoffman depended on in his law student came to be separated from and subordinated to masculine professional rules. Justice, in the market morality, became not a virtue but rather the product of a system. The new bar associations proclaimed professional rules that ignored or denied the connection between virtue and professional life. Time and strife and the promise of virtually unlimited wealth in a new world gnawed away at the first-order, white, male, Protestant, gentlemanly moral culture of the "golden era of American lawyers" (Hurst's phrase). Justice, both as a virtue and as the responsibility of the gentleman-lawyer, became a set of procedures (or the practice of procedures) for obtaining justice from the government. The political causes of lawyers and clients in the "golden era" became the representation by lawyers of the private economic interests of the robber barons.

The children of immigrants, who came into the profession in Justice Cotillo's day and later, heard the words of the gentleman-lawyer's ethic but what they saw was greed and hypocrisy. The lawyer stories we have from them—fiction such as Louis Auchincloss's and George V. Higgins's, biographies such as those of Louis D. Brandeis and Fanny Holtzmann—say that these immigrant lawyers were willing to follow the professional rules as they would follow traffic regulations; but they got their morals at home.

The children of Southern Italian immigrants are the principal example we propose to use. These lawyers' parents brought with them an elegant first-order moral culture. The immigrants were remarkably, bitterly poor, and they were routinely oppressed, but they put value on time well spent, on beauty, on enjoyment and decorous formality. (Still today, in an Italian city, one rarely sees a man who is not wearing a suit coat, or people carrying anything that is not wrapped.) They thought Americans mocked this natural order of things; Americans' language and bearing and manners were unrefined in comparison with those of illiterate peasants of the Mezzogiorno.[5] One immigrant, reflecting on how America looked to him, said, "Dignity had no place in life" here; he found America materialistic and revolting. Letters home from immigrants in those days said Americans were "colorless, unsalted ... without culture," cold and unemotional, "pickled in the sour juices of Puritanism." One Italian said, "Joy is a fruit that Americans eat green"—without flavor, *senza sapore.*

This immigrant culture did not believe in the American dream. Contrary to W.A.S.P. myths about Ellis Island, the Statue of Liberty, and the Fourth of July, Southern Italians, like other late immigrants, did not come here to escape oppression or to take on a new, liberated, American way of life. They came here for money; the Italians

---

5. "Middle of the day"—Southern Italy, where the sun shines.

came intending to return. They were not leaving their culture; they were trying to preserve it. About half of the Calabrian and Sicilian immigrants eventually decided to stay, but they did not decide to give up their culture. They knew from centuries of cultural memory that the way a community of people survives is to take care of its own, to adhere to *la via vecchia*. The highest value in their first-order moral world was (as it is among their grandchildren) the order of the family, the protection of the family, *l'ordine della famiglia*.

An Immigrant Virtue

> The possibility for a recovery of a coherent culture and rational agreement is dependent on not only philosophical argument, but also actually being embodied in the practices of ongoing communities dedicated to the virtues and to the common good.... [L]iberal society, morally bankrupt as it is, is not likely to develop such communities.
>
> L. Gregory Jones

In what remains of this chapter, and in the next chapter, Mary and I will explore this instance of moral formation in a culture, in a particular first-order moral world as Oakeshott and Meilaender describe it. We offer this as a discrete and neglected piece of applied ethics in the American legal profession—an example of first-order moralities brought to America by the late immigrants, an example one might call Italian-American legal ethics. Our project is, in terms of the agenda Jones sets (and with which we agree), a philosophical argument as (or as well as) the description of lawyers embodied in communities dedicated to the virtues. There are two reasons why such an example might be useful in late-twentieth-century legal ethics. It is, first of all, still capable of being described in first-order terms. Where descriptions of the gentle-manly first-order moralities of American Puritanism and of Jeffersonian republicanism seem remote and tenden-tious, the first-order moralities of the late immigrants are accessible even to personal memory, and they are (so far) relatively less infected with the ethics of choice than the "liberal" ways of thinking about morals that still dom-inate ethics in the American professions. And, second, the "ethnic" moralities of the late immigrants are in fact a moral force in American legal professionalism, although they are rarely recognized anywhere in the literature. (A trace of this influence is suggested in the developing lit-erature on the jurisprudence of Justice Antonin Scalia and in news reports about the combination of political conservatism and affability he displays among the judges and clerks of the federal supreme court, and in parallel political speculation from and about Governor Mario Cuomo.)

Our focus is a virtue for which Mary and I have used the Italian word *rispetto*.[6] Our understanding of *rispetto* is that it is a good habit, through which the person learns, practices, teaches, and remembers her member-ship in the family. "My family was an emotional support group and therapy center, with few secrets and frequent, open discussions about the range of human feelings, and their expression and resolution. Job fulfillment did not seem to be a priority; *fulfillment in family* was the ulti-mate priority."[7] The practice of this virtue is what allows

---

6. We avoid the English word "respect" because the use of that word in discussions about Italian Americans has been corrupted by stories of organized crime. Organized crime, of course, dogs Italian culture both in Italy and in North America; it is perhaps to the Italians what patronage and hubris are to the ethics of English gentlemen.

7. Emphasis added. First-person quotations that are not attributed, in this chapter and the next, are from interviews and letters we gath-ered from Italian-American lawyers. We offer comments by Italian Americans who are in law school, in law practice, and on the bench. Our request to them for comment presented broad, open-ended state-ments of subject matter roughly equivalent to the topic headings in

a modern American lawyer to be in and of her civic and professional community without loss either of dignity or of her sense of self.

Rispetto has to do with first-order moral community. It is the skill to accept love and to love. Its natural, organic location is in the family; the genius of Italian-American culture is its ability to extend the practice of the virtue beyond the organic community. If clannishness (Banfield's phrase was "amoral familism") was at first a fair description of Italians in America, it soon became evidence both of the ability of first moral orders to change and of the influences of the family on associations that appear to be products of choice. It became a skill practiced in an extended family that was founded less on blood than on place of origin in the Old Country—*paese*, from which comes the *American* Italian word *paesano*—and the moral value of *campanilismo*. The organic family is, though, the "community of memory" for *rispetto*, as it is the ordinary school for virtue and the place of initiation to moral reality, in any culture.

Among Italian Americans, the blood-related, nuclear, and extended family controls all serious analogical or metaphorical uses of the word "family" to describe neighborhood, *paesani*, town, parish, school, or professional association. The use of "family" to describe an association that is not a family is, for Italians, a moral claim. When Mario Cuomo uses the word "family" to speak of his aspirations for the State of New York, or for the United States, his use of the word seems to be serious, and different, and *Italian*. "Family" for Governor Cuomo seems not to mean what it means in an advertisement for an airline; nor does it mean the "community of man" of liberal social ethics. *The* family—his family—seems to control the Governor's analogies.

---

these two chapters. We did not provide our own hypotheses, and this book was not drafted when we contacted these lawyers. We endeavor to stimulate here a conversation with our helpers, well aware that our helpers will not in all cases agree with the social historians, nor with one another, nor with us. This is, after all, about Italians.

The social scientists and historians who describe Italian-American culture show how the social operation of the virtue of *rispetto* works. They describe how individuals are formed in the family, neighborhood, and church, and, because the virtue of *rispetto* is practiced there, are not swallowed up by these associations. They show also how the virtue, which is the good habit of exercising membership in groups, has affected the development of associations of Italian Americans and of older American associations (such as the legal profession) that now include Italian Americans. They show how Italian Americans exercise membership, how they go about belonging.

The constant in Italian-American life is the family. The family is described as the nursery of values in most cultures in America, but it has operated in the Italian immigrant culture in a distinctive, decidedly non-American way. (This is not an argument about the comparative importance of family values. We want to show in this chapter that the family was understood in Italian immigrant culture as formative of who a person was and was to be, rather than a place where a person was prepared to make moral choices.)

In contrast to the Italian-American family, the Puritan-republican American family in the nineteenth century, as the southern Italian immigrants found it when they came to America at the end of the century, was the product of a divisive "settlement" between men and women. The settlement defined a "woman's sphere" of domesticity and training of children in the individualistic virtues celebrated by Benjamin Franklin, and claimed for men control of the negotiations between the home and business, government, church, and voluntary civic organizations. Home was the woman's sphere. The world was the man's sphere.

This division was not characteristic of the Italians. Italian and Puritan-republican virtues were both home virtues, but training in virtue was a shared enterprise for Italian parents—shared across the immediate family, and

shared across generations. It could not, as we attempted
to show in our discussion of education in the last chapter, be entrusted either to American public schools or to
Irish nuns. Negotiation with the world outside the family
was a project for every member of the family. Respect for
the family, as the world looked at it from outside, was not
separated from respect for the individual who was respected in the family. The individual was the family for
most external purposes.

Impermanence and the insecurity of life was expressed in my mountain Western culture in frontier-
American terms; we were rugged individuals who left
home alone and overcame obstacles to individual
achievement. The Italian Americans met life—and meet
it—in a familial, even "tribal" encounter with commerce,
with the Irish-dominated Roman Catholic Church in the
United States, with the American social forces that draw
adult children away from the family, with the sort of
American politics that the Cotillo family overcame in
Harlem. In Cotillo's Little Italy, and elsewhere in the
U.S. and Canada, it was families, not individuals, who
developed collaborative forms of behavior, in school,
neighborhood, parish, recreational club, and even in encounters with organized crime.

Among Italian Americans, it was the family, not the individual, that moved from the highly protective enclave
of the old way to concern for place of origin and for the
broader associations that eventually resulted from a
steadily broadened community of concern.[8] It was the
family, in a web of *paesani*, not the individual, that
moved from this sort of "tribalism" to characteristic mu-

---

8. Zucchi notices two schools of thought among the social historians: (1) that *campanilismo* broke down in America and became a
consciousness of being either northern or southern Italians; and (2)
that *campanilismo* survived into the modern identification as being
from Italy—period. The social historians agree that the moral value of
loyalty within the family, among the *paesani*, and eventually among
Italian Americans, survived the change.

tual benefit societies, to eventual ethnic identification as northern or southern Italians, thence to identity as Italians in America, and finally to more typically American associations in local politics, parish, town, economic interest groups, and professions. None of these movements succeeded until Italian Americans came to the view (sometimes mistaken) that the movements could occur without threat to the health of the family, and that they could be undertaken from within the family and not outside it. Italians do not sacrifice their families to the common good; they love to belong, but they do not leave their families behind when they join up.

The social historians describe how change occurs in American Italian communities as an instance of the first moral order: Change is constant and it is managed within a stable community that can accommodate change. Given *l'ordine della famiglia* as the stable factor, the characteristic feature of the Italian community in America has been its tendency to reach out, to include, and to integrate. This tendency has reached through *paesani*, to regional identification, to the sense of being Italian in America (a kinship with other Italians who would not have been thought of as kin in Italy), to extra-ethnic companionship in work and in professional life. This way of dealing with change is, in Stephen S. Hall's phrase, an "unusual propensity to merge, rather than separate, the professional and the personal. Borrowing from a culture in which the extended family can easily include thirty to forty 'close' relatives, Italians thrive on community," he says. "They are accustomed to large numbers of people, and they seem to have developed an emotional facility in dealing with them. Even in large companies, they have a knack for keeping things on a human scale. 'The professional community,' explains one Italian-American psychotherapist, 'becomes the next family.' "

The disposition, characteristic, habit, or skill that has made this movement work without harm to the dignity of each person is *rispetto*. *Rispetto* is defined by Notari-

anni and Raspa as a way "to acknowledge publicly one's
position . . . and thereby to incur a set of obligations." It is
the claim and exercise of membership. One's position as
having incurred obligations is a position within and from
the family—so that the family, too, incurs obligations. It
is possible to incur obligations because one has learned
in the family the disposition, characteristic, habit, or skill
that makes it possible to be associated without loss of
self. The immigrant Italian family preserved unity as it
gave individuals a way to incur obligations without harm
to the family. *Rispetto* was a way for each member of the
family to be formed both in the ability to be in the family
and in the ability to be in the family without loss of self.
Such a formation makes it possible to be in other associations, and to be present there as the family (even when
one goes there alone), in an effective, realistic way, without loss of self, self-respect, or respect for the family.

This is a communitarian anthropology, but it is radically different from the individualistic, contractarian accounts of the person on which communitarian argument
rests in modern American jurisprudence and social ethics. (Most of modern legal ethics, as ethics, depends on
those accounts.) The individual's situation in the group
has focused, for Italian Americans, on (i) family, (ii)
paese, and (iii) ethnic group[9]—in that historical and normative order. The immigrants at first drew a curtain of
protection around their families. Later they expanded the
protection (and mutual aid) to include Southern Italian
immigrants from the same place in the old country; this
is the practice social historians call *campanilismo*.
(Friendship might be an English-Aristotelian word for it.)
And still later they came to think of themselves as Northern Italians or Southern Italians, and then as Italians in
America. This situation has not been interpreted, at any

9. If "ethnic group" is understood narrowly, Italians come from
more than one ethnic group. We mean to identify here the claim an
Italian American makes when she says she is an Italian.

point along this historical progression, as a product of negotiation and bargain, or in terms that might be used by
an *argument* for community. Italians did not consider
family membership, *campanilismo*, regional identity, and
ethnic identity as something the individual reflected on,
evaluated, traded for, or *chose*.

The preconscious or even subconscious "shared sense
of peoplehood" (Francis Femminella's phrase) that is be-
neath and prior to conscious identity as Italian is a given;
it is inevitable; it is fated. Common ways of thinking, be-
having, and feeling, from this Italian point of view, are
matters of fact—even burdensome matters of fact—before they are matters of either ideology or theory. One
copes with these givens in a web of relationships and, in
coping, learns to strive, as Erik Erikson put it, "for a continuity of personal character" and the "maintenance of an
inner solidarity." Femminella lists twenty elements in Italian culture which he calls "ethnic ideological themes."
Among these themes are several dispositions, characteris-
tics, or skills that provide insight into the way *rispetto*
has worked to bring about the movement of Italian-
American culture, from an exclusive focus in the family,
to a focus in the immediate community, thence eventually, as Leonard Moss put it, to "an accentuation [on]...
the contributions of the group to the broader host culture." These include:

(1) a sense of place (*paese*), an inheritance from the generation of immigrants who expanded the protection of
   the family to include fellow villagers (*paesani*);[10]

---

10. Identity as Italian is, for Italian Americans, a *consequence* of
adaptation to America; the immigrants were not consciously Italian
when they came here. They thought of themselves as Sicilians or Calabrians, or even as "citizens" of villages or neighborhoods. Italy at the
time they left it was imperfectly unified, legally a single nation for less
than a generation; and many of the immigrants or their families had
resisted unification and resented both the effects and the requirements of unification on the South.

(2) independence, the desire and skill to act on one's own "and in the event of a real need for help to go to one's family";[11]

(3) courage, for which Femminella invokes Dante—*seggendo in piuma in fama non si vien né sotto coltre* (fame does not come to one who lies on feathers under a blanket);

(4) *Fare bella figura.* Pride in meeting the world, with a sense that one meets the world *as* the family. "Pride and shame, self respect and disgrace are not only individual, personal matters; they always necessarily involve family;"[12]

(5) respect for the place of the outsider, when one is in the outsider's place, so that one does not flaunt one's own ways in the presence of strangers.

Italian Americans employ these and other elements of *rispetto* toward material and social goals. They have learned to take the regard of outsiders more clearly into account than the immigrants did, but to do that without loss of self, toward the future, and toward personal achievement. They became, Femminella says, more "responsible and hopeful, ... more mature, reasonable, and affiliative" than their immigrant ancestors were. The claim one can make for the moral value of *rispetto*, then, begins in an anthropology of the person as seen in earthy, given, fated association with other persons, and ends in an acquired (and inherited) skill for preserving self in community.

It is possible to build a theoretical claim on this social history. The reason for doing that would be to offer a first-order alternative to the thin and implausible anthro-

---

11. The family has not swamped the person but it has become the place where she both tests and protects her independence; and the family goes with her as she goes out into the community of strangers.

12. *Fare bella figura* is practiced within the virtue of *rispetto*; otherwise it becomes pretension—merely a matter of keeping up appearances. Within the practice of the virtue it can be seen as self-respect, which necessarily includes respect in and for the family.

pology of second-order morality, an alternative to the radical individualism that is implicit in what I described in chapter one as the legal ethics of choice. An Italian-American legal ethic, offered for this purpose, would begin with the organic, the given, and the earthy. It would dispute the notion we have from Enlightenment political theory that communities are the products of a social contract: You don't *agree* to be in an Italian family. It would say that our organic communities are the norm, and that the communities we agree to join are consequent, special, artificial, and secondary. It would then proceed to describe, in the same organic way, and from organic sources, skills for living in community: The person is formed, in her organic community, in the habit of membership. This formation does not suppress individual dignity; it *exalts*, *protects*, and *celebrates* it:

> My grammar-school dream of becoming a lawyer after the fashion of New Jersey's Attorney General . . . waned and my career goal in high school was shifting toward dentistry. My father wanted me to become a dentist; my dentist, also an Italian American, urged the same career—as his partner. Then I met Sam, also my father's lawyer. He not only hired me as an office boy . . . but also forever dashed any thought I may have had about dentistry with a quick, "Any shithead can be a dentist; you have to be smart to be a lawyer!" . . . (Our helper here later became Sam's law partner.)
>
> I really don't have the highest regard for Italy as a modern nation or its people. I'm proud for the Italian American who has busted his tail, not asked for any favors, nor cut any corners, and has become a decent person, an asset to our world. And I'm proud that such were the members of my family. The family—the most important societal unit in my world.
>
> "Family" during my early years was the blood family. Parties were family affairs, but any friend of a member of the family was welcomed as a member. My father's busi-

ness was the family business—a fuel oil and gasoline distributorship. It was started by one of his brothers, who took two other brothers in as partners. When the three decided to go into the automobile business they sold the company to my father and the husbands of his four sisters. Five brothers-in-law who stayed together for about fifteen years. Everyone worked for the company—everyone who didn't go to college. . . .

Over the past thirty years, the scope of the "family" has grown. Kinship by blood is no longer necessary. Identification as more than an acquaintance, or business or social colleague, is required, but the Americanization of the Italian American requires expanding out from the "blood" family.[13]

The Italian-American Lawyer's Situation

Italian-American lawyers are new to the legal profession and new to the influence that being a lawyer in America brings with it. Unlike the descendants of the Puritans and the nineteenth-century Protestant gentlemen-republicans, the Italians live within the personal memory of how their first-order moral culture was preserved and even revived in America while the older first-order moral cultures were being diluted by liberalism, market morality, and compromises with the robber barons.

Unlike the descendants of the other late immigrants—especially the Irish and Eastern European Jews—Italians did not quickly seize higher education as a ladder of vertical mobility; their children tended to stay away from school, to go to work young, and to contribute meager earnings toward a tenuous security for their families. Italians took this course for *moral* reasons. The Irish *sought* assimilation; the Italians feared it. The Jews resisted assimilation but managed to understand higher education

---

13. We would have said "the Italian-Americanization of the Italian American."

and entry into the professions as not assimilative; the Italians distinguished between education and training and claimed education for the family.

An Italian-American lawyer thus has a special moral heritage, one that, in the late twentieth century, is unique enough to be an example of how an "ethnic" moral influence in the legal profession makes a difference. In this section, we will first attempt a general description of where Italian-American lawyers come from, and then look at the way they and their families have dealt with the melting pot, with the insistence they and their families be like everybody else. The virtue of *rispetto* is a significant part of where these lawyers come from, as it has been significant in the way they and their families have felt, and still feel, about assimilation.

Most Italian-American lawyers are third-generation Americans. (Some few, such as Cuomo, Ferraro, and Scalia, are the children of immigrants.) They are the granddaughters and grandsons of poor farmers, unskilled laborers, and a few artisans from southern Italy (Calabria and Sicily predominantly), Judge Quilici said, "who sold their cattle and kitchen utensils, scraped, saved and borrowed money from their friends and relatives, packed their belongings in sacks, bundles, and handkerchiefs, and crossed the big pond wondering how much that they had heard, they would find to be true in America." Their old world is Sicily and the Mezzogiorno, "the place where the sun always shines, where it's always the middle of the day.... In the north is the industry, the education, the high culture, the refinement," Governor Cuomo said. "My people and Matilda's come from the Mezzogiorno, and things have not changed... much since they left."

Most of these lawyers were the first people in their families to reach the professions. Many were the first in their families to complete, or even begin, university education. Most of them were raised in an urban Little Italy and have lately moved to ethnically mixed suburban neighborhoods. From the perspectives of influence and prominence, these lawyers are visible in the second decade in which Italian Americans have gained, or will gain, prominence in law firms, on the bench, and in public elective office; their parents did not see Italian-ancestry contemporaries in high national executive positions, as ambassadors, university presidents, bishops, or baseball commissioners. By comparison, the descendants of Irish immigrants became influential half a century ago, and the descendants of late-immigrant Jews before that. Compare, for examples, Geraldine Ferraro with Al Smith, Antonin Scalia with Felix Frankfurter, Cardinal Bernardin with Cardinal O'Connell and other Irish bishops of sixty years ago. It became fashionable to be American and ethnic twenty or thirty years ago, but only in the last decade has it been fashionable to be Italian. "Now it's sort of neat to be Italian. Well, that's not how it was in the fifties and early sixties. It was neat to be Irish back then."

Italian Americans are no longer so much the objects of the public, even official, hostility and prejudice their immigrant grandparents and their American-born parents encountered. They are no longer so openly exploited, mistreated, and rejected. They have become patriotic, in peace and war. They have become consumers, watchers of television, and practitioners of American sentimentality. But this is not their deepest heritage; none of it was true before 1920. The immigrants' reaction to America was disgust and even horror. Italian immigrants did not come to America for culture. They were Italians in America; they brought their culture with them. Most of them did not come to find a new home. They came for survival—*pane e lavoro*, bread and work. They intended to work for a while, to save, and then to go home to Italy. Half of them did return: More than two million Italian immigrants were repatriated between 1899 and 1924. Those who changed their minds and stayed here did not care about becoming American or sending their children to American schools until years later, as they or their children gradually began to reconcile themselves to the fact that the new world was their home.

The immigrants lived in barracks and tenements at first, often in virtual peonage under Irish and Italian work bosses. They were frequently the victims of banks, steamship companies, and gangsters. Most of them eventually found blue-collar jobs and homes in working-class neighborhoods, and some moved from slums to more pleasant and less crowded areas. Often they had stores, shops, or businesses, such as the gelato and pastry shop Justice Cotillo's father owned in Harlem's Little Italy.[14]

Italian Americans in the second generation (first generation American-born) were more vulnerable to American culture than their insular parents had been. This generation balanced itself between two worlds. Some Italians, anxious to become American, even repudiated their parents and *la via vecchia*. They were like Auchincloss's Mario Fabbri, who "became an Episcopalian and treated his homeland as an exotic memory rather than a present-day inspiration." Humbert S. Nelli's *From Immigrants to Ethnics* says this group constituted a minority of the second generation, but it included the more ambitious members, and perhaps the ones most like the mythic melting-pot American child of immigrant parents. These were the second-generation Italian Americans who first became managers, professionals, white-collar employees, or (as in Fabbri's case) lawyers.

The first American-born generation had to be able to cope with both communities. Those who could cope skillfully enough were culturally prepared to enter the professions without losing their Italian character, although few of them did so. Eastern-European Jews and the Irish moved into professions much more readily.

---

14. Justice Cotillo was an example of what Humbert S. Nelli characterized as following the late-immigrant Jews in moving into the professions: Father owns a store or small business; sons go to college and become professionals.

Very few Italian professionals had emigrated from Italy. In 1902, less than one-half of one percent of southern-Italian immigrants had come from professional occupations in Italy. The few Italian professionals who emigrated found they were not able to work as professionals in America anyway, sometimes because their English was poor, or because of professional and cultural differences, but more often because Italians were excluded by W.A.S.P. and Irish prejudice from any but the dirtiest, dullest, hardest, and most menial work. Whatever status they enjoyed at home counted for nothing in America; they were "wops," and all wops were alike: "It was not unusual to find two men laboring shoulder to shoulder in a sewage ditch, one illiterate and the other with his head full of Dante and Virgil," Michael La-Sorte says.

Only toward the middle of the century did education become a feasible ladder of vertical mobility for working-class Italians—by then a ladder mainly for the children of immigrants—a practical, realistic, and acceptable alternative to blue-collar jobs and small businesses. The World War II "G.I. Bill" removed the choice between education for vertical mobility and acquiring property for business or home; World War II veterans' benefits provided both. After World War II, Italian-American men began to get an education, put on white shirts for work, and move to the suburbs. In this, the next generation, their daughters and granddaughters are also coming to law school.

In this way, the Italian family in America has moved into (and in some cases out of) an Italian-American way of life. The lawyers who helped us fall into three overlapping groups in this respect: Some show the ambivalence toward education that is said by the historians to be characteristic of the immigrants; some come from families that are, and are understood as, exceptional; and some show how, in the third and fourth generations, Italians have finally begun to climb the ladder—often, we think, at great cultural cost.

One of our helpers, an Italian-American lawyer who grew up in an Italian neighborhood in Brooklyn, is an example of the first group. He was the child of parents who emigrated from Abruzzi some ten years after their brothers and sisters came to Brooklyn. When this lawyer's parents got to Brooklyn, his uncles and aunts were already moving out of the Italian neighborhood there. He visited his cousins in suburban New Jersey, though: "When I first went to their homes, they were American homes. They looked like Walter Cronkite and his little Father-Knows-Best kind of families."

Although they were accustomed to the American way of life, many second-generation parents (first American-born generation) sent conflicting messages to their children: "Be successful but not too successful," and do not forget the old ways altogether. Richard Gambino calls this the "compound dilemma" of third- and fourth-generation Italian Americans, of whom there are some ten million living and working in the United States today. These Italian Americans, most of the current generation of Italian-American lawyers, are characterized in Gambino's *Blood of My Blood* as suffering from pressures from parents both to succeed and to adhere to traditional values. They are inspired by one pressure, hemmed in by the other. In a situation typical of the conflict, a second-generation, working-class couple gives their daughter who is in law school the message to "get an education" and "do better" while they express the fear that vertical mobility into the legal profession will "harm her morals." They want her to maintain the balance they have had to maintain between cultures—to juggle two cultures—and at the same time to keep pace with the current, relatively liberated generation of American women.

Gambino describes the second generation of Italian Americans as both ambitious and with less family and cultural guidance than their parents had. They had, in Gambino's view, less moral formation from which ambition could be pursued and defined than their grandparents had. Instead, second-, third-, and fourth-generation Italian Americans often cherish the cultural myths—Puritan rigor and frontier individualism—of the white-Protestant-American establishment that treated their immigrant ancestors as outcasts and criminals.

One of our contributing lawyers, thinking of his parents and their siblings who were born in America, says: "It has always made me laugh to read formula books on picking juries, where they say to pick Italians because they all tend to be warm and sympathetic. The attitude that a lot of my family would have sitting jury duty would be, 'What is this person trying to do by insisting that he is not guilty? Obviously he is guilty or he would not be here.' Or, in a civil suit, 'The guy must be lazy . . . and his quadriplegia has nothing to do with his not working.' "

It was not so in the immigrant generation: "When Pretty Boy Floyd was hiding out after the Union Station Massacre, my grandfather was sent for to cut his hair. He needed a good barber with discretion. When someone was stealing some motorscooters he rented, my grandfather wouldn't let a neighbor shoot at the young thief—better to lose the property than hurt the kid. Go figure."

Such changes in attitude are culturally significant; they are indicative of assimilation, of the way a first-order morality bends without breaking, and of the practice of membership in the family that is our focus in considering *rispetto*:

> I can remember overhearing heated discussions (which in a non-Italian family would have been flat-out arguments) in which certain of my uncles were promoting Franklin D. Roosevelt for sainthood, while others wanted him cast into the fiery depths. One of my uncles was as close to a Marxist as anyone I have ever known, and other members of the family were probably John Birchers. Interestingly, though, none of the political disagree-

ments affected the base of affection that everyone had
for one another. The trouble, of course, is recognizing
that a friendly discussion between Italians can often appear as quite close to open warfare when seen and heard
by persons of other ethnic backgrounds.

Political discussion, even heated discussion, displays
rispetto. Arguments over politics and religion, food and
literature, are (many of our helpers said) where Italians
become voluble and their W.A.S.P. neighbors become silent, because polite people do not talk about politics and
religion. Assimilation is a deeper and more painful issue,
particularly in an immigrant culture which brought with
it the ideas that the most important thing in life is to
preserve the family and that the only way to preserve the
family is to erect a cultural barricade around it and exclude the strangers.

Assimilation became a family issue and an intergenera-
tional testing place for *rispetto* on the questions of
whether adult children should go to school to get ahead,
and of whether they should leave the family to succeed
in business and the professions. As the helper we quoted
at the beginning of this chapter put it, the big question
was whether fulfillment in the family was secondary to
prosperity and fulfillment in the job. This was an issue,
an argument, and a testing ground for the virtue of belonging, that occurred in a national culture that believes,
with the Puritans, that the good are prosperous and, with
the Jeffersonians, that the prosperous are good.

An issue for professional ethics, within the practice of
the virtue of *rispetto*, is this issue about belonging:
whether success demands that one move his deepest dependence on others to an individualism that is practiced
outside of the family, and without the family. To return,
then, for a moment, to the situation of the ambitious
child who is both held onto and inspired upward by her
Italian-American culture, and who must find form and

nourishment from the culture for the skills she needs to negotiate the tension:

> I never intended to be a lawyer. As far back as I can remember, I wanted to be a librarian, because I loved books and spent most of my free time reading them or daydreaming about the stories in them. Although I always did very well in school, I was not particularly ambitious or competitive. This may be attributed in part to my background. My father was the youngest of nine surviving children of two Italian immigrants. I was the first of twenty-two grandchildren to go to college (my brother and sister being the second and third). My parents always encouraged me in my school work, but I never got the feeling it was the most important aspect of life. In fact, clearly the most important thing in life was family; family affairs were like Holy Days of Obligation—required.
>
> Almost from the start, I hated law school. People were openly competitive (something I had not experienced at Colgate) and the subject matter was difficult for me. I felt very out of place at Columbia, in law school; most of my classmates seemed to me to come from wealthier and better educated backgrounds and to be highly competitive rather than socially and family oriented. Although I interviewed at some of New York's big firms, I did not feel comfortable with the idea of working at such a place. My first summer I didn't even do legal work; my second year and summer I worked for a tiny customs-import specialty firm. I had decided that labor law was the most attractive area to me, and after law school I went to work for a medium-sized firm specializing in the representation of airline management in labor disputes.
>
> When I called up my father to tell him I had a job offer, and how much they were paying me ($26,000—far less than most of my classmates but a large sum to me) he started to cry. I had only seen him cry twice before— once when he left me at college for the first time and once when he left me in London after flying over for a

visit. He said, "That's more money than your mother or I ever made in our entire lives."

Throughout this time, I considered myself very Italian American. I studied Italian in college, and made two trips to Italy to visit relatives and soak up the atmosphere. I felt far more at home in Italy than in America; even the body language was eerily identical to my parents'. I constantly corrected the pronunciation of my last name, and usually the first information I would give someone was that I was Italian American. I began to go to the opera (my maternal grandmother had been a devotee); I often cooked Italian food for myself and friends; I spent a great deal of time with my family.

At the same time, I felt constantly divided between my professional life and my personal life, with my professional life impinging on the latter. My parents simply did not understand the enormous pressures created by my career. I remember a bad fight the day I had to work on Mother's Day, and my mother's angry question, "Doesn't your boss have a mother?" I remember my parents' incomprehension of my irritability, my unavailability, my hyper behavior.[15] As for me, I grew to resent the pressure and the devotion the profession demanded. In addition, I disliked the competitiveness and the combativeness. I wasn't cut out to be someone's warrior. I tried changing firms, to see if that was the problem, but, after working in three different places (always doing labor law or litigation), I became so unhappy that I knew I couldn't continue. Law was too harsh, too demanding, and too draining. I felt trapped. I did a great deal of soul searching. I decided I just didn't want to make law my career. I felt I had sacrificed a personal life to something that really did not give me much satisfaction. I looked for a

---

15. One of the members of the ethno-therapy groups formed by Drs. Sirey and Patti was more aggressive: "It's like you want to scream at them, 'This is what you really wanted. Don't you recognize it?'.... We are super women... but they don't know it.... When I go back to them I'm still a little kid wanting their approval."

scaled-down legal job which would allow me the time
and energy to pursue other interests and live like a human being.

I now work forty hours a week, which in my firm is
about half what all the other associates work. I told the
firm from the beginning I wasn't interested in partner-
ship, and wanted time to pursue personal goals. Although
I didn't have the excuse of a family and children, my
terms were accepted. I enjoy the intellectual stimulation
of my current position, shudder at the pervasive atmosphere of tension and pressure, and leave at five without
a moment's regret. The values of my culture—of interpersonal relationships, of family, of music, art, enjoyment—appear to me irreconcilable with practicing law.
It is these cultural values which have become more and
more important to me as I grow older, and which I am
no longer willing to sacrifice in the name of "success."

Political discussion and the pressures of assimilation
are two rather different places to observe how the virtue
of *rispetto* works in an Italian-American family. Political
(and religious and gustatory) arguments are carried on
within the family; they are no doubt where a child learns
what belonging is like. (The Italians are hardly unique in
training children in skills of inclusion and friendliness,
but we think Italians have a special way of doing it.)
Working out the stresses of assimilation is different; it operates outside the family—or, rather, as our helper the
labor lawyer has determined, belonging to the family operates in moral contexts that would seem, to one whose
morals are more Puritan or republican or liberal, to have
nothing to do with the family.

The practice and the memory of membership in the
family is put to a stark test when the agenda is the material ambition in America that involves skills and credentials gained in schools. A young professional woman in
the Sirey-Patti group had less success than our labor lawyer did: "I have to do a whole intellectual number with

myself to try to get back there.... I love them.... I'd like my mother to acknowledge who I am.... Just having her in my house would be fine.... I would just like having her around.... She loves me so unquestioningly.... But she doesn't consider the price... I've had to pay to be who I am." Coming home from school is a challenge to *rispetto*; prosperity is a stressful case. We turn then, again, to the formal education of Italian-Americans, to see if we can describe how formal education was seen differently among the Italians than among other late-immigrant groups.

American Schools and Italian-American Families

As late as the 1960 census, the median years of school completed by immigrant Italian Americans was 5.9 years, as compared to 8.5 years for all of the foreign born. The median for the second generation was 10.9 years for Italian Americans who were fourteen years of age or older, well short of a standard American high school education. The conventional account has it that there are two reasons why Italian families used schools less than, for example, the Irish or late-immigrant Jews: (i) the belief among Italian-American parents that school did not have as much economic value for the family as going to work did; and (ii) cultural hostility to formal education.

The economic-value account has it that Italian immigrant families saw the best financial promise in vocational training after elementary school, maybe because that was the system in Southern Italy. Skilled jobs gained with vocational credentials (such as acknowledged apprenticeships) were attractive—they paid more and they were relatively novel and promising for Italians; immigrants who had skills but no vocational credentials had been almost relentlessly excluded from such jobs in America. Italian-American families also placed a high and competing value on obtaining ownership of the land on which their homes and businesses sat. The use of the

earnings of teen-aged children to support the family and
to buy land for the family was the practice in Italy, and
such earnings were no doubt an attractive resource for
Italians in the United States, as they were for other
immigrants.

Even those who disagree with the thesis that Italian
immigrants were culturally hostile to formal education
admit the economic argument: The cultural historians
generally agree that the majority of Italian immigrants
came to America to find work; they intended to return to
Italy with money they could not earn in Italy, and nearly
half of them did. The possibility that later immigrants
were more cordial to formal education, and the fact that
second- and third-generation Italian Americans gradually
lost their aversion to schools, are explained by the one
camp as assimilation and by the other as evidence that
Italians were not hostile to formal education in the first
place.[16]

The argument that Italians were hostile to formal education begins with the fact that late nineteenth-century
Italian formal education was inflicted on Southern Italy
as a device in the drive from the central government in
Rome for nationalistic unification, and was imposed in
a biased, class-based manner. The traditionally clannish,

---

16. Briggs and Nelli are principal sources for an argument that the
first Italian Americans were not hostile to formal education. They
point to the early Italian-language American press, which encouraged
the immigrants to send their children to school and usually argued
from motives that included the non-economic—e.g., American patriotism, loyalty to the culture of the old country, support for Italian-
immigrant communities. Briggs argues that Italian Americans resisted
or rejected American formal education, when they did, for specific,
situational, political reasons—because the activities of the school
were aimed at the preservation of class or narrow professional interests—"to preserve the class structure, secure the future of the children of the already privileged, and prepare the rest to function
efficiently and quietly in their preassigned places in the individual order." Italian-immigrant parents recognized that the school was being
used as a "cultural weapon and resisted its influence." This aversion
was no doubt related to the central government's use and abuse of the
public schools in Southern Italy.

suspicious, and difficult Calabrians and Sicilians consequently resented and avoided state schools when they were available and resented their absence when they were not available. The southerners did accept five years of elementary education and some further vocational training but they made a distinction between education and instruction. Education was moral formation and initiation into the culture and tradition. It was the responsibility and the preserve of the family; an attempt by the central government—which, to the Calabrians and Sicilians, meant the North—to impose formal education, in this cultural sense, was an assault on *l'ordine della famiglia*. It was resisted in the same ways (largely apathy and avoidance) that the Southern Italians had used for centuries to overcome the corrupt influence of alien invaders, *gli stranieri*.

Instruction, as distinguished from education, was useful economically and, when confined to training for work, was acceptable to the southerners. The standard Italian system, at least for peasant children, had been five years of elementary schooling, followed by vocational training and, by about the age of thirteen, entry into the labor market. The principal complaint of the peasant South, on this score, was that such instruction was often not available to their children. Formal instruction, in either country, was not perceived by Southern Italians as economically useful, beyond that age.

Formal *education* was not only economically useless; it was also dangerous. Italians who came to this country discovered that the dominant Anglo-Saxon-Protestant culture was as inimical to traditional Southern Italian moral values as the central government in Rome had been. American culture was even more materialistic, crude, and corrupting than Northern Italian culture. America undermined the family and challenged the family's claim to be the exclusive source of moral formation—of education in the cultural sense. Roman Catholic parochial schools drew as much hostility from the Ital-

ians as public schools did: they, too, were strange to
Southern Italian experience; Southern Italy did not have
parochial schools.

Church schools in America did not even carry the traditional authority of the Italian Church—such as that
authority might have been among the frequently anticler-
ical Southern Italians. American parochial schools were
dominated by the Irish, who discriminated against Italians, and who had not resisted Americanization. In fact,
Irish Catholics put their faith in institutions (including
the church) that Southern Italians had learned to resist.
The Irish wanted their political and religious associations
to make assimilated Americans of them. If the Italians did
not generate hostility to schools out of their own experience and culture, the schools and the civic and religious
communities that ruled the schools provoked Italian
hostility.

Teachers in American schools showed contempt for
Italian family customs; they punished Italian children for
what their parents had trained the children to do. (One
of Gambino's examples is the shamefulness of accepting
carità, charity—"any aid from someone not a member of
the extended family. The person who accepts such aid is
considered to disgrace himself and his family.") A large
proportion of children in the first two generations of
American-born Italian Americans did not go to school at
all. The level of illiteracy in Italian-American communities must have been about what it was in Southern Italy.
There was little chance, for this reason and for deeper
cultural reasons, that Italian-American school children
would fall under the influence of supportive teachers,
counselors, pastors, or relatives who could guide them to
universities and thence to professional schools.

Prior to World War II, six percent of all Italian Americans went to college. After the war, as educational benefits began to flow under the G.I. Bill (along with, and not
instead of, Veterans Administration loans for homes and
businesses), that number increased to twenty per-

cent. The ability to afford college—and, beyond that, to afford college without risking avoidable economic dependence outside the family—was doubtless a factor here, but the culture changed, too. Italian-American culture came to accept and to seek education. Our friends showed us how that worked and how painful it sometimes was. The helpers we quote here all felt strongly about higher education. They have not come, as perhaps the lawyer-descendants of the Irish and the late-immigrant Jews have, to take it for granted that children of the suburban middle class go to college (and probably beyond). Within that relative seriousness, we notice that most of our helpers have been beneficiaries of the Italian-American acceptance of education as a ladder of vertical mobility. They seem here to fall into the three groups we mentioned above: Some remember and even feel the pain of accepting the assimilation that comes with going to universities in America; some marvel at parents that seem to have been exceptions to the attitudes the social historians describe; and some have come to feel as descendants of other late-immigrant groups have come to feel: They seem to take it for granted that going to college is what prosperity in America means and requires. This last group, we think, shows that prosperity in America is a morally expensive enterprise.

> Because my father had no education, he insisted that I get the best education available. To my dad, that did not mean the local public or parochial school. He went to his own lawyer to get a recommendation on the grammar school I should attend. The result was a private Catholic academy located about fifteen miles from our home. Every day, from K through eight, my mother would drive me to school and either my mother or father would pick me up. The school was known as the best Catholic grammar school in Buffalo. And because my father had little, if any, contact with business people from Ivy League backgrounds, he never heard about the private secular

schools which may have had a better academic reputation than the Catholic academy.

After grammar school, I again went the private, Catholic route to a Jesuit high school, also located about fifteen miles from home. Until I obtained my driver's license, my mother or father chauffeured me to school every morning. My father encouraged me to interact with children from professional backgrounds and made it a point to take me with him to meetings with his own lawyer, stockbroker, or insurance agent, to give me the exposure. He always told me that he wanted me to work with my brains, not with my hands.

When the time for college came, my dad went to a business friend, a manager with Bethlehem Steel, and sought his counsel as to what school would be best for me. Dad knew his own limitations, and he wanted to ensure my future through the finest education he could provide.

* * *

Although my parents were very proud of me, they also were apparently threatened by the education I was receiving. My first two years were punctuated with remarks like, "Now that you're a big shot in college, I guess you can't talk to us." Since I felt no shame in my parents, at first I didn't know how to respond. After a while I just made it clear that I was proud of them and had no intention of denying or abandoning my cultural heritage just because I was being "educated." Nevertheless, I felt during this time a social schizophrenia, having to be one person at college and another at home, and not feeling totally comfortable with either.

* * *

There wasn't a lot of emphasis on education in any of the families in my neighborhood. My father was just hooked on education, even though he wasn't educated himself. He figured it out somewhere along the line that education was the key; all four of the boys in our family went to college; my older brother is a lawyer also. When I look at my cousins, though, I don't know if you'll find another college degree. One of them is married to a lawyer, although she didn't go to college. They didn't see education as worth the effort, or the financial commitment. When you got out of twelfth grade in Brooklyn, if you were a man, you went to do some physical labor; if you were a woman, you had children and made pasta.

* * *

I don't know where my dad's thrust for education came from. It totally went against the grain of our community; it was not a high priority there. But I never knew a time when my parents didn't talk about "when you go to college [or]... when you finish college." They had not finished high school. They were nineteen and seventeen when they got married. Maybe education was a unique kind of chemistry that they put together; none of their siblings were much into education. I have thought about it a lot. My mother told me, after I applied to Notre Dame and Holy Cross, "If you can't get into one of those two schools you can work in the shoe store with your father."

* * *

I knew no professionals, with the exception of the two doctors who had their practice in my little town. My father had profound respect for those doctors and considered both of them friends. They were the only people I knew who had college degrees, who could provide me with some idea of what college was all about.... The high school was oriented toward teaching industrial arts, since most of the graduates entered the work force. Only a small number of students were college-bound. Counseling was almost nonexistent. You pretty much had to make your own way and figure out what the future entailed for you. . . . I discussed college with some of the teachers I knew in high school and even had a conversation with one of the doctors.

* * *

On my father's side of the family, there seemed to be less emphasis on going to school; however, a lot of that has to do with the ages of my older cousins coinciding with the draft age during the war. On my father's side, I am the only lawyer, aside from some second and third cousins who are attorneys in Italy. It should be understood, of course, that an attorney in Italy is less often a lawyer, as we think of it, but is more of a government bureaucrat. Despite the fact that on my father's side there was less of a tendency to attend college, my father always put an emphasis on going to school. He dealt with several business people who had law degrees as a background. My father was always fascinated by courtrooms and the legal profession. His theory was that to go to law school was the best thing one could do.

* * *

Dad became a merchant tailor and had his own business of making tailor-made men's suits, until the end of World War I introduced mass production of men's clothing after the companies were geared up for the manufacture of uniforms during the war. My father then was selected as a deputy coroner of Allegheny County and became in a short time a known expert in legal medicine, dealing with homicides and suicides, although he was neither a lawyer nor a doctor. He was soon elevated to the position of chief deputy coroner, a post that he held during thirty of his thirty-three years in the office.

There is no doubt that my father's participation in the law was an inspiration to me to study law. My brother became a physician; my sister served as assistant dean of women at the University of Pittsburgh following graduation there. My father's two sisters, who also settled in America, collectively produced two lawyers, one dentist, one engineer, and one dental hygienist. Only two of their children did not graduate from institutions of higher learning.

Rispetto and Prosperity

We are comparing the contexts in which *rispetto* is practiced, in family disputes ranging from intense, not-merely-recreational political argument to family decisions about marriage, vocation, and most of what we mean when we talk about personal "destiny." *Rispetto* usually operates comfortably—that is, habitually—in those contexts. Italian Americans know how to argue, how to claim and confer dignity without surrendering truthfulness. The conventional understanding of the Italian-American family as insular and patriarchical ("loyalty to the father and the family before the state," as Joe Martori puts it) is not, we think, challenged by our understanding of how *rispetto* works in such family disputes. *Rispetto* is not a virtue of obedience or subordination; it is, rather, a way to negotiate issues about obedience and subordination without loss of self, as it is also a way to negotiate disobedience or insubordination and at the same time honor authority.

Family arguments do not push the virtue of *rispetto* to the narrative prominence that would show what virtue is like when the daily habit, formed in small matters, becomes evident because the virtue is tested, displayed, and described. *Rispetto* then becomes like other virtues in American lawyer stories—courage, truthfulness, or friendship. In such stories, virtue becomes clear as it becomes vivid in moments of dramatic crisis. The crisis that appears useful for examining *rispetto* is formal education.

The social historians' account is that formal education was seen among Southern Italians and Italian Americans to be an external force. It challenged moral reliance on the family, and moral reliance on the family was how Southern Italian culture survived. A young professional woman in the Sirey-Patti group said, "I went away to college and found out there was more to life. People in New Haven acted as if they could change the world.... They also acted as if they were in charge of their lives. Which were two very different things [from] what I grew up with.... But, you know, I felt ashamed to be an Italian.... That's where I started feeling this big split.... I got into counseling.... I learned a lot, but I had to come home." From an Italian point of view she was cured of an illness.

Rispetto is tested in such a context, and that testing gives us an opportunity to describe what we mean when we say that *rispetto* is a virtue in and through which the person learns, practices, and teaches membership within the family. The heart of the educational crisis for the Italian-American family, as for other late-immigrant families, is assimilation. This is the general conclusion among the social historians and is evident also among the lawyers who helped us. The culture the Italian immigrants brought with them resisted assimilation with unusual moral force. Assimilation involved survival as well as identity; *la via vecchia* and *l'ordine della famiglia* were how Southern Italy had survived physical, violent, corrupting invasions for thousands of years. The Southern Italian immigrants were a powerless, poor people; they survived by building a wall of indifference around the family and then evaluating external events in terms of their effect on the family. The allure of American culture—prototypically formal education—tested *rispetto.* The moral issue was, again and again, how to come to terms with that allure and retain the deepest—and often the only—communitarian values that made sense, the values Italians had and treasured in their families. To become American and remain Italian, to be Italian in America, in that deeply significant way, was an issue on which *rispetto* was tested, displayed, and described.

CHAPTER SEVEN

Rispetto and the Community

> A self-controlled person seems self-indulgent in relation to an insensitive person and insensitive in relation to a self-indulgent person, and a generous person extravagant in relation to a stingy person and stingy in relation to an extravagant person. This is the reason why people at the extremes push the person in the middle over to the other extreme: A coward calls a brave person reckless and a reckless person calls a brave person a coward.
>
> Aristotle

The structural possibilities of the number three appealed to Aristotle, as they have to every generation of speculative thinkers. He used three to describe what a virtue is: Virtue is the mean, the middle way between excess and deficiency. Courage is the middle way between cowardice and recklessness; self-control is the mean between insensitivity and self-indulgence; generosity is the mean between extravagance and stinginess; high-mindedness is the mean between vanity and small-mindedness; honesty is the mean between boastfulness and self-deprecation.

"There are, then," he said, "three kinds of disposition: two are vices (one marked by excess and one by deficiency), and one, virtue, is the mean. Now, each of these dispositions is, in a sense, opposed to both the others: The extremes are opposites to the middle as well as to one another, and the middle is opposed to the extremes."

In the moral life, so described, the skills to see and to say what is going on are necessary for the virtue that is in the middle. The insensitive person looks at someone who exercises virtuous self-control, for example, and accuses him of self-indulgence. The self-indulgent person looks at the same person and accuses him of insensitivity. Neither sees what is going on; neither is truthful, and neither is likely to develop the virtue of self-control until he is able to be truthful. Aristotle not only taught the middle way as the way of virtue; he also taught that the skills of truthful description were necessary to the middle way, so that skills of description are not only necessary for understanding; they are also a moral art.

Rispetto as an Aristotelian Virtue

In this middle way, and in this disciplined attention to what is going on, *rispetto*, the disposition to practice (to learn, to teach, and to remember) membership in the family, is (i) the mean between surrendering identity to the group and exhibiting a destructive independence from it; the mean between the deficiency of conformity and the excess of individualism. And it is also, necessarily, (ii) the disposition to describe truthfully where one is situated in the community. The practice of the virtue requires more than the passive comfort of custom within a secure group and conventional accounts of what is going on:

> One negative and one positive remark: The negative one is that I have always felt that there is too much of a we-versus-them attitude about Italian families—a sort of nationalism as described by Benedetto Croce, and that I never liked. If prejudice toward outsiders is the counterpart of internal cohesiveness, then I'd prefer to be less cohesive.

The positive remark is a little story that enabled me to see an Italian family through the eyes of an outsider. When I was in college, my best friend and I were guests at a nearby women's college during one of their weekends, and one of our dates took us to her Italian family home. We had a pleasant time, exchanged a few jokes, had good and abundant food, and then I picked up an accordion that was there and we all sang some of the standards of the day.

Later when we were driving home my friend observed that I "fit in so easily" to that family, and I said that it was no problem fitting in because things were very much like that when I was a kid. He told me that his upbringing was very austere; his father was a police captain, and they were never intimate; they never sang songs or told jokes. Well, I said, you probably did other things—better things, *intellectual* things. I asked him whether he really thought that the afternoon at the Italian home was all that big a deal. His reply startled and saddened me enormously. He said, "I've never before had such a feeling of happiness."

Our helper's story illustrates both points about *rispetto* as an Aristotelian virtue—both the middle-way method of description and the dependence of the virtue on the art of seeing and saying what is going on. The deficiency that helps place *rispetto* as a virtue is suggested by the self-effacing conformity that caused our helper's friend to have had an austere childhood. One of the Patti-Sirey's group members noticed an instance of the deficiency in the problem an Italian-American woman has when "she cares a lot about her family, but she doesn't care a lot about herself." She is, we think, rather like our helper's friend; in Italian-American terms she is assimilated. By contrast, another member of that group suggested the place of the virtue, rather than the deficiency, when she said of the family she grew up in: "There's an acceptance. You don't have to do anything.... [when] you're home; you're home.... You can

never get thrown out of an Italian family. I can't imagine
getting thrown out of an Italian family.... You can always
go home and I didn't understand how important that was
until I realized that some of my [non-Italian] friends really couldn't go home.... I think that's very important—
to have that sense of being loved and accepted, just for
being."

This young woman discovered the virtue of belonging
as it is practiced in the family. Congressman Peter Rodino
described it outside the family. He defined the virtue of
rispetto as the practice "of personal worth and dignity
independent of" marks of external rank and status (such
as being a policeman, or being a captain, or being an
adult in the presence of a child, or being an elder partner
in a law firm, or being a member of the United States
House of Representatives).

The excess that places the virtue, and the importance of truthful description of excess, are illustrated
by our helper's distaste for a "we against them" defen-
siveness among Italian Americans (many of our helpers
mentioned it). The excess is too much concern for
what Robert Viscusi (in Juliani's anthology) called "respectability"—"the manufactured simpers of the well-
established, upwardly mobile, endless aspirant dullards
we [Italian Americans] are likely to become if we insist
always upon putting our dignity before our conscience
or our desire to be accepted before our desire to tell
the truth."

The word "dignity" is important to these descriptions
of *rispetto*, but the way the word is used by Mr. Rodino
(as part of the virtue, as a synonym for "self respect") is
not the way Professor Viscusi uses the word (as a synonym for respectability). The comparison is confusing,
but the confusion is useful: Like the English word "respect," dignity signals both a virtue (*rispetto*) and the
vice of excess (respectability). Mr. Rodino understands
dignity to be the self-regard necessary to *rispetto*; dignity

is, in that sense, necessary as well to Aristotle's under-standing of truthfulness, or to the self-regard on which depend such moral principles as the Golden Rule (love your neighbor as a person like yourself) or Kant's second formulation of the central moral imperative (act so that you treat humanity as an end, and never as a means only).

But Professor Viscusi understands dignity to be a claim on others for deference, as the consequence and manifes-tation of respectability. It would probably be more lucid to translate Rodino's meaning of dignity as virtuous self-regard and Viscusi's as a vicious ethic of honor and shame. There is a sense in which a person should *seek* honor as consequent on and necessary for virtuous self-regard. Thus Femminella describes *fare bella figura* as an aspect of *rispetto*. But such seeking of honor becomes an ethic of honor and shame when it loses its perception of what is going on.

This comparison of understandings, by two Italian Americans, of what dignity means is an illustration of the practice outside the family of the virtue of belonging. What is important in the discussion is that both Rodino and Viscusi understand also that the skill for being a member is a skill learned in *l'ordine della famiglia*, a product of the Old Way, and that it is practiced in a local and national community that continues to insist on as-similation as the price of success. It is in that way, in the face of that pressure, that the issue of dignity comes up.

The occasion to make some such translation of the no-tion of dignity is instructive in describing *rispetto* in pro-fessional ethics, in that it shows the extent to which *rispetto*, which depends on dignity as virtuous self-regard, is an *Italian* and *American* virtue—neither Ital-ian nor American—to be distinguished (in Aristotelian fashion) from the excess of the modern Italian social practice of respect for status, but distinguished as well from the self-effacing deficiencies of Protestant American culture.

Fran Claro's memoir of her childhood in Italian-American Queens illustrates what we mean to claim when we say that *rispetto* differs as much from class-based deference in the Old World as it does from New World individualism. Miss Claro is a third-generation (second generation born in America) Italian American. Her mother Mary seemed to Fran to despise Italianness; Mary sought to be an assimilated American, through association with her Irish neighbors. And, of course, to assimilate well, Mary had to learn to deny what she was. She rebelled against Italian soap operas and street festivals as she rebelled against Italian Catholic spirituality and Southern Italian family custom.

Mary's daughter, Fran, perhaps out of adolescent rebellion at first, resisted assimilation. She speaks of standing to the side, but as close as her mother would allow her to stand, when the Italian-American neighborhood celebrated its annual *festa*: "Oh, how I wanted to be part of that parade. I wanted to be on that float. I dreamed about pinning bills on The Saint. But my mother was becoming an American. 'That's not for you,' she would say. 'Even when you're old enough we're not gonna let you do that.'" Mary preferred Irish-Catholic religious culture, helping the "fine ladies" of the Rosary Society at the parish bingo games. "She thought the way they let their ice cream melt in their coffee was very stylish. She admired their appearance, so different from her very dark and very Italian beauty."

Aristotle might have explored this contrast as an attempt to locate excess and deficiency and thus to describe a virtue. Italian-American lawyers often express, as Fran Claro did, the contrast between their two cultures as inter-generational—as a social phenomenon, a "generation gap." It is, they say, an ambivalence within each Italian American; they give us an opportunity to describe the middle way personally, as they also give us a way to show that *rispetto* is an American virtue. (We should notice again that these lawyers think of themselves as beneficiaries more than as victims of the sort of moral struggle Fran Claro describes.)

When I was in law school, I tried to run away from my heritage, including marrying a person who knew nothing about the traditions and values. Of course, the marriage was a disaster, as was my attempt to deny my emotions, thought processes, and style of life. Fortunately, the damage was reversible and we now have a wonderfully understanding relationship. We have two Italian-American children and my in-laws live ten minutes away. The children see their grandparents regularly and are becoming more and more aware of their heritage.

* * *

Italian women are not encouraged to go to school. I didn't think that's what I wanted for my future. I hoped that my wife might be someone educated, who might share more of my interests and also share as far as the family would go. When I went to Notre Dame, I'd been dating a girl. The thing that soured the romance was that she wouldn't go to college, and I just couldn't understand that. I couldn't believe that we would have enough in common, given that choice. So we broke up.

* * *

Today I have a much different attitude about my Italian background. While, as a youth, I wanted to assimilate and have parents who were like everyone else, today I feel a sense of pride about my background. My wife and I visited Calabria on our honeymoon. I saw the house where my mother was born and lived as a child. She has a sister there, and we visited with her. We went to my father's village and visited with his brother and sister. I have a large family in the New Castle area and we continue to keep in touch with them. We gather at the old homestead on major holidays, but enjoy only a few of the Italian dishes that were so prevalent when my mother cooked. My sisters and brothers have married non-Italians. . . . My wife is German and French.

* * *

I ended up getting my first job with a five-person Italian law firm in New Haven; I was very happy there for
the three years that I stayed. Eventually I left to go on my
own, or, that is, with a partner my own age, in the suburb
of Wallingford. I felt that's where I wanted to settle. I
wanted to raise my children there, where they could have
tremendous educational opportunity. In terms of clients
for myself, in terms of being almost midway between Boston and New York for cultural purposes, and, generally, in
terms of rustic atmosphere—I always thought of myself
as wanting those things.

* * *

If you're inculcated with the values of a group, then to
reject, to challenge, to give them up means a conflict of
loyalty—a kind of disloyalty. You're being untrue to your
family, your parents, and your ancestral heritage. That is
true of many ethnic groups. But to make that break is perhaps more of a trauma for Italian Americans than for
other groups.

* * *

I cannot tell you that I had formal exposure or training
in the art of being Italian when I was younger, because I
did not. However, the intrinsic values of Italian Americans
were transmitted to me, my siblings, and my raft of cousins. There was a certain dignity that one was to maintain
because if one did not maintain it, it reflected poorly on
the family and that was perhaps the greatest sin that one
could commit. There was also a special bonding of the
family entity (and this includes the entire family and not
just the immediate family) that prompted each of us to
help the other when that was necessary. In a sense this
reflects the "we against the world" situation that the
older Italian-Americans were faced with when they came
to this country. They could only depend upon one another. While I think that is less so today, there is still a
significant element in my family of being responsible to

the family and for the family. Just before my father died, he made it clear to me that I was responsible for this family in his absence. He made it clear to me that, while I had my own life to live, I should never stretch myself so thin that I would not be available for the family should I be needed. Even though I live several hundred miles from my family, I maintain continuous contact with them in an effort to try and keep the promise that I made to my father before he died.

* * *

I remember when I was a child, going to numerous weddings of cousins and other relatives which were very "ethnic." Like the opening scenes of *The Godfather*, but ours were done a lot cheaper. On the other hand, my son has been to more *bar mitzvahs* than he has been to Italian weddings. I have no problem with this. I want them to have a broad range of experience and cultures; however, I would like them to know something about their ancestry and take some pride in having an Italian last name.

* * *

I love having Italian genes, but regret that assimilation has been so complete that genes are about all that is left. I enjoy Italian food and nineteenth-century Italian opera (particularly Donizetti), but know nothing of Italian literature or language. What little is left in me is likely to die with me. With my children, the transformation is complete. All they possess is part of a gene pool, and a diluted one at that, since their mother does not share in it. Before I joined the bench, my practice included federal Indian law. There the interest of tribes in preserving their cultural identity was paramount. Assimilation was akin to genocide. In a very real sense, the powerful forces of assimilation have resulted and will inevitably result in the loss of any identifiable persons in North America as Italian Americans. I feel a little special because of it, a member of an endangered species.

* * *

I grew up in an immigrant parish, served by priests
from the Italian Precious Blood order, a unique Italian
neighborhood, isolated from the rest of the Italian-
American experience, centered around this one parish
and surrounded by Irish parishes. The priests were Italian
missionaries. The pastor I had is still alive; he lives in Italy now. A missionary parish didn't have the same priorities as a diocesan parish, and now the parish is
completely gone. The building was sold and is now a
Baptist church. An area of four blocks square was my entire neighborhood, surrounded by the Chicago mix of
other ethnic groups. There was a Lutheran church nearby,
with classes in German. The missionary priests did not
see themselves as assimilators; they were a step behind.
The people in the community, on the other hand, were
very interested in assimilating, partly because of a remote
feeling. They felt the lack of other Italian parishes around
them. Their neighborhood was not like other areas, not
like the Little Italys in New York, or even on the west
side of Chicago. They felt very isolated, and everyone
was very interested in becoming American.

Our parish maintained a lot of customs—the big feast
for Our Lady of Mount Carmel, for example, an evening
procession with the statue of the Virgin carried through
the streets. It wound up at the parish school yard, where
the local bakery sponsored a fireworks show. There were
also processions for St. Ann, St. Rocco, and St. Gerald.
Each of the saints had a society that backed them. Pretty
typical. The St. Rocco di Potenza Society still exists. I
never belonged to any of them. My family had no involvement in any of them.

Rispetto as a Virtue of Italians in America

Hell is what a person does to himself when he
goes against the grain of his own character.

Helen Barolini

The sentimental movie *Moonstruck* tells about three generations in an Italian-American family. It shows how the sense of family operating in an Italian-American neighborhood reaches out to include the grocer around the corner, business customers, suitors and the rivals of suitors, and even a potential mother-in-law on her deathbed in Sicily. At the end of the story, tensions in temporary abeyance, suitor, rival, grocer, and all three generations of blood relatives toast their stubborn harmony with good red table wine, as they say together: *Viva la famiglia!*

There is much that is distinctively Italian in such a story, but much of the distinctively Italian is characteristic more of Italians in America than of Italians in Italy. There is a sense in such a story of (a) tradition being held on to (centrally, stereotypically, *l'ordine della famiglia*); (b) traditional peculiarities being rediscovered, as if an American from the suburbs who had an Italian surname came upon an ethnic food festival and discovered an atavistic fondness for *sanguinaccio*; and (c) deeper values being noticed and (as Michael Novak would have it) being not so much chosen as come home to. All three of those ways of describing tradition—retention, discovery, and return—are Italian-American experiences.

We think such experiences are characteristic of being Italian in America and that, in a characteristic way, they show that *rispetto* is a virtue of Italians in America. It is not the product of roots alone; it is the product of growth from roots. *Rispetto* is the result of being both Italian and American. It is for that reason that its practice displays something valuable for conversations about community in America. It illustrates the ability of a first-order moral culture to change and to become more inclusive.

The retained, discovered, and revived ethnic values are not the moral values the Italian American's immigrant grandparents had—at least not when this third-generation moral maturity is described by an Italian

American who earns her living in a modern American profession and raises her family in a modern American suburb or in a gentrified urban enclave. The good habit of practicing membership in the family (and in associations for which the metaphor of family is claimed and claimed seriously), the virtue of *rispetto*, has a quality about it that is distinctively Italian *in* America. Richard Gambino, in what is likely the most widely read of all books in English on Italian Americans, *Blood of My Blood*, illustrates the argument we want to make when he talks of the directions an assimilated Italian American has before her in the late twentieth-century United States.

"Three stages of the journey," Gambino calls these. "First, there is the stage in which a group almost totally lacks access to the larger society. This stage characterized the immigrant period of Italians...." Rosemary Santini's interview of a three-generation family in Queens shows this first group as grandparents waiting for their teenaged grandsons to visit them and eat some of the grandmother's homemade *fettucine*—the teenagers "tall, solid, muscular young men who say they want to live farther out on Long Island, near the sea, in a house complete with a boat ... an office nearby in town, and lots and lots of privacy." The grandparents would, even if these grandsons did live in such a place, still be waiting in the Italian neighborhood in Queens, to feed and to be visited, "eating vegetables in garlic oil with fresh Italian bread, waiting for the third generation of the family to be available from their busy life." While the grandparents wait, the grandsons are "swimming in the beach-club pool, clowning with their friends, listening to rock music, drinking soda pop, eating frankfurters, oblivious to the lifetime of dedication and hardship represented by the plates of rare and delicious *fettucine*...."

In between the grandparents and the boys at the beach club is the first American-born generation of parents. This, Gambino says, is "the stage in which a group blames itself. It feels guilty about its differentness, shies away from contact with its heritage, and deferentially subordinates itself to the larger society." Gambino's "second stage" describes the situation of Mary, Fran Claro's mother, who as a child retreated to her room, by herself, away from the street celebrations of the annual *festa*, and read to herself from *Rebecca of Sunnybrook Farm*. As our helpers indicated to us, though, the situation of the first American-born generation is ambivalent. The author Pietro di Donato, American-born son of immigrants, says with fondness, "My father took me to the Metropolitan Opera when I was five, and he had concrete on his shoes."

The third generation is different: The grandsons in Queens are able to enjoy the *fettucine*: "My grandfather—and almost all of his friends—dug," Claro says. "I was never really sure just what they dug, although I knew it had something to do with buildings.... His heavy shoes would be caked with mud and plaster. His hands were hard and brittle, like plastic. His complexion was almost Indian red. On the way home from the subway, he would joke with us, half in English, half in Italian. My grandfather smiled most of the time. He liked to play with us, and he felt proud when we walked with him. We loved being with him. But what I found charming about him, his daughter—my mother—found embarrassing."

The fidelity of the grandparents and the trauma of the parents are present in the grandchildren, present because, as Faulkner said, the past is not dead; it is not even past. These cultural forces are focused morally in the grandchildren who dream of a house on the beach, whose highest ambition in life is a moored boat and lots and lots of privacy. The forces are formed as well in the attentive grandchildren, who walk with their grandfather. The grandchildren can also foresee the comfort that comes from being in a profession in America; but Gambino and Viscusi might say of them that they do not foresee the moral differences in the paths their lives

could take. They may, Gambino says, "let old values die
and become jellyfish Americans, transparent souls in sur-
face pursuits." Aspirant dullards, as Robert Viscusi calls
them, pursuing active, chatty careers. "Or they may revi-
talize their traditions and contribute them in new form to
an enriched American culture" (Gambino). The argument we wish to make here for *rispetto* is an argument
for the moral importance of tradition. It is as present in
the boys at the swimming club as the rock music and the
sense of possibility. It is a memory, something formed in
them that will influence the apparent choice of direction
their professional lines will take; and it is a skill they will
require in their effort to contribute something Italian to
American culture.[1]

No one, as Isaac Bashevis Singer said it, is "just a human being." Each of us comes from somewhere. Part of
the formation of the virtues that each of us has is formation in memory; it involves the *practice* of memory. This
is true perhaps of all the virtues, evidently so of friendship, civility, and justice. The practice of memory is significant in this way in the formation of the virtue of
rispetto, as we attempt here to describe it. The virtue has
to do with being—with remembering—Italians *in* America, including the struggle for *pane e lavoro* among
grandparents, and the subtle, painful ambivalence of parents. Memory is part of the formation of the good habit of
teaching, learning, practicing membership in family; and
this memory is the memory of being Italian *in* America.

Rispetto is an Italian-American virtue. We non-Italians
know this from stories; the distinctive quality of remembering how it is to be an Italian in America is something Italian Americans know from experience, but they
also know it from stories. They and we know from
narratives, biographies, and novels, from drama and the

---

1. We and our Italian-American helpers take more optimism from
Santini and Gambino than they perhaps intend to provide.

recollections of Italian American friends. Such sources are primary in our evidence, but they need not exclude studies that purport to be more scientific—studies such as Rocco Caporale's "profiles" of members of the professions in America and in Southern Italy, and his conclusions about the differences between modern-day professionals in each of these blood-related communities.

Italian and Italian-American Professionals

Caporale studied professionals in Sicily, Calabria, and Lucania, and Italians in America, in the period 1929–1979. Teachers, physicians, dentists, lawyers, the clergy, and business managers in Southern Italy are, he says, "more clearly motivated by the ethics of particularity and individual interest" than their American cousins, who "show greater sensitivity for the exigencies of more universalistic and rational modes of relating to one's own profession and to society."[2] Caporale was curious about the relative extent of "amoral familism" (Banfield's phrase for the preference for family security and prosperity at the expense of a broader common good) among the two professional groups; at the attitudes the two sets of professionals had toward the Roman Catholic Church; at where higher education conferred status and where it confirmed status; and at involvement in politics by members of the two sets of professional groups. He noticed a deep cultural morality that, on our evidence, is as strong

---

2. The Italians demonstrate "values of sophistication, political savvy, and survival capability," Caporale says, while Italian Americans have "managed to absorb to a great extent the ethos of a democratic and national social order and translate it in a mature form to professional behavior." I argue with "absorb" in that conclusion, and I think that "mature" is a tendentious judgment. We believe the Italian American's civic virtue has more to do with its formation in *la via vecchia*, in America, than it has to do with the English-Protestant culture's instilling the American "republican" vision in the Italian immigrants and their children. But Caporale also noticed an important difference, and we want to exploit it.

among Italian Americans as he says it is among modern
Southern Italians—"profound attachment to the family,"
for example; at least nominal affiliation with the Roman
Catholic Church and remarkably little defection from this
affiliation; and *campanilismo*, "a strong identification
with the local community." Caporale seems to have concluded that these three traditional values are weaker in
America than in Southern Italy. Caporale also found indicative professional differences. Two are important to
our argument that *rispetto* is a virtue formed by Italians
in America: (a) relative isolation and (b) professional
status.

Relative isolation was probably the most evident difference that Caporale reported. Professional groups in
communities in Southern Italy practice what Caporale
calls "conspicuous exemption from demands and obligations to which all other common citizens are subject.
Thus a professional will seldom be expected to queue up
in lines, to wait to be served in his turn at restaurants
and offices, to follow routine in applying for public services," he says. "Exceptions in his favor are an everyday
event, most frequently from class subordinates, but also
from fellow professionals in the form of mutual exchange
of favors.

"*Il professore, l'avvocato, il dottore, il reverendo* are
different people, entitled to priorities and exceptions,
without necessarily eliciting envy or resentment in the
lower classes. This system of conspicuous deference and
exemption is effectively enforced by the professional
class, albeit in a smooth and unassuming way. I have
never observed a single case where a professional would
turn down differential treatments. . . . " Mary agrees:

> I observed a similar system of respect and conspicuous
> exemption in Tuscany. According to this system, every-
> one is deserving of civility and an outward show of re-
> spect, regardless of class. Thus the woman who sells
> bread to the local doctor's wife is treated with gentle re-

spect and formality by the doctor and his wife when they come into the bakery, and she returns their polite pleasantries. But when she sees a long line with the doctor's wife at the end of it, she indicates to her to scoot around to one side of the counter, and fills her shopping bags with the freshest bread. The woman at the bakery does this not out of friendship—between the two classes there could never be friendship—but out of deference. And the other people in the bakery don't resent this special treatment for one of the town's professionals.

Caporale located a startling social effect of this deference and exemption in Southern Italy: It *deprives* the professional person of civic power. It puts the professional in a markedly different situation from that of his counterpart in America—where, for example, lawyers are and have always been a republican aristocracy—and leaves him in a favorable position for narrow exploitation of his professional position (something American professionals have always denied they want):

> On the one hand the professional is prevented from exercising independent leadership, especially in the direction of change and needed reforms; on the other hand the informal system of deference and privilege granted the professional class reinforces ... exploitative tendencies [in] ... Southern Italian society. ... The presence of a well educated group of professionals, highly respected by the population, made no difference as regards the solution to serious problems affecting the community. All political activity was carried out by the professional group mainly as a form of self-serving interest through a political party. The idea of the common good has as little appeal to the professionals as to the common peasants. Common good is pursued only when it coincides with the individual's interests.

And the interests of his family—which is what Banfield's WASPish sociological label, "amoral familism," was meant to suggest.

"In contrast," Caporale says, "the Italian American professional, though deprived of the sophistication and class-consciousness of his Italian counterpart, appears much more committed to a universalistic attitude and a sense of equality and rational political action. . . . " Caporale admits that his Italian-American subject "retained" what he called "a certain amount of timidity and provincialistic in-groupness that makes him identifiable as not-quite all-American." (This suggests the nuance we would claim for *campanilismo* among Italian Americans. I think of it as friendship in the Aristotelian sense.) But the Italian American has managed to develop "a firm commitment to rational professional standards both in his behavior and in the exercise of his skills."

(b) *Professional Status.* One way to have put this last conclusion of Caporale's would have been to say that the Italian-American professional practices in the community a skill he learned from being a member of his family. *Rispetto* has become a way to function in an influential and influenced way in the community and in professional associations. The contrast would then be (and we think Caporale's observations support this way of saying it) between (a) the professional person in Southern Italy, who bargains for membership in a professional fraternity, and maintains a position in the fraternity through a system of exchange; and (b) the Italian American whose place in a profession is somewhat analogous to her place in her family—maintained less by exchange than by friendship.

> Among the Italian-American professionals . . . friendship was found to be less demanding and involving, but at the same time more enduring, fair and reliable; its lack of depth was compensated by less ambiguity and fragility. The Southern Italian professional remains at all times a political animal, keen for his personal interest and that of his family; the Italian-American professional's image is that of a social participant, less intense about his status

and goals, and more open to a variety of communitarian endeavors of human import, wider than his personal interest and political sphere of influence.

The fraternal involvement of the Italian-American professional is also relatively generous: "The obligations to family and profession are given almost equal consideration," Caporale says. But in America "the case of conflict between the two roles is not infrequent. The male professional in particular is expected to participate actively in various institutions," he says—and we think first of the typical cases of Italian-American professionals such as Salvatore Cotillo, and Geraldine Ferraro, Mario Merola, Mario Cuomo, John Pastore, Antonin Scalia, and generations of Italian-American mayors, whose first arena of public service was an immigrant version of *campanilismo*, service in and for the surrounding Italian-American community. One of the skills necessary for such service is the skill to negotiate the conflict between *campanilismo* and fidelity to the family, and it is, of course, our suggestion that such a skill is learned in the family, learned through negotiating loyalties within the family. Its ethical nursery is *l'ordine della famiglia*.

In education, the obvious difference is that school became a ladder of vertical mobility for the Italian Americans, but has not functioned that way in Southern Italy. In America, education confers status. In Southern Italy, it confirms status. In America, education "has molded the children of unskilled manual workers into full-fledged members of the professional community, often socializing them into ways of thinking, relating, and producing that characterize a socially different group than the one in which they were born," Caporale says. In Italy, "higher education was the seal and confirmation of the privilege of belonging to the professional middle class in virtue of family tradition.... The basic ethical requirements (confidentiality, meritocratic system, ongoing self-improvement, rational judgment, criteria, etc.) were considered unrelated and unnecessary for professional status; but an appropriate lifestyle, one that came close to a semi-aristocratic pattern, was considered indispensable (spacious living, distinctive furniture, valuable paintings, etc.)."

Across all of these categories, as we see it, the experience of Italian professionals in America has become more communitarian than experience in Southern Italy. This, we think, had at first to do with the fact that Italian immigrants settled into America in Italian communities, and began then to practice and to teach the importance of broadening the defensive bulwarks of *la via vecchia* to include neighbors from the same place in Italy. Helen Barolini's immigrant heroine, Umbertina Longobardi, had little sympathy for what the dominant culture in America in the late nineteenth-century thought of as its republican communitarian vision: "Her concern was only for her family, not for some abstract common good." But, still, "she despised those [not in her family] who broke strikes in order to work for low wages, who didn't speak up their grievance, were self-denying, and still dependent on a *padrone*." Her struggle for *pane e lavoro* in America became a struggle for her fellow immigrants, as it had been at first a typically Calabrian struggle for her husband and children. Umbertina did not announce a theory for this gradual change, but her behavior came to describe the Old World protection of family in a way that included people who were not in her family.

In one indicative episode in the novel, a fellow immigrant, Domenico Saccà, had been politically active in the upstate New York community where Umbertina and her family settled (with Domenico Saccà's help). As often happened among early-day Italian American political leaders, Domenico, a cobbler, became discouraged at the lack of response from other Italian Americans, who were more interested in fellowship and small material gain than in reform of the structures that kept the Southern-Italian immigrants poor. Then,

> something happened that seemed to Umbertina another great lesson of life. Serafino [Umbertina's husband] burst

into the store one day, excited and flushed, to say that he had just heard ... that Domenico Saccà was at the station about to board a train to leave the country and go back to Italy. Domenico had been brooding for months over the end of his *Circolo Socialista*, which had come about when the old members defected and set up a new club, the *Società Castagnese* [named for their home village in Italy, rather than for a political cause], which was strictly social with no politics allowed. It hurt Domenico, and ... he had decided to return to Italy.

"*Imbecille*," said Umbertina in disgust at such a senseless act. At the same time she was moved, for despite the aggravation he provoked in her, Umbertina knew they all owed their start to Domenico. Serafino was beside himself at the thought of the shoemaker's leaving.

"Run to the station!" he shouted at Ben [his son], who was in the midst of dealing with a salesman from New York. "Keep him from getting on the train! Bring him back!"

Somehow Ben did it, reaching Domenico on the platform and persuading him to return with him to the store.

"*Pazzo*," Serafino greeted him gruffly, but there were tears in his eyes as he put his arm around the shoemaker's shoulder. "Were you going off to spite yourself? Stay so that you can tell your grandchildren how the stupidest thing Serafino Longobardi ever did was to send his son to the station to keep you here so you could go on insulting him at Scalise's."

Italian-American lawyers have similar stories to tell:

The family was an emotional support group, and therapy center if necessary, with few secrets and frequent, open discussions about the range of human feelings, their expression and resolution. The family was also a recreational forum, where siblings and cousins played together every week, adults played cards, and everyone played music and danced. And despite our modest financial circumstances, there was always food, and plenty of it. Everything one needed was in the family: This was the code by which we were raised, and until adolescence, this was reality.

Coupled with this tribal sense of family unity came a clannishness and close-mindedness towards the outside world. Friends of the family were few and carefully chosen. They were either neighbors also raising children, or families from around the corner who helped out at church functions. There were no friends from work, friends from college, or friends from the Knights of Columbus. First-generation Italian Americans in the 1950s and 1960s huddled together for protection and support, distrustful of outsiders.

This family self-sufficiency and distrust of outsiders is significant with regard to the Italian-American view of the working world. My father and all of my uncles were blue-collar laborers; they worked with their hands and had regular union hours. They were always home at dinnertime, the whole family ate together each night, and they were always home on the weekends, which were devoted to household chores on Saturdays and family gatherings on Sundays. Women of my mother's generation were raised to be, and seemed content as, housewives. The Italian-American community, and certainly the extended family infrastructure, placed great importance on motherhood, and approval for raising babies was readily available and freely given. Job fulfillment in my father's generation did not seem a priority; fulfillment in family was the ultimate priority.

Professionals such as doctors and lawyers were respected in the abstract as accomplished members of society; there were none in the family, and none that we knew in the first and second generation Italian-American community in which we lived. Role models were not readily available. Politicians were distrusted, disrespected, and assumed to be crooked and corrupt. Likewise, businessmen who had accumulated conspicuous amounts of wealth quickly were assumed to have achieved prosperity dishonestly, through deal-making, bribery, etc. The mob, a

distinct presence in New York's Italian-American community, were disrespected for their sins and refusal to earn a
living honestly. The religious values of our family and
community segregated, with one broad stroke, corrupt
politicians and businessmen, mobsters and other criminals, from the work-hard, insular family model that ordered our lives.

My teenage years, in a more heterogenous religious
and economic community during the Vietnam era,
brought with them much internal questioning, a predict-
able amount of rebellion and a gradual blurring of the
black and white lines which so clearly set the moral
boundaries of my upbringing. Still, the daily examples of
parents who attended church religiously, who worked
hard for an honest living, and who impressed upon us the
importance of doing the same, had their effects. I expressed my own feelings about being a Christian through
volunteer work in service to the community; helping
mentally ill, handicapped and aged members of the community was Christ-like, I felt, and although my high
school experiences with volunteer work were mostly in
the guise of high-profile high-school politics with many
social perks, the underlying hands-on work with less for-
tunate members of my community brought me genuine
fulfillment. My college years saw the evolution of a more
personal, less publicized but ultimately more fulfilling
form of volunteer service to my community which became my metaphor for living as a Christian.

These experiences with volunteer work are germane
to my decision to study law for two reasons. The Catholic
school boy grown up, as a young man, believed that being
a Christian meant being like Christ with the lepers, the
blind, the dying, etc. It was necessary to do something to
make society better by helping people similarly situated.
My hands-on, physical contributions to those in need—
e.g., reading to those who couldn't, helping with physical
therapy of cerebral palsy victims, playing the piano for
hospital patients—translated to an intellectual ambition

vis à vis a career. I would become a lawyer so I could help other people, and change society for the better. The second connection between volunteer work and law school was the appearance of positive role models. Several attorneys were involved in the volunteer organization I worked with in high school (I was in Key Club, they were in Kiwanis) and these individuals seemed to me good citizens, making a difference to people's lives.

* * *

Since graduating from law school I have gone into the practice of law and live now in the city in which I work, Chicago. I like to think that even though I'm supposed to be a professional person I still work in a 'blue-collar' fashion. I consistently strive to bring the type of work ethic to my job that my parents, aunts and uncles, and grandparents demonstrated throughout their lives.

* * *

I think my background would have created in me a sympathy for the underdog even if my own father had not gone to prison when I was fourteen. My feelings were set by then. I have never felt that people who violate the law are inherently evil—particularly those who commit nonviolent, economic crimes. I think many Italian Americans feel that they must be insensitive and prosecutorial as a reaction to being in a minority group that is historically associated with organized crime. I sometimes catch myself feeling that; I'm not sure it may not be warranted in some cases. Here is an essay I wrote at the age of nine:

"When I grow up. When I grow up I want to be a lawyer. I would like to be a lawyer because I could really be enforcing the law. Sometimes innocent people are punished because of unjust jurists. To be a good lawyer you must know this. Just because a person is at the scene of a crime before anyone else does not necessarily mean he committed it. I wouldn't want a person to be punished because he couldn't employ a private attorney. I would take that person's case for little or no money. I would defend the poor man as much as a rich one. I would try to make this country of ours a better place to live in."

*   *   *

Mario Cuomo (in his *Diary*):

The whole religious experience of Catholics like myself... painted for us a world of moral pitfalls that needed to be avoided in order to earn an eternal peace. It was as though God had created the world as a kind of hard passage to eternity....

Of course, that's not the way it was supposed to be. Those who were learned enough or wise enough saw in our religion even 40 years ago the kind of joy and hope and affirmation that is apparent now every Sunday morning at mass. But for the simple folk of South Jamaica, in Queens County, who came from behind the grocery stores and from the tenements and from the little houses on Liverpool Street, it was often a world of guilt and repentance and renewed effort to avoid the final defeat....

I see things a little differently today. So do the modern young altar boys who have been freed from having to stumble through the *Suscipiat*. But I am sure that I will never be totally free of the tentativeness, the concern— even, from time to time, the twinges of guilt—that accompany anything I might be tempted to regard as material success....

There is also a bright side to our old-fashioned religion, for those disposed to see it. It was the joy of giving, as compared to the joy of having. If you wanted to earn that carrot and avoid that stick, you could do it by sharing, contributing, helping. That's why they called them—those marvelous, inscrutable women, those faces surrounded in starched white linen and flowing black— the Sisters of Charity. Their whole mission at St. Monica's and elsewhere was to teach that while you were suffering the pains of denying yourself temporary and superficial

delights, you could also earn yourself an occasional moment of warmth and even, my God ... self-satisfaction!
You could do it by helping the sick, feeding the hungry,
comforting the bereaved.

It is this part of my background that has always made
it difficult for me to accept the so-called conservative
idea that, when it comes to government's redistributive
function, "God helps those whom God has helped, and if
He's left you out, who are we to presume on His will?"
And ten years of Vincentian training at St. John's Prep and
St. John's University, only reinforced my conviction that if
St. Francis of Assisi were alive today, and was reckless
enough to get involved in politics, he would be fighting
for some kind of progressivism that sought to help people
improve their lives. I just can't see him arguing for the
kind of social Darwinism that has been thrust upon us in
recent years. (That some of the current believers in "survival of the fittest" were altar boys with me nearly 40
years ago, or were my schoolmates, never ceases to sur-
prise me.)

Rispetto in the Community

The communitarian argument in jurisprudence, in
social ethics, and in professional ethics, has an anthropological difficulty: A communitarian argument is not persuasive when it is made to people who do not perceive
that they are in a community. The presence or possibility
of community in America is not evident enough to support the argument that we have moral obligations outside our domestic lives; nor is it evident enough to
support the premise or assumption that we are communal creatures who ought to find or revive or somehow
create such a community.

Neither of the two prevalent positions on communitarian jurisprudence and ethics acknowledges the anthropological difficulty. The argument for community-
by-agreement, from the individualistic philosophy that

dominates modern American jurisprudence—our intellectual inheritance from the Enlightenment and its doc-
trines of abstract duties and abstract "rights of man"—
lacks confidence in the earthy substance of human
communities. And the response from the American republican vision—the vision that led the freethinking
Thomas Jefferson and Benjamin Franklin to think of
America as a biblical community, "God's new Israel"—
lacks both history and sincerity; there is too much disap-
pointed aspiration in it, too much shopworn optimism, to
have confidence in a moral anthropology that perceives
the human person as essentially a creature who comes to
be in relationship with other human persons.

An anthropology of rights (if we may be allowed to use
that as shorthand for the philosophical, theological, and
political inheritance of the Enlightenment) is not persuasive on the question of community. It seems always to
depend on the premise that the human person is funda-
mentally alone. "How can one account for or legitimate
the existence of a society made out of individual persons
each of whom by the very nature of personhood 'is at
heart an anarchist'? . . . It is difficult if not impossible to
give any account of society, communion, or unity between the social atoms of modern individualism other
than of an artificial and external joint venture of convenience," as Jefferson Powell says it. "The most benign
type of community conceivable on individualist terms is
an ethical accord between individuals well disposed to
one another; the more likely community is an arrange-
ment based on mutual agreement or convenience."

All that such an individualist anthropology can come
up with by way of describing human community is contract or (in theology) civic covenant. Such a perception
of reality would—to put the test in the most realistic
terms—have been of no interest to the Italian immigrants we have been describing, and it is not plausible to
those of their descendants who have helped us. In more
analytical terms, individualist anthropology is the percep-

tion of loneliness and despair; and in consequentialist terms it is a predicate for nihilism. Its account of freedom "must be seen as a false or illusory freedom, since to the extent it is exercised it necessarily leads to an incoherent history and thus to a diminished or disrupted person-hood," Powell says. As a matter of ordinary common sense, this individualism is an anthropology which can account for organic communities—most radically the family—only in terms of choice: Its weakness as a foundation for jurisprudence and ethics "is amply illus-trated by how it has led us to forget that the family has traditionally not been rooted in contract but in biology," Stanley Hauerwas says. "Relations in the family have come," as a result, "to resemble relations in the rest of society—namely, a relationship between friendly strang-ers.... Ironically, this kind of family, which was justified in the name of intimacy, now finds intimacy impossible to sustain."

"The moral language our culture supplies," he says, "tends to distort the very experience we are trying to describe" when we speak of the family. "Nowhere in con-temporary ethical literature is there discussion of the simple but fundamental assumption that we have a re-sponsibility to our own children that overrides responsi-bility to children who are not ours. Although [this is] a powerful assumption, there is no adequate account in contemporary ethical reflection of why we hold it or if it is justified. Instead, the best my colleagues can offer is the doubtful thesis that children ought to have rights." Barolini's Umbertina would probably say that her chil-dren were well out of a school that could do no better than that.

The American republican vision is more attractive than the "liberal" understanding of the person as the sub-ject of his own lonely tyranny, but it is no more persua-sive. In the "golden era of America lawyers" (Willard Hurst's phrase) who were our natural aristocrats before the late immigrants came here, cultural America aspired to be a nation of self-sufficient farm and business families who would give of their lives and of their property for the common good. Popular culture in America managed to entertain such an aspiration despite the facts of slavery and the subjugation of women, and held on to it and at the same time imposed virtual genocide on the American Indian, apartheid on the freed slaves, and brutal exploitation on the late immigrants and their children. It is the case, I think, that the republican aspiration never counted for as much in the American conscience as prosperity, imperialism, and regional economy did. Americans, as Abraham Lincoln said, are God's almost chosen people. In any event, by the time the late immigrants got here, the republican vision was little more than hollow hypocrisy—and the earthy Calabrians and Sicilians saw it for what it was: Americans hid the preservation of privilege behind the rhetoric of millennialism and opportunity. They were to be kept away from Italian children.

Notarianni and Raspa provide an image and an example of the contrast between a culture that made the American republican claim and the culture of Italian Americans: The Mormons in Helper, Utah, built neat, symmetrical houses on neat, symmetrical plots of land, along orderly streets and roads. When the Italian-immigrant miners became prosperous enough to buy some of these Mormon houses, they improved them (particularly in the back yards) with gardens, vineyards, smokehouses, and chicken coops, in chaotic, untidy ways. Their aesthetic disarray seemed to say that "to acknowledge publicly one's position in the universe... and thereby to incur a set of obligations... [was, to the Italian spirit the acquisition of] limited good, [a sign of] the absolute finiteness of material and spiritual resources," this in contrast to Mormon millennialism, which claimed power over nature, which was building the Kingdom, and which confidently claimed divine authority for what it did. The Italian miners looked at this Mormon world, and decided not to tempt Fate with order.

Since neither of the prevalent jurisprudential arguments is persuasive, the communitarian argument in legal philosophy and in ethics has to choose between being uselessly abstract and dealing truthfully with the possibility that America is not a community to be communitarian in. (We do seem to have some communi*ties*, although any we can think to mention are daily reported to be falling apart.) The alternative, in our view, is to take into account the evident and commonsense primacy of organic groups, to see if we can build plausible common-good arguments there and from there.

Perhaps the ardent individualist would concede that we human persons have in us a disposition to love and to want to be loved, and that each of us is incomplete when she is alone. If that much territory is given up from the individualist side of the anthropological debate, perhaps we communitarians would make some earthy concessions from our side—that we find other people troublesome, even, with Sartre, hellish. It takes a virtue such as *rispetto* to put up with them. We might also concede that philosophy and politics have always reserved the communitarian excuse for the crudest human tyrannies. Our ability to argue about community without being burned at the stake, beheaded, or hanged for being wrong owes something to Enlightenment individualism, even if we will not allow the fact to influence our anthropology. Thus a minimum of reciprocal scholarly respect might return the communitarian argument to the question of whether modern America has a community to be communitarian about, and then to the question that question depends on: whether it ever has had.

I argue that such questions should be taken up in an earthy way, by turning to the primacy of the earthy communities we cannot help belonging to; to the communities that grew up at the places we come from and around the times when we were there. To our families, prototypically. The argument can then move out in two ways: We can move, in one way, being as truthful as we can, to the groups we seriously describe with family metaphors (in the typical American—and maybe Western—experience: neighborhood, town, religious congregation). We should probably stop from time to time in this process and find out how serious we are prepared to be in our use of family metaphors, before we reach the sort of hypocrisy from which politicians and advertising agencies insult the families we remember as well as the families we have. We should move cautiously but purposively when we talk about companies, agencies, religious denominations, law firms, bar associations, universities, and civic clubs as if they were families.

We might not ever be able to move beyond these relatively interpersonal associations. I doubt that we can move truthfully to the modern nation-state, for example. To the extent we cannot move to political orders, we may have to look more seriously than most of my colleagues today do at the importance of the "mediating associations" that justify describing themselves with family metaphors and that can stand between the person and the jurisdictions in which law and the accidents of geography place him. Even if our communitarianism never gets beyond these mediating associations, we will have described extensions of friendship in which the virtues can be practiced. One of these might, if it is described very carefully, be some version of a legal profession.

The critical moral question in this appropriation of organic metaphors is less doing it than how it is done. That is the issue of the second way of moving out from the truthful description of the community we cannot help belonging to. The how-to issue is a matter of skill and disposition—itself a matter of virtue. We suggest of course that the Italian Americans, who formed in their children the habit of learning, teaching, remembering, and practicing membership in the family, can teach the rest of us something about disposition and skill in the truthful use of metaphors.

CHAPTER EIGHT

The Community
of the Faithful

We need a communal instrument of moral
reasoning in the light of faith precisely to defend the decision-maker against the stream of
conformity to his own world's self-evidence.
Practical moral reasoning, if Christian, must
always be expected to be at some point subversive.

John Howard Yoder

American legal ethics has its roots in English common
law and the American republican vision. Most of the
lawyers who carried the spirit of one or both of these
traditions from one generation to the next—beginning
with the colonial lawyers' earliest consciousness of
being a profession—were Christians. Many of them
(Judges Sharswood and Jones, for examples) were apparently devout. Others (David Hoffman, for example) were
industriously curious about the Bible. But there is little
indication that the principal influences in the development of legal ethics in America were thoughtfully or
even consciously rooted in the moral teachings of Moses, or of Jesus, or of the eighteenth-century English
clergy.

That is curious. It cannot possibly be the case that
American legal ethics grew up without religious influence. The gentleman-lawyer of chapters two through

four must have seen, been moved by, and been interested in the turbulent movements among Christians in America that were evident all around him. He and his neighbors were in the middle of them: stresses and schisms among Calvinists, from 1620 on; waves of revival, beginning in the middle of the eighteenth century, much of it legalistic in style and some of it led by lawyers; the growth of Methodism from John Wesley's stint as a missionary in Georgia to the circuit-riding lay preachers in the South and Midwest; the energetic, pervasive Sunday-school movement; the Great Awakening in the middle of the nineteenth century; the immigration of Jews and Roman Catholics with their alien, Eastern European, Mediterranean, and Hibernian superstitions. These religious currents must have affected the gentleman-lawyer, but there is almost no evidence that he thought of them when he wrote down his thinking and his teaching on how to be a lawyer and a good person. Being a gentleman was what he talked about, and he kept to himself whatever there was in his faith that bore on his being a gentleman.

The other lawyers' community from which American lawyers come (chapters five through seven) is not any clearer as a source for a theological legal ethic. Lawyers who were daughters and sons of the late immigrants went into the law from their immigrant communities; their view on how to be lawyers and good persons came more from those communities than from the common law or the republican vision. That is evident, for example, in the way Salvatore Cotillo acted, as a lawyer, legislator, and judge, to preserve Italian culture in New York City. The immigrant communities were, as much as the American gentleman's community was, communities of faith; they were not usually communities where lawyers, or anybody else, kept their faith to themselves. Professionally significant moral values such as the "Mediterranean cynic's" friendship or the Jewish immigrant's impulse to reconciliation were and are religious values.[1] Stories about these lawyers evidence a moral theology; theology is more accessible in them than in stories about Protestant gentlemen-lawyers, but it is difficult to get a moral theology from them because it is virtually impossible to separate what is precisely theological from what is ethnic in stories about the late immigrants.

I need a starting place from which to describe a religious legal ethic without cultural trappings—not, now, an anthropology so much as a *theological proposition*. The theological proposition is this: Faithfulness to the tradition of Israel and of the Cross means that the lawyer stands in the community of the faithful and looks from there at the law. Faithfulness means that a lawyer imagines that she is first of all a believer and is then a lawyer. She is a person who has come to suggest (or to hear the suggestion) that one of the many things a Jew or a Christian can do in the world is to qualify for the legal profession. She then goes out, from the religious community and with encouragement from the religious community, to learn and practice law.

When the study or practice of law becomes painful or confusing for her, she returns to the community of the faithful, and talks there, in that religious community, about her professional life. She considers what she is thinking and doing, and in some sense "decides" what to think and what to do, as much as the autonomous actor imagined in our liberal political philosophy does, but she "decides" *in* the religious community. Her continuing to practice law is the continuing determination of the church that such an occupation is consistent with her life in the church.[2]

---

1. I am thinking here of George V. Higgins's Jerry Kennedy stories, and of Fanny Holtzmann's law practice in New York and Hollywood. I spent a lot of time on these two sources in my *Faith and the Professions.*

2. It is embarrassing (if necessary for a Christian theological proposition) to have to use the word "church" to include Jews. What I am attempting to describe is something I have noticed among Jewish

What does "church" mean in such a notion? How does a gentleman-lawyer or an immigrant lawyer stand there? Does he leave his gentleman's or immigrant's community? "Church" is part of the theological proposition, but it has to mean something concrete or the theological proposition will not work. "Church," then, means the place where the connection between faith and work is developed, talked about, described truthfully. It might be a religious congregation. It might be shared faith in a family. It might be a Bible-study group or the regulars at a series of prayer breakfasts or the *minyan* at a synagogue. It might be shared study and elaboration of guidance from an authoritarian source, such as, say, a pastoral letter from church leaders about the American economy in which a lawyer practices law and from which she is made prosperous. It might even be a personal guru of some sort (a religious substitute for the psychoanalyst maybe). The church as a place to stand will, certainly, often, be the conventional religious congregation within an ethnic community or in a gentleman's community, and it may occasionally be a movement across such communities.

If I were asked to say what *my* church is for this purpose, I would say it is the circle of believers I live and work with, some close by, some who talk to me on the telephone or in letters, who take seriously the enterprise of being Jews or Christians in the American legal profession. This is or is the largest part of my "community of meaning" (to use Josiah Royce's phrase). It may become, for a time, and from time to time, a cultural force as well as a literal and literally available circle of friends; I sometimes have the sense that believers all over the country are of one mind about something, and I sense, then, that the church is speaking out. (That must have been the way the Great Awakening felt to Judge Sharswood, a pious Christian and a Sunday-school teacher; I don't know

---

teachers, colleagues, and students, as much as among Christians.

why he didn't say anything about it in his legal ethics.)
Many of the believers I know who are teachers, colleagues, and students in the law in America have such a
place to stand; it is where their *real* legal ethic should
come from.

The church as a place to stand, and from which to
look at the law and the legal profession, has the advantage for this book, and at the end of it, that we normally
find from changing perspective, even if both the place to
stand and the act of standing there are propositions and
not an anthropology. In the American law of church and
state, for example, law students (even in law schools run
by churches) learn the law of church and state from appellate opinions issued by federal courts and essays written by law professors who are or who pretend to be
agnostic on questions of theology. Law students are
trained in this way to look at the church as an intrusive
subculture. They are trained to look at faith as if the critical issue were how much religious eccentricity the
American democracy can tolerate. The principal constitutional cases involve Jehovah's Witnesses, Anabaptists,
and Mormons—sectarians, in all senses of the word.

Because of this pedagogical bias, we lawyers look at
the community of the faithful—even when it is our own
community—as if it were outside of our lives as lawyers.
And not only outside but *consequent* on our lives as lawyers. It is as if the community of the faithful is legitimate
only when the state approves of it. It is as if our political
founding fathers gathered our ancestors together and set
up a legal order, and then the church came along to tor-
ment and test their creation.

And *then* it is as if the *modus vivendi* was worked out
not between that republican, common-law legal order
and the community of the faithful, but between the legal
order and the individual. The American constitutional ar-
rangement accommodated the religious community sec-
ondarily and derivatively. The legal order does not
address the community of the faithful at all. What the law

says, and all that it says, is that the state has to respect the individual's right to choose a religion, if he wants one. We have communities of believers in America only because these free individuals somehow meet one another and agree to be together for agreed-upon religious purposes.

I propose to proceed as if this training as church-state lawyers had not occurred or had been different—or as if we American lawyers are able to set it aside and to look at American law, and the ethics of American lawyers, as if the community of faith comes *first*.

A Particular People

The community of the faithful, in the Hebraic religious tradition in our culture, has not understood itself as consequent on political order. It has not understood itself as a collective exercise of individual theological preferences, nor as a subculture that asks to be taken into account by liberal-democratic, republican government. It has understood itself as a particular people formed by a sequence of facts, and as the custodian of an ancient story. The business of this particular people is to remember its story. (We sang about it in the Baptist Sunday School I grew up in: "Tell me the old, old story.") In this sense, as Dietrich Bonhoeffer said, theology is the memory of the church. The community of the faithful, the particular people, is not a world within a world, not a *constituency*. Its vitality is to preserve in memory—in teaching, ritual, calendar, and narrative—what Michael Goldberg calls its "master story." Jews, Goldberg says, remember the Exodus in this way, and Christians remember St. Matthew's Jesus as the new Torah.

The community of the faithful, this particular people, strives to be self-conscious in preserving the story for its children and for others who are willing to hear it. This fact puts the community into tension with those who do not share its self-consciousness. The community of the faithful, the particular people, thus looks outside of itself and sees what it has come to call "the world," or "the nations," or "the powers." In America, this world outside, the world with which the particular people is in tension, includes the law and the legal profession. Charles Grandison Finney, a giant in the early nineteenth-century American Revival (and a lawyer), said to his converts: "You will be called eccentric, and probably you will deserve it."

The tension comes about for two reasons: (1) The particular, remembering people is wary of circumstances that might obscure its memory or impair its ability to teach what it remembers. And (2) one of the things the particular people remembers is what it knows of the destiny of human persons. Julian N. Hartt covered both the wariness and the claim of knowledge (the "epistemology," as philosophers call it) when he said:

> The church does not behave faithfully when it tries to make the Resurrection somehow intellectually digestible, if not exactly palatable, for the refined sensitivities of contemporary man (who has buried enough victims of his modernity to have little stomach for meeting them face to face sometime). Rather, the faithful church interprets what man is and ought to become in the light of the Resurrection. If someday we must all be confronted by every last one of our victims, many of whom we could not name if we wanted to, it is only because God who brought Jesus Christ from the dead, loves them and loves all with the infinite love which will prevail even over our mortal guilt.

My own community of the faithful talked to me once about my being legal counsel for a Nazi. Later, it talked to me about accepting court appointment to represent a man who had been convicted of raping a child. My sister and brother Christians who talked to me about what I was doing in those cases were conscious of our memory of the Resurrection. They knew that the memory of the

Resurrection defined the destiny of the defendant in the rape case, and of the Nazi, as well as my destiny, as it also defined the significance of the American constitutional law I would use to represent my clients. What the community of the faithful did, with me, was look out, *from* the church, at these people and at the account of human existence that is to be found in American constitutional law. We looked at the people and at the law and talked about them, in the church, and then we kept on living out and living within professional undertakings that are related to such legal accounts—related not because America is "God's new Israel," but because God finds us where He put us. We talked about this in the church and then I went on downtown and tried to do something as a lawyer for my clients.

* * *

Here is a story and a picture: The children of Israel are assembled on the borders of Canaan. Moses says to them: "You are a people consecrated to the Lord your God; of all the peoples on earth the Lord your God chose you to be the treasured people" (Deuteronomy 7:6). This is a people chosen by God and formed by centuries of desperation and powerlessness—by discord, a generation of wandering and living hand-to-mouth in the desert, and the ambivalent memory of four centuries of slavery. One of its two principal leaders, Aaron, is dead. The other, Moses, is dying. Moses in his frail old age tells these feeble, fractious people that they are to *consume* the more numerous and prosperous people who live in Canaan. They are to take over the Canaanites' land and hold it as a treasure and a promise from God Himself.

They will, as it will turn out, live among the Canaanites. But, Moses said to them, should that come about, they were not to give up their particularity: "You shall not intermarry with them.... You shall tear down their altars, smash their pillars, cut down their sacred posts, and consign their images to the fire.... You shall not worship their gods.... You shall consign the images of their gods to the fire; you shall not covet the silver and gold on them and keep it for yourselves... for that is abhorrent to the Lord your God" (Deuteronomy 7:5, 16, 25). Israel was to continue to be—as it had been in Egypt, and as it is—a particular people in Canaan and among the nations. The Jews who later became the Christian church laid claim to this particularity. Their story and their picture is the Cross, which is a symbol both of what the nations do to Jews and of what people do to one another in the name of the law.

Jesus before the power of Roman law and Moses at the borders of Canaan are signs of insistence on particularity. They are not signs of insistence on power. My theological proposition is not about an interest group or a constituency. Power is God's business. Moses told Israel at the borders of Canaan to remember that the Lord brought them out of slavery and to be wary of the idols they would find as they went on into a new place. The purpose of their testing in the desert was not military; it was to teach them to depend on Him. He told them the occupants of Canaan would be dislodged only little by little. As it turned out, the Canaanites were not destroyed so much as they were assimilated (which is what happened to the Romans too), but Moses did not say they were to be destroyed; he said they were to be consumed. Assimilation takes a while; it involves negotiation and the development of government and law; it mixes cultures; it made the warning about Canaanite idols perennial.

Idols in this imagery are things the Canaanites make with their hands. They are idols because of what people do with them. I think of the little wooden figure Herman Melville's savage seaman Queequeg carried into his room at the inn on Nantucket (in *Moby Dick*). Queequeg seemed to pray to this thing. Ishmael, his roommate, watched him in horror: Ishmael had a biblical Christian's wariness of idolatry. Ishmael was on the borders of

Canaan, listening to Moses, in the room at the inn. Ishmael tried not to be curious about Queequeg's little wooden figure, but he did not need to stifle his curiosity if the little figure was not an idol. Ishmael could be curious about the little figure—he could ask about it and talk to others in the inn about it—if it was not a god, or after it stopped being a god. What made it a god or not was what Queequeg did with it.

There came a time, after Israel was established in Canaan, when Israelites dug up or found or bought Canaanite artifacts and wanted to keep them as antiques and mementos (as our fathers and uncles, home from World War II, kept Nazi and Japanese military decorations). Some of these Canaanite artifacts had been idols, which might have meant the Israelites had to get rid of them. The Rabbis—the ancient lawyers of Israel—had to decide whether these things fell under Moses's injunction at the borders of Canaan: Their ruling was that a Canaanite artifact could be kept by the Jew who had it, even if it had been an idol, if it could be determined that it had been repudiated by the person who had held it as an idol. The artifact could be kept only if the Canaanite who had once worshipped it had turned from worshipping it. If it appeared that the figure had been an idol, the rabbi was commissioned to check and to see if the figure had been repudiated. For example, he looked to see if it had been mutilated; mutilation was favorable evidence of repudiation.

We believers who are also lawyers look at American law as the Rabbis looked at the Canaanite artifacts: We look out from and with the community of the faithful; we are wary of the law in Canaan, because it may be an idol, or it may have been an idol and we need to find out if it still is. The way to find out whether the law is an idol is to see if the people for whom it is the law have come to put it where God ought to be. If they have not begun to do that, or if, having begun, they have stopped, the law is

then much like other activities that are available to use
our time and effort as we live in the world, among the
nations. Law, when it is not an idol, or after it is repudiated as an idol, is not the subject of Moses's urgent and
perennial warning at the borders of Canaan. It is then
possible to be a believer and a lawyer in America, although, even so, we should keep checking the artifacts.
Theological legal ethics is, among other things, what we
do when we check the artifacts.

The mood and rhetoric of the 1986 Roman Catholic
Bishops' pastoral letter on the economy is an example of
a theological ethic formed in the community of the faithful. In this case the artifact was our "free enterprise" cap-
italist economy. The Bishops seem to have found, after
checking, that the economy is not an idol. If it has been
an idol in the past, there is evidence of mutilation; they
give many examples (as does Robert E. Rodes, Jr., in his
Law and Liberation). They invite the particular people
they advise to talk in the church about whether Christians should go out into the economy, but they add their
own advice that it seems to be safe—and even a good
idea—to do so. One can serve her neighbor in the American economy; one can feed the poor and help the
helpless; one can be a trustee for honest labor and the
products of honest labor. The Bishops speak of this as
going out from the church into the marketplace in
America.

The Bishops emphasize that the particular people
must continue to guard its particularity; it must continue
to check the artifacts. Their vision is rabbinical: "The
church is not bound to any particular economic, political
or social system; it has lived with many... evaluating
each according to moral and ethical principles." They
have checked the artifacts for us; the signs of mutilation
they looked for, and found, show that, for the present, the
American economy can accommodate an array of particular Hebraic understandings—that human dignity is a
higher value than prosperity or individual rights; that

community is a higher value than autonomy; and that the minimum for every person in a just society is not economic freedom but material and personal participation in common life.

I propose now to talk about two broad aspects of a lawyer's wanting to stand in the community of the faithful while she considers being a good person and a lawyer: One aspect has to do with the community of the faithful itself: How does it continue to be able to identify the signs of mutilation? The other aspect of doing legal ethics from the community of the faithful is how to go about destroying the idols in Canaan.

The Community of the Faithful Seeing to Itself

> The Christian life is a mediated life. That means that persons committed to growing as Christians do not make their decisions in isolation, but in consultation with the sense and insight of those they consider wise in the Christian community.
>
> University of Notre Dame Campus Ministry

What did Israel say for itself at the borders of Canaan? What did the Christian church say for itself when it appropriated for the Gentiles the particularity of Israel? What does the church at the University of Notre Dame say to itself as it invites nineteen-year-olds to talk with those who are considered wise?

The first thing to notice about these questions is that the answers to them, if Israel and the church are faithful, will not be claims of power. What Israel and the church say in these situations is that they will be people who remember. Israel *hears*, in the classic prayer of the Jewish tradition. Israel hears and remembers what God has done and what He has insisted upon—Exodus, Sinai, the Promised Land. The community of the faithful does not *assert* jurisdiction (not when it is faithful). Nor does it boast of accomplishment; it does not report that the faithful have fulfilled what God requires of them. Jews pray, on the Day of Atonement: "We are not so arrogant and stiff-necked as to say... [that we] have not sinned." The particularity of the people of God is normative; it is a way of life; it is a priestly commission for the benefit of all of humanity; but it does not include a score card from God. Karl Barth described this particular people as "a fairly fragile and not very impressive minority... aliens, exiles, and pilgrims... a lonely bird on the house-tops... the people and community of His witness to all other men."

Israel and the church have failed; their particular history is a history of failure, of disobedience, and of abandonment. Moses said to Israel at the borders of Canaan, "From the day that you left the land of Egypt until you reached this place, you have continued defiant toward the Lord." The particular people is stiff-necked, as Jewish Scripture and Christian Scripture say; but, still, it remembers. Still it is a particular people. When the children of Israel worshipped the golden calf, God said He would destroy them and would give to Moses a new people. But Moses argued with the Lord: What would a *new* people be like? This people was the only people the Lord had; Israel alone among the nations had been willing to take the burden of the Torah. What would a new people be like—for God? What would the nations say about what God did to His old people? Moses argued successfully that not even the Lord could disown this particular people, as fragile and not impressive as they were; that faithfulness of the Lord, and that claim on the faithfulness of the Lord, is the memory of the particular people.

The particular people can forget to remember. Then, until it remembers to remember, it loses its ability to be a place to stand, a place from which to look at the world, at the nations, and at the law in Canaan. From a "sectarian" point of view (and it is important for "mainline" believers to consider that the "sectarians" may be right), Israel surrendered its particularity when it demanded a king; the early church surrendered its particularity when it baptized the emperor and then made a deal with him. The "sectarian" argument is that the particular people in such cases was corrupted by power; it turned its particularity over to the government—as the medieval church did, with its pagan theories of church and state; and the congregational church of the Reformation did when it turned its procedures over to magistrates and, in the name of order, abandoned the procedures it had discovered in the New Testament. The "sectarian" argument is that the particular people forgets to remember its particularity when it becomes responsible for the government and lets the government be responsible for it. It is not then a place to stand and look at the law in Canaan.

The particular people is thus not dependent on an establishment, on any sort of institution guaranteed by coerced order, for what it knows. The community of faith depends for its preservation of memory on its members listening to one another, on what Yoder calls "the communal quality of belief." Its assurance of political soundness, as well as its knowledge, come not from a democratic "marketplace of ideas" but from the presence of God in the community: "For this Law that I enjoin on you today is not beyond your strength or beyond your reach. It is not in heaven, so that you need to wonder, 'Who will cross the seas for us and bring it back to us, so that we may hear it and keep it?' No, the Word is very near to you, it is in your mouth and in your heart for your observance" (Deuteronomy 30: 11–14).

Destroying the Idols in Canaan

We American lawyers learn to look *at* the community of the faithful, rather than *from* it. We stand in the courthouse looking at the church. We see the particular people, even when we claim to belong to it, from the point of view of the government. When we are able to change the place where we stand, when we walk across the street and look at the courthouse from the church, we notice a couple of things about the way the government in America regards the community of the faithful.[3]

First, what the American government has usually wanted to do about the church and about particular communities of Jews is to appropriate their energy—to turn religion into civil religion. James Madison's theory of the first amendment to the federal constitution was that democratic government here could not survive unless the government could appropriate the energy of the church. Beyond that, and to the extent that such an appropriation of the church's energy is not promising, the government wants either to control the church or to render it irrelevant.

Communities of faith in America have cooperated with these political processes of appropriation, submission, and privatization because they have forgotten what they are. They have acted as if Moses told the spies who checked out Canaan to ask the Canaanites what they thought about Israel's mandate from God. They act as if Moses should have negotiated on the matter of the idols—as he would have, surely, if he had been interested in being responsible for a peaceful and religious public order. Some accommodation on the matter of idols would have saved the successors of Moses from war, civil strife, and apostasy: It would have served the evident interests of both law and religion, and it would have made a lot of legal sense.

What Moses did did not make legal sense, nor did the behavior of the first Christians. There was a sort of security investigation of potential converts in the primitive church, in which the person seeking baptism was asked if

---

3. I have seen this happen, during my life as a Christian and a lawyer, among groups as various as the Baptists I grew up with, the Roman Catholic Bishops of the U.S., and Jews in legal education.

he had anything to do with the Roman government—whether, for example, he was a soldier or a judge. If he had anything to do with the government, he was told to give it up; if he wanted to keep his valuable imperial contacts, he was denied baptism. It would have made sense, as it did after the conversion of Constantine, to have baptized a few key military officers and as many judges as possible. But the primitive church saw the issue as Moses saw the idols of Canaan: The memory of the church is here the celebration of its oddity, not a basis for civil religion.

But the converse of that may not be true. If the church is to make sure the government leaves it alone, it does not follow that the church is to leave the government alone—our civil religious myths of the "wall of separation" to the contrary notwithstanding. Here the particular people will remember that it is a priestly people; it has its particularity for the benefit of all of humanity; it is not to hide its light under a bushel; it is to bear witness to its faith in the Lord Who is the Ruler of the Universe, and to bring the nations to praise Him.

Of course it must not compromise what it remembers. It has to be sure that what it does by way of witness does not amount to bowing down to the idols of Canaan. The community of the faithful will insist on its capacity and commission to determine what is an idol and what is not. The refusal to bow down is a significant limitation for participation in American liberal democracy, a limitation that has been—in my opinion—often ignored by believers. It was Jefferson who referred to America as "God's new Israel"; some Jews and Christians have agreed with that notion, but they are, I think, the ones who have forgotten who they are, and in their lapse of memory they have risked bowing down to the idols of Canaan. Legal ethics is an example.

David Hoffman, the founder of American legal ethics and an eloquent Jeffersonian, as well as a Christian, spoke of American law as a temple and of lawyers as priests who served in the temple—"ministers at a holy altar," he called us. Some of the excesses of the late revival, particularly the notion that American democracy *was* the church, were even worse. (Hoffman left possible the inference that he was being metaphorical.) This is not a quaint or entirely historical issue; it has been the moral and political substance of the long, careful pastoral letters that have issued from virtually all of the "mainline" Christian denominations on the subject of nuclear weapons. Bowing down to idols is the moral and theological issue discussed in those documents.

One familiar, biblical way to clear the idols out of Canaan is the way of the priest. This way first appropriates the particular people's most ancient understanding that it is a priestly people: Israel and the church are chosen to bring the one Lord to all of humanity. The community of the faithful is among the nations for purposes of atonement and witness. As faithless as it often is, the community of the faithful is capable of turning because it is capable of remembering its covenant with God, of remembering that it is a priestly people. It atones, when it does, for itself as well as for the nations. It atones as Moses did: Through fasting and argument, Moses changed the mind of God.

The particular people is prophet as well as priest; it sees and says what is going on and reminds the nations of what their values cost. In its manifestations in America— the Social Gospel movement, for example; Catholic social action; the "Christian realism" of Reinhold Niebuhr; pastoral statements that speak to America, rather than within the church—the particular people may assume or state that there is an American political theology that can be appealed to as the prophets of Israel appealed to the Torah. In this way in America the prophet speaks of values his hearers know and need to hear. The existence of a common political theology is perhaps more doubtful as secular America leaves the twentieth century than it was when America left the nineteenth century. It may never have been there; it may have been there and have faded from memory as Robert N. Bellah and his colleagues argued in *Habits of the Heart*; there may be enough of it left to work with as Jeffrey Stout argues in *Ethics After Babel*.

I suppose that there is enough possibility for prophetic witness in America to justify the particular people in trying to get something going—even in the legal profession, even in legal ethics. The important thing is to keep checking the artifacts—to remember that what the prophet appeals to is the memory the particular people tries truthfully to preserve and not the myth of America as a "righteous empire" or "God's new Israel," not a civil-religious American *volksgeist*. My friend Stanley Hauerwas says, for example, that his test for the Canaanite artifact is whether the political institution that solicits the adherence of the particular people is one which claims "that Christians . . . must be willing to choose sides and kill in order to preserve the social orders in which they find themselves." If we join in that effort, he says, "it surely means that we are no longer the church that witnesses to God's sovereignty over all nations, but instead we have become part of the world," bowing down to Canaan's idols.

Most lawyers who see the profession and the law from where they stand in the community of the faithful deal with the idols in Canaan by quiet witness to the memory of the particular people. I explore the promise of their way in reference to an example: the situation of a lawyer who has gone out from the community of the faithful to do useful work for the communities in America that aggregate wealth, build empires, and employ people for the production of goods and services—the business corporations. I chose the example because these communities of work *are* communities—so that the lawyer I am talking about goes out from one community and into another—

and because most of the energy of American law teachers is given to training lawyers who serve these corporate communities.

Very little of our teaching energy is directed to showing these lawyers how to work in business communities with quiet witness. If our graduates do it—and many of them do—it is, for the most part, in spite of their law teachers rather than because of them. Prophetic witness is discounted in law teaching. Our part of the academy, more than any other, has systematically discouraged and disapproved of invoking the religious tradition as important or even as interesting. It ignores the community of the faithful so resolutely that even its students who have come to law school from the community of the faithful learn to look at the particular people from the courthouse, rather than at the courthouse from among the particular people.

Suppose, though, that both the business manager and her lawyer are persons who might be influenced by the faithfulness of the particular people, by remembering both that they are not to bow down to the idols of Canaan, and that they are a light to the nations. These are people open to the possibilities of quiet witness; they regard the business corporation and the law office as enterprises that can be seen, thought about, and gone into from the community of the faithful.

Every business lawyer I have observed confirms the impression I got from being an apprentice business lawyer in the early 1960s—that business people are subject to moral influence from their lawyers. The manager I imagine, who comes out from the community of the faithful to do useful work in a corporation, is not only open to moral influence; she is looking for it (although she is also alert not to bow down to the idols of Canaan). She is open, for example, to the particular people's saying to her that her work in business is a *vocation*, a calling; and that what she is doing is administering wealth that has been assembled by and from the labor of others—

that she is a *trustee* for the wealth and the labor of others. She is open to being reminded of that even by her lawyer.

But Canaan has idols for corporate life and idols in the law: "In the U.S. *law*," the Catholic Bishops said, "the primary responsibility of managers is to exercise prudent business judgment in the interest of a profitable return to investors. But *morally* this legal responsibility may be exercised only within the bounds of justice to employees, customers, suppliers and the local community. Corporate mergers and hostile takeovers may bring greater benefits to shareholders, but they often lead to decreased concern for the well-being of local communities and make towns and cities more vulnerable to decisions made from afar."[4] The argument the Bishops make is both witness in American politics and a proposal for discussion in the community of the faithful. In both places the Bishops describe the vocation—the calling—of business managers and their lawyers. In doing this, the Bishops here are also reporting on their rabbinical examination of the artifacts of Canaan.

Teachers in the community of the faithful (and that is what our pastors, rabbis, and bishops are) are agents of memory. In this instance the teacher bids manager and lawyer to remember that the corporate business enterprise is itself a community; the influence exercised through the manager, when she talks about her useful work in the corporate community, is a communal influence. She remembers what a community is; she knows how to want to be in a community with those in her business enterprise, because the community of the faithful has been a community for her (or for her lawyer, or for both). Her influence is that she remembers how it is

---

4. David Gregory and Christopher Axworthy show how American labor law, in a similar development, reduced the legal status of labor unions from communities of workers to commodities. American public law, governed largely by democratic liberal political theory, destroys communities.

to act for the welfare of a community. (The broadened
context for the practice of *rispetto*, as Mary and I described it in chapters six and seven, is an instance of this
sort of action.)

Teachers in the community of the faithful have an exact quarrel here with American law: The law encourages
the corporate manager to undertake an immoral course
of action. She was sent out from the particular people to
be a trustee for those whose labor has produced the
wealth she manages. Some of these are employees; some
are customers; some live in towns where her business
operates; and some have invested their money in the
business. These participants in the enterprise are in communities, are often communities themselves, and are in
the community of the enterprise. The manager's vocation
as trustee is to be faithful to all of her beneficiaries. To
prefer one and neglect the others is to betray her trust.
When her lawyer indicates that betrayal is safer than being faithful to her trust, because the law encourages betrayal, she should see Canaan asking her to bow down to
an idol; in this case the idol is money. (This seemed to
me, during sixteen years on the board of a "Fortune 500"
public corporation, to be the situation and the effect of
federal regulatory law and judge-made corporate law on
the duties of corporate officers and directors.)

The notion of business manager as trustee is one that
can be found, here and there, in American business law.
"Not for him the morals of the marketplace," Cardozo
said. "His the punctilio of an honor the most sensitive."
The difference between the fiduciary notion in business
law and the notion of trustee that is being argued by
teachers in the community of the faithful is that the particular people is less influenced by indications of safety.
It remembers that any useful work may bring suffering to
the worker and to those she serves. Being a trustee in
corporate business involves the ordinary, daily, bitter suffering that comes from laying people off, from asking
workers to take less and do more, from deciding against a

dividend the investors need and investment analysts and
fund managers will punish the corporation for not making. Faithfulness to trust involves ordinary suffering such
as this; Israel and the people of the Cross know about
that because their memory is a memory of suffering
more than it is a memory of triumph.

The contrast suggested by this example is perhaps the
sort of thing a prophet might notice—between the law's
rejection of the possibility of community in a business
enterprise and the yearning for community that comes to
a business manager because she remembers the community she comes from. In this case, law's coercive support
of "the market" (meaning the market in corporate shares,
which, when dominated, gives power to determine who
the managers are) exalts the idol of money and rejects
the possibility of community—as it has in legal theories
of free speech, civil liberties, labor law, land development, and contract.

Lawyers who come into the courthouse (and law office) from the community of the faithful do not, finally,
depend on the law to encourage them to do what they
can in and with the law. The operative theology for those
who look at the law, and go into it, from the community
of the faithful, is a theology of hope and of faithful witness. The children of Israel, as they paused on the border
of Canaan, are the scriptural model: They listened to
Moses remind them of who they were. They heard him
warn them to be wary of the idols of Canaan. And then
they went on across the border.

NOTES

In most cases references in the text will lead from the text to the bibliography. These chapter notes are meant to provide for cases in which that is not so—and to offer extended discussion on a few tangential points. I abbreviate here references to my own work: "OBCL" for *On Being a Christian and a Lawyer*; "ALE" for *American Legal Ethics*; and "F&P" for *Faith and the Professions*. I distinguish between single-author and multiple-author work with commas: "Smith and Jones" is one work; "Smith, and Jones" are two.

Chapter One: Legal Ethics After Babel

Accreditation of law schools and the teaching of ethics. Law schools in the U.S. are accredited by the American Bar Association; the A.B.A., in exercising this function, has somewhat more clout that other professional school accreditors do because of court rules or statutes in most states that require a law degree from an A.B.A.-accredited law school as a condition for the license to practice law (along with passing performance on the bar examination in most cases, and demonstration of good moral character). The A.B.A. is and always has been a voluntary national organization of lawyers, a club and not an arm of the government, but in this function it exercises what amount to governmental (judicial) powers. The *A.B.A. Standards* for accreditation thereby become a sort of rule book for what schools have to provide so that their graduates can obtain licenses to practice law; thus the post-Watergate *Standard* requiring instruction in "professional responsibility" is perhaps more significant than other sources of professional opinion on whether law students should study ethics.

Drinker. My research assistant, Dan Semmens (Notre Dame law class of 1991) said of Drinker: "What strikes me the most about him is the scope of his learning. He was a great lawyer, ethicist, and musicologist. (I do find it disturbing, however, that many of his clients are known as pillagers of the environment—Kennecott Mining Co., for example.) . . . The Drinker family is also of some note, Henry's father being fairly widely published and his wife being published and accomplished in music. . . . " Dan lists among Drinker's publications, besides his *Legal Ethics* (1953), legal treatises on interstate commerce, the first amendment, business associations, and evidence; books on the music of Brahms, Bach, Schubert, Wolf, Schumann, and other composers; several books on playing instrumental music; and at least two about the Drinker family.

One leg shorter than the other: Mary provided me her own translation of a piece of Italo Svevo's novel *La Coscienza di Zeno*. Zeno is talking to his friend Tullio about the fact that Tullio has one leg that is shorter than the other:

> His illness . . . was his main distraction. He had studied the anatomy of the leg and foot. Laughing, he told me that when you walk with a rapid step, the time it takes for one step is no greater than half a second and that in that half a second no less than fifty-four muscles move! Startled, I was immediately distracted with thinking about my legs and finding this infernal machine. I thought I'd found it. Naturally I didn't find fifty-four devices, but rather an enormous complication that lost all order as soon as I turned my attention to it. . . . A few days later I was struck by a more serious malady . . .

which diminished the first one. But still today, as I write about it, if someone watches me while I'm moving, the fifty-four movements get all mixed up and I just about fall over.

There is nothing new in the tendency among American lawyers to define issues as technical rather than moral. Maxwell Bloomfield's work on nineteenth-century American lawyers, particularly his essay on David Hoffman, is a useful source on the point. Mark DeWolfe Howe's review of the history of the Cravath firm, particularly his distinction between a cause and a client's interests, is a concise way to think of the development. (See also Horwitz, and Hurst's *Growth*.) Schudson's work traces the development of American professionalism in journalism and, to some extent, in business, as well as in law. I trace it in materials for classroom discussion in *ALE*, and more carefully (largely from Schudson) in my *Vanderbilt Law Review* piece. See Thomas's *Youngest Science* for medical parallels.

Feminist religious ethics. I consulted several sources from as-yet unpublished papers given at the 1990 annual meeting of the Society of Christian Ethics. Indicative published sources on which I also rely include Ruether, Fiorenza, and Holden. Parallel work in jurisprudence is in Matsuda, Menkel-Meadow, Okin, Rhode, Sherry, and West.

Socrates on law teachers: The chapter on schools in *F&P* develops admonitions in the *Gorgias*, more fully than I do here. I am indebted to James Boyd White's work, particularly to *When Words* and to his essay on the *Gorgias*.

Killing Ethiopians for the Italian state, particularly in Ethiopia. The best story I know is Marina Warner's splendid novel, *The Lost Father* (1989). My friend and former student Vito Gagliardi, whose family comes from the part of Italy Warner wrote about (Bari, just above the heel of the boot), was also in my mind: "My father's father came to this country in 1927, from his home in Molfetta . . . ,"

Vito wrote. "Mussolini was head of the Fascist Party, but was not in power yet. He was speaking in a nearby town and my grandfather went to hear him speak. When Mussolini got up to speak, my grandfather declined to take his hat off. Two of Mussolini's thugs in the crowd didn't take kindly to this and took my grandfather into an alleyway and beat him. That made up his mind. And at age sixteen, without telling any of his brothers and sisters or his parents... he came to this country." Chapters five, six, and seven discuss the fact that Italians of Vito's grandfather's generation were more likely to think of themselves as citizens of their place than as the sort of nationalistic Italians Fascism sought to develop. Other sources: Barolini, Briggs, Davis, Nelli (1983), Vecoli (1972), Zucchi, and especially Saladino.

Moral sensitivity. It is part of the gentleman-lawyer's ethic to claim "heightened moral sensitivity" for lawyers (Harry W. Jones), partly, I suppose, as a matter of noticing that lawyers in America are in positions of moral leadership, so that heightened sensitivity is as necessary for their work as, say, for the work of the clergy—and partly as a claim for the effect legal education and work in the profession has on character. Jones (in his Villanova lecture): "Most lawyers, I think, are certainly more sensitive in their personal ethics and perceptions of justice than the mine-run of humanity.... The restraining influence that good lawyers have had on even their most avaricious clients is a significant story that should be told far more often than it is...." Burt Louden suggested in a letter to me that both aspects of the claim are cordial to Aristotelian *phronismos*; I do not mind the resemblance. In other useful comments on this manuscript, both he and Harlan R. Beckley, along with lawyer-advisors Fernand Dutile, Robert E. Rodes, Jr., Daniel Semmens, and Steven Pepper, said they think my distinction between rights arguments in ethics and virtue arguments is overstated; the bibliography provides references to their own more guarded discussions. My principal sources in academic ethics are Fish, Hauerwas, Meilaender, McClendon, and MacIntyre; see also Brosnan, Bush, Geach, Post, Sandel, and Toulmin. Beckley's essays on Rawls and his and Swezey's anthology on Gustafson are useful on the other side of the issue on rights arguments in ethics, as is Childress's criticism of Hauerwas (*Interpretation*). Several other sources are listed in my *American Journal of Jurisprudence* review of recent books on narrative.

The anthropological argument—that we get our morals from our culture. Any interesting communitarian argument rests to a certain extent on intuition, which is easier for a poet than for a professor, and on what Michael Goldberg calls a "master story." My principal reliance here is on Greenhouse, who in turn depends significantly on Huizinga. Carr's *Time, Narrative* is also useful.

"Intuition" is very difficult for me to describe. C. G. Jung (in *Analytical Psychology*) listed intuition as one of the four psychic functions (thinking, feeling, sensation, and intuition) and said the prevalence of intuition varies inversely with the strength of sensation. Intuition has to do with perception; he called it "seeing around corners." I mean to include that sense of the word, but to include as well the articulated and unarticulated and half-felt movements of our minds that have to be attributed to our communities, traditions, and ancestors (including what Jung called the collective unconscious). It could be that I would be better off leaving the word undefined; I am grateful to John Howard Yoder for helping me think about it. See also Simon, Redmount, Lindbeck, and Dworkin.

Chapter Two: The Gentleman's Community

On the use of "gentleman" in obituaries and salutes. Douglas B. Faver (Carroll Kilpatrick), *Washington Post*, Mar. 25, 1984, p. B–7 (quoting Katharine Graham); William H. Harbaugh (John W. Davis), in his *Lawyer's*

Lawyer: The Life of John W. Davis (1973), quoting a 1955 *Washington Post* obituary; James Reston (Averell Harriman), *New York Times*, July 27, 1986, p. E–23; Tom Shales (Cary Grant), *Washington Post*, Dec. 1, 1986, p. B–1; Ray McAllister (Lewis Powell), "The Southern Gentleman," *A.B.A. Journal*, April 1, 1988, p. 48; Jung to Freud, quoted in a letter to me from Peter B. Seldow, M.D., Mar. 6, 1985. Two references not quoted in the text: (i) Douglas J. Coleman (Dr. Gurdon Corning Oxtoby, late professor at San Francisco Theological Seminary): "a fine Christian gentleman... super-scholar... gracious host... roistering musical impressario.... The radiance of his genius brightened the pathway for many a Christian pilgrim." (ii) "A gentleman is a man who is clean inside and out; who neither looks up to the rich or down to the poor; who can lose without squealing and who can win without bragging; who is considerate of women, children and old people, who is too brave to lie, too generous to cheat and who takes his share of the world, lets others have theirs" (a matchbook from D'Iguazia's Towne House, Media, Pennsylvania).

Mensch (mensh) (mentsch): The suggestion comes from my friend Monroe Freedman. The references: Hyman Bookbinder, letter to the editor, *Washington Post*, Mar. 25, 1984, saying that Clarence Mitchell, "even when fighting relentlessly for specific goals, never abandoned civility and tolerance and respect. In every respect, he was a giant of a *mensch*." See also Harris, Patai, and Scarpaci.

General Lee: The classic and still standard biography is Freeman's. Flood's more focused treatment of Lee after the war, and Coulling's charming book on Lee's daughters, are pictures of the general as a college president in a little Virginia town.

Atticus Finch: A colleague once told me he admired an academic who read a novel and then made a career out of it. Atticus is in all of my books, extensively so in *ALE*. My assertion that people the age(s) of my students (from

1963 until now) know that novel better than they know the Bible is based on personal observation.

Dr. Craig: An episode similar to Dr. Craig's interview with the rejected heart-transplant patient is in the movie *Broadcast News*.

Chapter Three: Class and Professionalism in the Gentleman's Community

The gentleman's community as a sub-cult of Christianity. The argument is Mason's. Mary, when she helped me with this chapter, was interested in making a more extensive point: "The nineteenth-century English gentlemen were not as involved or interested in the Cross as their gentlemen forefathers had been. This is a part of the ethic that is left over from its roots.... [Mason] was trying to explain the gentleman's ethic by understanding its roots, but he was not condoning or condemning the fact that later generations weren't necessarily as Christian as in the days of yore.

"Being Christian was a safety valve for the original gentleman's ethic: Where the ethic fell short or didn't demand enough of gentlemen, Christian education took over; it accounted for any gaps in the ethic. I think Mason points out what this eventually evolved into—a sub-cult of Christianity—as he is saying that later generations of gentlemen could not be assumed to have Christian values, and therefore the old safety valve and stop-gap would no longer work. He is pointing out a *real threat* to the ethic of the *modern* gentleman!

"This is an interesting point when you look at the figure of the Christian knight—in Chaucer, Boccaccio, other medieval literature, and even into the Renaissance and Castiglione (not forgetting the Crusaders!). They had a license literally to get away with murder because they were counted on to be good Christians, above all else. This leaves lots of room for irony.... "

The situation of women in this Victorian culture is discussed in Rose, and Wijesinha, as well as in Letwin and in C. P. Snow's study of Trollope. Rhode (*Justice and Gen-*

der), and Okin relate the cultural history to the law. Sally Purvis's and Jean Myers's contribution to feminist theology are in papers they read, which are as yet unpublished, at the 1990 meeting of the Society of Christian Ethics.

Robert E. Rodes, Jr., does not agree with my treating the English Church as Protestant—and he is certainly an expert on that subject. I persist in the face of such good advice because my focus is influence on American lawyers, and that is largely from the nineteenth-century English church (the subject of Rodes's third and final volume on the English establishment); my reading of Trollope's ecclesiastical novels, as well as of Austen and Eliot and other Victorian writers, is that the church as the gentleman met it in urban parishes in London and in the demesnes of the squires in the country was low (in the ecclesiastical sense) and determined to remain so; I mean by "Protestant" what was translated into the southern Episcopal and Methodist culture that is potent in the formation of the American gentleman-lawyer.

* * * *

Honor. My argument that honor is not a virtue is Aristotelian (Book One, *Nichomachean Ethics*); Newman (see Mason) makes the argument, as do Wyatt-Brown and C. S. Lewis. The premise in the Aristotelian argument is that the virtues are teleological, and honor, depending as it does on the approval of others (usually peers) is not oriented to a goal and is therefore not subject to the discipline that asks, "Where am I going?" Without the discipline of a *telos*, moral reason slides into fatuity, moral life slides into fashion, and moral perception is lost—as with Thomas Mann's Gustave Aschenbach (*Death in Venice*):

> He had been young and crude with the times and by them badly counselled. He had taken false steps, blundered, exposed himself, offended in speech and writing against fact and good sense. But he had attained to honour, and honour, he used to say, is the natural goal towards which every considerable talent presses with whip

and spur. Yes, one might put it that his whole career had been one conscious and overweening ascent to honour, which left in the rear all the misgivings or self-derogation which might have hampered him.... It seems that a noble and active mind blunts itself against nothing so quickly as the sharp and bitter irritant of knowledge.

Childress, in surveying thinkers who have discussed the morality of honor, in his and Macquarrie's *Dictionary*, distinguishes between honor given and honor sought (rather different moral categories), and, within honor sought, notices the theological proposition (Aquinas, Barth) that honor sought is disciplined both by clear perception and by purposes other than egotism. Lewis, in saying that there is no honor in Gethsemane, adds the scriptural argument against the ethics of honor, one that is rather like the ascesis of the "preferential option for the poor" in modern Roman Catholic social ethics. (My source for the "preferential option" is the Bishops' letter on the economy; Robert E. Rodes's developing "liberation jurisprudence" has come to identify the moral teaching there as an ascesis; see his and my essay, "A Christian Theology for Roman Catholic Law Schools," 14 *University of Dayton Law Review* 5 [1988].)

The curious dynamics of self-deception. Fingarette is the classic source, and the one I depended on mostly in analyzing Auchincloss's *Timothy Colt*, in *ALE*. But it is useful to expand Fingarette's psychoanalytical account of self-deception into consideration of the professions in social ethics; my favorite source on that is Stanley Hauerwas's and David Burrell's essay on Albert Speer, in Hauerwas's *Truthfulness and Tragedy*. This body of learning is essential, in my view, to an adequate appreciation of the "new" ethics of virtue in and out of the subdiscipline of legal ethics; I think I could defend the criticism that MacIntyre, James Boyd White, and Kronman neglect the Hauerwas-Burrell argument, but the poets do not.

The Stanley Report. Virtually every state and local bar association, and many law reviews, have found it necessary to publish discussions of professionalism. Few of these discussions are interesting for ethics; some exceptions: Stanley (*Montana Law Review*); White (*Cumberland Law Review*); Brown, Rotunda (three pieces—the *Illinois Bar Journal* one quoting Martha Barnett); and Freedman (*Two Fables*).

Chapter Four: Power, Tragedy, and Suffering in the Gentleman's Community

Orley Farm. I deal with this story much more fully in OBCL.

Judge Horton. I deal with him more fully in OBCL. His story was the subject of a television drama called "Judge Horton and the Scottsboro Boys," that I sometimes rent for my ethics classes. The story, in brief: Patterson (see Patterson and Conrad, and Carter) was one of a group of poor, young black men who were arrested on a train in Alabama and put to trial for the rape of two white women. All were tried and sentenced to death; several were retried after the federal courts reversed convictions on federal constitutional grounds. They were again found guilty and sentenced to death. None was killed by the state, but most of them spent years in prison. Patterson was tried before Judge Horton, convicted and sentenced to death, but Judge Horton then set the verdict and sentence aside and ordered a new trial—an act that ended his promising judicial career and resulted in Patterson being tried, convicted, and sentenced a second time. Horton's opinion on the motion for new trial is printed as an appendix to the opinion in *Street v N.B.C.*, 645 F.2d 1227 (6th Cir. 1981).

Hauerwas. The quotation is from his *Peaceable Kingdom*. His theory of tragedy is in *Truthfulness*.

Hamilton. His jury speech in the Zenger case is in Schroeder. See also Bailyn and Hench, and Schlesinger.

Adams. The standard account of Adams in the Boston Massacre case is in Bowen's biography.

Rabbis. A brief summary of the rabbinical teaching on Deuteronomy 21: 18–21 (capital punishment for the disobedient son) is in Rabbi Hertz's annotated *Pentateuch and Haftorahs* (2nd ed. 1987), at 842: "The Rabbis tell us that this law was never once carried out; and, by the regulations with which the infliction of the death-penalty was in this case surrounded, it could not be carried out.... Its presence in the Torah was merely to serve as a warning, and bring out with the strongest possible emphasis the heinous crime of disobedience to parents." See also Cover, Epstein, Heschel, Passamaneck and Brown, and Patai.

Saul and Agag. The Bible story is at 1 Samuel 15; Weisel's discussion is in *A Jew Today*.

Professionalism. Robert E. Rodes, Jr., gave me these two notes as he finished reading this chapter in manuscript:

(1) "I wonder if A.B.A. professionalism isn't in part a refuge from the vice you have discussed here in the gentleman's ethic, that being the argument that the gentleman cannot bear that others suffer." Rodes referred to a case he often uses in teaching legal ethics: "Remember my story of the student intern ... who was asked to represent an abusive mother in a child-custody case, when all other lawyers in town refused her? I asked him whether he wanted to accept responsibility for her losing her child without representation, or for her gaining custody. He chose the former. But the A.B.A. doctrine on professionalism is that neither responsibility is his." See Peter Brown, Bush, Ellmann, and Rotunda.

(2) "Is not taking the Cross seriously a way of revising the gentleman's ethic out of its own internal resources, and therefore an answer to the question you say you cannot answer?" I think the answer to that is yes; I try to work it out in chapter eight. Neither Rodes nor I would make a distinction between the "internal resources" of

the gentleman's ethic and the ethics of the Cross. The problem is that the gentleman, hewing more to honor than to the implications of his tradition, as Mary says, failed to take account of his internal resources. My hope for the gentleman's ethic, in this regard, is that it still has the internal resources to correct its failings. See Brueggemann ("Passion and Perspective"), Cooper, and Meilaender.

Chapter Five: Between the Gentleman's Community and the Other Community

Cases. *Reynolds* v. *United States*, 98 U.S. 145 (1878) (Mormon marriage); *Employment Division* v. *Smith*, 58 U.S.L.W. 4433 (1990) (hallucinogens); *Gordon* v. *Weinberger*, 475 U.S. 503 (1986) (yarmulke); *Repouille* v. *United States*, 165 F.2d 152 (2nd Cir. 1947) (mercy killing); Petitions of Rudder, et al., 159 F.2d 695 (2nd Cir. 1947) (cohabitation without marriage); *Schmidt* v. *United States*, 177 F.2d 4350 (2nd Cir. 1949) and *United States* v. *Manfredi*, 168 F.2d 752 (3d Cir. 1948) (prostitutes); *United States* v. *Francioso*, 164 F.2d 163 (2nd Cir. 1947) (marriage to niece); *In re Spenser*, 22 Fed. Cas. 921 (D. Oregon 1878) (crime for which applicant had been pardoned by the governor). Periodical discussions of the immigration cases are in the Notre Dame note ("Aliens"), the Marquette note ("Jurisprudence") and Joseph O'Meara's and my essay on the *Jacobellis* case.

Immigration statute. Immigration Act of 1924, 8 U.S.C., Sec. 145 ff. (repealed 1952). See Cordasco and Cordasco, DiFranco, DiStrasi, Lopreato, Moquin and VanDorn, Thompson, and Vecoli.

Individualism. Robert E. Rodes, Jr., has misgivings about my sharp distinction between American law's protecting the vulnerable community and its protecting individuals. He reads the Mormon marriage case (*Reynolds*) as imposing (English Protestant) Christianity on the Mormons—a culture being imposed on a culture—

rather than as dealing with the rights of individuals. He
has in his work (particularly in the essays *Sub Deo et
Lege* and on the Christian civil magistrate) found more of
a common Christian culture in mainline America than I
have. See the Gelpi anthology.

Civil rights lawyers. My principal sources are Kluger,
Tushnet, Rhode ("Class"), McNeil, Franklin and Meier,
and Bell. I am grateful, as to the argument on participa-
tion, for the scholarship on Dean Houston of my Wash-
ington and Lee colleague Steven Hobbs. Participation as a
constitutional argument is developed in Glendon and in
Kommers; it is prominent as a moral argument in the
Bishops' letter on the American economy (United States
Catholic Conference); see also Gelpi, Beckley (Ryan),
Burt (Parables, and Dred Scott), and Lindbeck.

Camelo. We got on to Nick Camelo from Briggs; the
stories we quote were in *L'Avvenire* Nov. 10, 1900, Jan.
11, 1902, Jan. 10, 1903, Sept. 12, 1903, Feb. 10, 1904,
June 11, 1904, and Aug. 26, 1905; and in *La Luce*, Jan. 10,
1903.

Education. See the sources cited in the notes to chapter six.

Modern Italian-American leaders. My sources include
diaries and autobiographies: on Cuomo, Boyte; on Ferraro, Hughes and LaVeness, LaVeness and Sweeney, and
Schneider; on Scalia, Adler, Fein, Nagareda, and two news
stories published without bylines: "The Supreme Court
with a Smile," *U.S. News and World Report*, Jan. 12, 1987,
p. 23, and "New Kid on the Block," *A.B.A. Journal*, Aug.
1, 1986, p. 20. On other leaders: Gallagher's biography of
Carlo Tresca, Hall, Henderson, Krase (Community),
Meyer, Paolini, Pane, Parker, Pugliese, LaGumina (on Senator Pastore), Angell, Briggs (1978), and Quilici.

The social situation of Italian Americans is discussed in
Ferber, Mariano, and Henderson, as well as in LaSorte,
and Musmanno and in sources noted on immigration, in
the notes to chapter six. The Center for Migration Studies
pictorial book is our source for images and cartoons; the

prejudice illustrated there has by no means disappeared. It surfaces, for example, in political discussions of candidates for national office; e.g., the unsigned editorial, "Italian Men," in the *National Review*, Nov. 2, 1984, and D. Keith Mano's editorial, "Geraldine Ferraro," in that periodical, March 28, 1986, p. 67. More subtle manifestations are discussed in Judith Ann Warner's study of the media, an unpublished doctoral dissertation titled "Marginality and Selective Reporting." See also the notes on politics in the chapter notes to chapter six.

Chapter Six: Virtue in the Other Community

Adversary ethic. The second-order legal ethic of the American profession as the daughters and sons of Italian immigrants began to enter it is sometimes generalized under the phrase "adversary ethic" (see my Vanderbilt essay); Durkheim's "market morality" is broader and more descriptive (see Schudson, and Harry Jones). See Ellmann, Hazard, Hazard and Rhode, Luban, and Wolfram. The way it has been received by the descendants of the late immigrants is the subject of chapters in *ALE* and in *F&P*—discussing not only Higgins's novels and the Italian immigrants but also the practice of immigration law and the children of Eastern European Jewish immigrants. See Pane, and Pugliese.

Italy today. See the notes for chapter five, Harrison, and Governor Cuomo's diaries; the point that is usually made about the ethos of the Mezzogiorno in these sources is that it is little changed from the days when the late immigrants left; Gambino, Krase (in Juliani), and D'Andrea discuss comparisons of family life among Southern Italians and Italian Americans, as Caporale discusses the professions. See the notes to chapter five for sources on the situation in Southern Italy between 1860 and the period of extensive emigration. The "conventional account" of Southern Italian disdain for education is in Mariano and Covello. See also Egelman, Perlmann, and

Weisz. The modern Italian American's sense of ethnic identity is the subject of the Sirey-Patti book and of their videotapes of therapy sessions; see Harrison also.

Women's sphere. Our sources include Chafe, Herman, Kerber and DeHart-Matthews, Welter, and Woloch. Jurisprudential insights are in Matsuda, Menkel-Meadow, Okin, Rhode, and Sherry; and theological insights in Cahill, Fiorenza, Holden, and Ruether.

Second and third generation Italian Americans. Gambino is our principal source, but many of the essays cited in the bibliography (notably D'Andrea and Femminella) deal with the subject. See also del Russo and Tropea, and C. L. Johnson, and the discussion in chapter five and the sources noted for that discussion. Herberg's *Protestant, Catholic, Jew* deals with this in a broader American "ethnic" context: The third generation, he says, is trying to remember what the second generation forgot; we believe the same can be said, among Italian Americans, of what the fourth and fifth generations are trying to remember. Barolini's *Umbertina* is a powerful story of these differences among four generations of Italian-American women.

Anthropology. I am persuaded that every ethic has its anthropology. The anthropology of second-order moralities is "thin." Ethical accounts of these moralities (especially the ethics of autonomy) tend to avoid describing their anthropologies; these accounts are, for that and other reasons, inadequate. This is the argument of those who attack "decisionism" in religious ethics, particularly Hauerwas, Goldberg, Murdoch, Pincoffs, MacIntyre, McClendon, L. Gregory Jones, and Jefferson Powell. It is what influences most of these writers to prefer Aristotle and Aquinas (and, for that matter, Moses and Jesus) to Kant, Rawls, and the Scots Enlightenment. See also Brueggemann, Dworkin, Gelpi, Glendon, Lindbeck, Simon, and Walzer. The debate between Beckley and Gregory Jones is instructive on the differences. My understanding of the anthropology of "liberal" ethics is what a person of normal liberal education understands about Hobbes and Rousseau (human life as insulated, savage, brutish, and short; human associations as the products of self-interested agreement). Bellah and his colleagues show how both the biblical and Jeffersonian "republican" visions in America are at odds with that liberalism. My present quarrel with modern manifestations of liberalism in ethics and jurisprudence is anthropological, in part empirical and in part a matter of seeing and saying as moral arts (Murdoch, Fingarette, Fish, Hauerwas, and H. R. Niebuhr): That the ethics of choice (or of autonomy) does not account for organic associations is only part of the argument. Robert E. Rodes, Jr., maintains a steady and characteristically incisive disagreement with me on this point. "It seems to me that when you build a theoretical claim on a first-order morality you are creating a second-order morality," he says. My view is that *any* ethic is a theoretical claim built on a morality: Ethics is thinking about morals. Beyond the level of words, the difference between first- and second-order ethical theory that we mean to explore in this chapter—by looking closely at a first-order morality—is that first-order theory takes into account what Hauerwas calls "moral notions" (and Murdoch "morality") (see Lindbeck, and Goldberg) and second-order ethical theory for the most part fails to do that. (This is, by the way, the meaning of feminist ethics' insistence on examining experience and of Martin Buber's insistence on describing relationships rather than individuals.) Rodes gave me permission to use an aphorism he invented when reading this chapter in manuscript: "A person whose moral reasoning doesn't support what his mother taught him has either a bad mother or a bad mind."

Education. See the Caporale anthology, Briggs, Covello, Egelman, Green's study of the Italian-American novel, Lopreato, Perlmann, Sartorio, and Weisz. The idea among early immigrants and their children, that American education would corrupt *la via vecchia*, is suggested in what one of Joe Martori's characters says in *Street Fights*: "The biggest threat to our families has always been the... educational system in this country. The vast majority of Italian immigrants wanted nothing more than a new setting in which to continue their old traditions. But this Anglo society had other ideas. Supposedly, the purpose of the public school system was to ensure an educated citizenry for the survival of democracy. But the sudden influx of southern and eastern Europeans gave the system a new goal—Americanize the foreigners! Our response was resistance. Italian children brought into their homes ideas that threatened centuries of honored tradition.... So we invented a new way out: passive aggression. We avoided Americanization. We strengthened our bonds to our families."

Broadened understanding of community. General references include Barton, Briggs, Cavaioli, del Russo and Tropea, Eula, Femminella, Ferber, Gallo, Gambino, Glazer and Moynihan, LaGumina (especially *Steerage*), LaSorte, Lopreato, Meloni, Moss, Nelli, Notarianni and Raspa, Sandler, Schiro, Tricarico, Velikonja, Venturelli, Vicusi (Juliani), Wilson, and Zucchi. On attitudes among the newcomers, see DiFranco, DiStasi, Gambino, LaSorte, Perlmann, Nelli, Thomas and Moran, Thompson and sources in the Cordasco and Cordasco bibliography. On women and on the family, see Birnbaum, Caroli et al., D'Andrea, Gabaccia, Gesauldi, Harney, Tomasi, C. L. Johnson, Juliani (anthology), Krase, Maglione and Fiore, Vezzosi, and Viscusi (Juliani). On the Roman Catholic Church, see D'Andrea, Krase (Juliani), Meloni, Miller and Marzik, Moss, Santini, Swiderski, Tomasi, Tricarico, Vecoli (Miller and Marzik). On politics and the professions, see Cavaioli, Cuomo, D'Andrea, Ferber, G. Ferraro (and LaVeness), Hall, Krase, Meyer, Quilici, Paolini, Pugliese and the sources noted in the notes for chapter five... On neighborhoods, see LaGumina (all of his work), Tricarico, and Velikonja... On organized crime, see T. J. Ferraro, Martori, Meloni, Tricarico, and the sources noted in the notes for chapter five ... On "amoral familism," see Gesauldi.

The Italian-American lawyers who helped us with this chapter and with chapter seven include Ruggero J. Aldisert, Benedict V. Aspero, Anthony T. Bruno, Marie Butarazzi, Anthony M. Calderone, Joann M. Calderone, Philip D. Calderone, Joseph A. Camarra, Philip F. Cardarella, Henry J. Catenacci, Richard D. Catenacci, Henry G. Ciocca, Paul Collella, James J. Conte, Anthony D'Amato, Anne D'Errico, Philip S. DiMatteo, Lawrence D. DiNardo, Richard H. Farina, Vito Gagliardi, James D. Ghiardi, Peter J. Ippolito, John J. Jiganti, Steven J. Madonna, Paul J. Maganzini, Alfonso A. Magnotta, Frederick J. Martone, Joseph P. Martori, John F. Mezzanotte, Fred M. Morelli, Jr., Patrick F. Pacella, Joseph R. Pagano, Anthony J. Palumbo, Jr., Anthony Patti, Richard Sandy, Steven J. Talevi, Joseph Turzi, and Frank G. Verterano.

Chapter Seven: Virtue in the Other Community

The communitarian argument we make here is made from the moral cultures we have described in chapters two through six. I do not mean it to be a "natural law" argument, although it is for the most part consistent with the natural-law politics and jurisprudence I have learned from my friend Rodes, when I was his matriculated student at Notre Dame (1958–1961) and ever since (see his *Legal Enterprise*). I am aiming at a more modest target, at a moral anthropology that has to do with describing excellences in our moral culture. The criteria I mean to apply are cultural criteria (see Cooper, and Meilaender). I am not depending on assumptions about human nature. (Rodes insists that, if I read Margaret Mead carefully, I would do so.) Nor do I mean to argue, as H. Richard Niebuhr did in his *Responsible Self*, that human communities build from Buber's (or Royce's) understanding of one-on-one human relationships, in a way I would describe as contractual. The morally significant cultural communities are, in my view, products of the fact that, as Karl Barth put it (in his *Ethics*), God will find us where He put us. "Bloom where you're planted," as the poster said in the 1960s. See Burt, Gelpi, Glendon, Lindbeck, Schneyer, Walzer, and Watson.

I admit that whatever ethical generalizations are possible from moral anthropology are culturally relative and even, as the story theologians say, narrative dependent. Mary and I have been content to attempt to describe a culture that has functioned, and can function, as a school for the virtues that have to do with the internal goods of the practice of law in the United States in the 1990s. (Those terms will be familiar to readers of Alasdair MacIntyre, although he has not focused his argument about "practices" on professions, let alone on the American legal profession.)

Christianity in the United States: Clebsch, Dawson, Gaustad, Hatch, Hostetler, Marty, McNemar, and T. Smith.

* * * *

The republican vision as a culture. Robert E. Rodes, Jr., suggested to me that the morality with which I contrast a communitarian morality in this chapter is itself a communitarian morality. (See also Fish, Millon, and Sherry.) The culture Harper Lee and William Faulkner described in their lawyer stories, for example, was a communitarian morality of the sort I attempted to describe in chapters two through four. So, probably, were the lawyer-story cultures of Auchincloss and Howells. If Rodes is right, moral anthropology should take care to try to describe this community (as, I think, Bellah and his colleagues do), rather than to treat it as an abstraction (or, worse, a straw man). I do not perceive such a community across the United States; I do perceive communit*ies* in America, one of which is the one Lee and Faulkner described. (See Bellah, and Hostetler, and Bellah and Sullivan.) Their culture was specific (regional, denominational even) in its recognition of complicity in evil. It was not a republican culture, although it did recognize and celebrate excellence in its lawyer-aristocrats. It was not distant in memory or in conscious attribution from its Old-World roots, which roots were ethnically English (see Cash) and theologically Methodist (see Harper Lee's description, in the novel, of the pedigree of Finch's Landing).

Quotations. The Hauerwas quotations toward the end of the chapter are from *Community and Character*. The Powell quotations are from unpublished theological work: Powell, already eminent as a law teacher and constitutional scholar, is at present studying and teaching theology (as well as law) at Duke and is turning at least part of his astounding energy to Christian ethics. He is in many ways a disciple of Hauerwas's, but retains (in correspondence with me and in helpful comments on my manuscripts) more respect for liberalism than Hauerwas and I have. It is Powell who referred me to Zizioulas, which is a powerfully helpful source for communitarian anthropology.

Chapter Eight: The Community of the Faithful

The "sectarian" argument. This chapter was originally a paper given at one of Richard Neuhaus's gatherings in New York, and is published in its original form in his *Law and Our Life Together*. There was a spirited discussion of the paper during that gathering, involving such eminent and incisive thinkers as James T. Burtchaell, Robert Bork, Lynn Buzzard, Martin Golding, Edward Gaffney, Mary Ann Glendon, Frank Alexander, Neuhaus himself, and many others. My argument, there and here, is "sectarian"; I admit that, but do not see that such an argument is out of place in an argument to Christians and Jews or in an argument from Christians and Jews to secular communities in America. (The fact that my modest paper provoked such a wonderful conversation seems to prove the point.) "Sectarian" has a narrow meaning among theologians (see Clasen's discussion of Anabaptist Ethics and on Mennonite Ethics, Long's article on Modern Protestant Ethics, Childress's article on pacifism in the Childress-Macquarrie *Dictionary*, and Max Stackhouse's presidential address to the Society of Christian Ethics, published in the Society's 1987 *Annual*); the term is often used as what seems to me an anti-intellectual putdown for the work of Yoder, McClendon, and Hauerwas (see Hauerwas's response in the *Theology Today* essay, and Yoder's presidential address to the Society of Christian Ethics, published in the Society's 1988 *Annual*). I am not worried about my argument in this chapter attracting that characterization; I am in good company. I aim here at an argument that is narrower and more radical than may seem consistent with my own rearing in "mainline" (American Baptist) Protestantism and my present allegiance to American Roman Catholicism. The important thing, I think, is that the Yoder-Hauerwas-McClendon moral argument (which is also an argument one can find in the Rabbis and in the religious life of religious Jews in America today [see Lis Harris]) be taken seriously in the mainline church and among Jews, and that lawyers take seriously its usefulness in legal ethics. Beckley's work on Rawls and on Gustafson is helpful here, as is a new volume of his on Reinhold Niebuhr, Walter Rauschenbusch, and John Ryan, that will probably be published at about the time this book is. Michael Goldberg's essay on corporate communities is also helpful; it will be in the proceedings of the 1990 Notre Dame symposium on business ethics.

Jurisprudence. Is it necessary for a lawyer who is also a believer to take his ethical stance outside the law, in order to remain in the community of the faithful—or even in order to avoid idolatry? A different description of the community of the faithful would avoid these issues (see Dawson, Gustafson's *Theocentric Ethics*, Stackhouse, and Barth's final fragments for the *Church Dogmatics*);

but those theologians who would prefer to argue differently would not disagree with me about the seriousness of idolatry as a moral issue. Idolatry is still a discussable issue in the mainline church and in the left wing of modern American Judaism (see my Hebraic Jurisprudence essay).

The artifacts of Canaan. The rabbinical source is the Talmudic tractate *Abodah Zorah*, especially 41a, 42a, 53a, and 53b. See also the two-part essay by E. E. Urbach of Hebrew University, Jerusalem: "The Rabbinical Laws of Idolatry in the Second and Third Centuries in the Light of Archaeological and Historical Facts," in vol. 9 of the *Israel Exploration Journal* (1958–1959).

The Cardozo quotation is from his opinion in Meinhard v. Salmon, 249 N.Y. 458, 164 N.E. 545 (1928).

BIBLIOGRAPHY

(Several anthologies of essays on Italian Americans that are listed here are published annual proceedings of the American Italian Historical Association; these are listed according to the names of the persons who edited them, and in each case identified as A.I.H.A. proceedings. References to the volumes are made to the names of editors and A.I.H.A. Several of our sources are also excerpted in my *American Legal Ethics* [1985]; where the excerpt is substantial, I have indicated that here with the letters "ALE.")

Adler, S., "Live Wire on the DC Circuit," *American Lawyer*, March 1985, p. 86.

"Aliens—Naturalization—Good Moral Character As a Prerequisite," 34 *Notre Dame Lawyer* 375 (1959).

Angell, Roger, "The Sporting Scene" (on A. Bartlett Giamatti), *New Yorker*, Aug. 22, 1988, p. 50.

Aquinas, St. Thomas, *Summa Theologica* (Benzinger ed., Dominican Fathers trans., 1947).

———, *Treatise on the Virtues* (Oesterle trans. 1966). (See Maritain.)

Aristotle, *Magna Moralia*, in *The Works of Aristotle Translated into English* (1915).

———, *Nicomachean Ethics* (Martin Ostwald trans., 1962) (ALE).

Auchincloss, Louis, "The Fabbri Tape," in *Narcissa and Other Fables* (1983) (ALE).

———, *The Great World and Timothy Colt* (1956).

Axworthy, Christopher X., "Corporation Law as If Some People Mattered," 36 *University of Toronto Law Journal* 392 (1986).

Bailyn, Bernard, and John B. Hench (eds.), *The Press and the American Revolution* (1980).

Ball, Milner S., (et al.), "Law, Metaphor, and Theology: A Frances Lewis Law Center Colloquium: Law Natural: Its Family of Metaphors and Its Theology," 3 *Journal of Law and Religion* 141 (1985).

———, *Lying Down Together: Law, Metaphor, and Theology* (1985).

Banfield, Edward C., *The Moral Basis of a Backward Society* (1958). (See Gesauldi.)

Barolini, Helen (ed.), *The Dream Book: An Anthology of Writings by Italian American Women* (1985).

———, Umbertina (1979).

Barth, Karl, *The Christian Life* (Church Dogmatics, vol. IV, part 4; Lecture Fragments) (G. Bromiley trans., 1981).

———, *Church Dogmatics* (T. and T. Clark ed., 1961).

———, *Ethics* (1928–1929) (G. Bromiley trans., 1981).

Barthold, Clementine, Walter H. Gladwin, Paul B. Rava, and Ephraim Margolin, "Judges and Lawyers: First Generation Success Stories," 25 *Judges' Journal*, Spring 1986, p. 5.

Barton, Josef J., *Peasants and Strangers: Italians, Rumanians, and Slovaks in an American City, 1890–1950* (1950).

Beckley, Harlan R., "A Christian Affirmation of Rawls's Idea of Justice as Fairness," *Journal of Religious Ethics*, vol. 13, p. 210 (1985) and vol. 14, p. 229 (1986).

———, and Charles M. Swezey (eds.), *James M. Gustafson's Theocentric Ethics: Interpretations and Assessments* (1988).

Bell, Derrick A., Jr., "Brown v. Board of Education and the Interest-Convergence Dilemma," 93 *Harvard Law Review* 518 (1980).

———, "Serving Two Masters: Integration Ideals and Client Interests in School Desegregation Litigation," 85 *Yale Law Journal* 470 (1976).

Bellah, Robert N., and William M. Sullivan, "The Common Good," Tikkun, July–August 1988, p. 29.

———, (with Madsen, Swidler, and Tipton), *Habits of the Heart: Individualism and Commitment in American Life* (1985).

Bellow, Saul, *The Adventures of Augie March* (1953).

Berkman, Ted, *The Lady and the Law* (1976). (On Fanny Holtzmann.)

Bird, Caroline: See Bradwell.

Birnbaum, Lucia Chiavola, "Education for Conformity: The Case of Sicilian American Women Professionals," in Pane (A.I.H.A.).

Bloomfield, Maxwell, *American Lawyers in a Changing Society, 1776–1876* (1976).

——, "David Hoffman and the Shaping of a Republican Legal Culture," 38 *Maryland Law Review* 673 (1979).

Bolt, Robert, *A Man for All Seasons* (1962).

Bowen, Catherine Drinker, *John Adams and the American Revolution* (1950).

Boyte, Harry C., "The Politics of Community," *Nation*, Jan. 12, 1985, p. 12.

Bradwell: Myra Bradwell v. The State, 83 U.S. 130 (1872); Caroline Bird, *Enterprising Women* (a Bicentennial Project of the Business and Professional Women's Foundation 1976), at 106.

Brandeis, Louis D.: See Frank, Mason, and Vorspan.

Briggs, John W., *An Italian Passage: Immigrants to Three American Cities, 1890–1930* (1978).

Brosnan, Donald F., "Virtue Ethics in a Perfectionist Theory of Law and Justice," 11 *Cardozo Law Review* 335 (1989).

Brown, Harold A., and Louis M. Brown, "Disqualification of the Testifying Advocate—A Firm Rule?" 57 *North Carolina Law Review* 597 (1979).

Brown, Louis M., and Edward A. Dauer, *Planning by Lawyers: Materials on a Nonadversarial Legal Process* (1978).

Brown, Louis M., and Thomas L. Shaffer, "Toward a Jurisprudence for the Law Office," 17 *American Journal of Jurisprudence* 125 (1972).

Brown, Peter Megargee, "Professional Responsibility: Has the Rise of Megafirms Endangered Professionalism?" *A.B.A. Journal*, Dec. 1989, p. 38.

Brueggemann, Walter, "Covenant as a Subversive Paradigm," 97 *Christian Century* 1094 (1980).

——, "Expository Articles: Psalm 100," 39 *Interpretation* 65 (1985).

——, "II Kings 18–19: The Legitimacy of a Sectarian Hermeneutic," 7 *Horizons in Biblical Theology* 1 (1985).

——, "Passion and Perspective: Two Dimensions of Education in the Bible," 42 *Theology Today* 172 (1985).

———, "Vine and Fig Tree: A Case Study in Imagination and Criticism," 43 *Catholic Biblical Quarterly* 188 (1981).

Buber, Martin, *Eclipse of God: Studies in the Relation Between Religion and Philosophy* (Humanities Press ed., 1979).

———, *I and Thou* (Kaufmann trans., 1972).

———, *The Knowledge of Man* (Smith trans., 1965).

———, *On Judaism* (Glatzer trans., 1967).

Burt, Robert A., "Constitutional Law and the Teaching of the Parables," 93 *Yale Law Journal* 455 (1984).

———, et al., "Dred Scott and Brown v. Board of Education: A Frances Lewis Law Center Colloquium, What Was Wrong With Dred Scott, What's Right About Brown," 42 *Washington and Lee Law Review* 1 (1985).

———, *Taking Care of Strangers: The Rule of Law in Doctor-Patient Relations* (1979).

———, *Two Jewish Justices: Outcasts in the Promised Land* (1988).

Bush, Robert A. Baruch, "Between Two Worlds: The Shift from Individual to Group Responsibility in the Law of Causation of Injury," 33 *U.C.L.A. Law Review* 1473 (1986).

Cahill, Lisa Sowle, *Between the Sexes: Foundations for a Christian Ethics of Sexuality* (1985).

———, "Feminist Ethics," 51 *Theological Studies* 49 (March 1990).

Caporale, Rocco (ed.), *The Italian Americans Through the Generations* (1986). (A.I.H.A. 1982)

———, "The Value System of Southern Italian and Italian American Professionals," in Pane (A.I.H.A. 1979).

Caroli, Betty Boyd, Robert F. Harney, and Lydio F. Tomasi (eds.), *The Italian Immigrant Woman in North America* (1978). (A.I.H.A. 1977)

Carpenter, Farrington R., *Confessions of a Maverick: An Autobiography* (1984).

Carr, David, *Time, Narrative, and History* (1986).

Carter, Dan T., *Scottsboro: A Tragedy of the American South* (1969).

Carter, Henry, *The Methodist Heritage* (1950).

Cash, W. J., *The Mind of the South* (1941).

Cather, Willa, *My Antonia* (1918).

Cavaioli, Frank J., "Chicago's Italian Americans Rally for Immigration Reform," in Juliani (A.I.H.A. 1980).

Center for Migration Studies of New York, Inc., *Images: A Pictorial History of Italian Americans* (1981).

Chafe, William Henry, *The American Woman: Her Changing Social, Economic, and Political Roles, 1920–1970* (1972).

Childress, James F., "Scripture and Christian Ethics: Some Reflections on the Role of Scripture in Moral Deliberation and Justification," 34 *Interpretation* 371 (1980).

———, *Who Should Decide? Paternalism in Health Care* (1982).

———, and John Macquarrie, *The Westminster Dictionary of Christian Ethics* (1986).

Chroust, Anton-Hermann, *The Rise of the Legal Profession in America* (1965).

Churchill, Larry R., "The Professionalization of Ethics: Some Implications for Accountability in Medicine," 60 *Soundings* 40 (Spring 1977).

Claro, Fran, "South Brooklyn, 1947," in Barolini's *Dream Book*.

Clasen, Claus-Peter, *Anabaptism: A Social History, 1525–1618* (1972).

Clebsch, William A., *American Religious Thought: A History* (1973).

Cooper, John M., "Aristotle on the Forms of Friendship," 30 *Review of Metaphysics* 619 (June 1977).

———, "Friendship and the Good in Aristotle," 86 *Philosophical Review* 290 (1977).

Cordasco, Francesco, and Michael Vaughn Cordasco, *The Italian Emigration to the United States, 1880–1930: A Bibliographic Register of Italian Views, Including Selected Numbers from the Italian Commissariat of Emigration, Bollettino dell'emigrazione* (1990).

Cotillo, Salvatore A., *Italy During the World War* (1922).

Coulling, Mary P., *The Lee Girls* (1987).

Covello, Leonard, *The Heart is the Teacher* (1958).

———, *The Social Background of the Italo-American School Child: A Study of the Southern Italian Family Mores and Their Effect on the School Situation in Italy and America* (1967).

Cover, Robert, "Obligation: A Jewish Jurisprudence of the Social Order," 5 *Journal of Law and Religion* 65 (1987).

———, "Nomos and Narrative," 97 *Harvard Law Review* 4 (1983).

Cuomo, Mario M., *The Diaries of Mario M. Cuomo: The Campaign for Governor* (1984).

D'Andrea, Vaneeta-Marie, "The Ethnic Factor and Role Choices of Women," in Pane (A.I.H.A.).

———, "The Social Role Identity of Italian-American Women," in Juliani (A.I.H.A.).

Davis, John A., *Conflict and Control: Law and Order in Nineteenth-Century Italy* (1988).

Dawson, Jan C., "The Religion of Democracy in Early Twentieth-Century America," 27 *Journal of Church and State* 47 (1985).

del Russo, Carl, and Joseph L. Tropea, "Identity and Contradictions," in Juliani (A.I.H.A. 1980).

"Developments in the Law: Conflicts of Interest in the Legal Profession," 94 *Harvard Law Review* 1244 (1981).

DiFranco, J. Philip, *The Italian Americans* (1988).

DiStasi, Lawrence (ed.), *Dream Streets: The Big Book of Italian-American Culture* (1989).

Duclos, Nitya, "Lessons of Difference: Feminist Theory on Cultural Diversity," 38 *Buffalo Law Review* 325 (1990).

Dworkin, Gerald, "Autonomy and Behavior Control," Hastings Center Report, Feb. 1976, p. 23.

———, "Moral Autonomy," in *Morals, Science, and Sociality* (1978), at 156.

Edman, Victor Raymond, *Finney Lives On: The Man, His Revival Methods, and His Message* (1951).

Egelman, William S., "Italian American Educational Attainment," in Caporale (A.I.H.A.).

Ellmann, Stephen, "Lawyering for Justice in a Flawed Democracy," 90 *Columbia Law Review* 116 (1990).

———, "Lawyers and Clients," 34 *UCLA Law Review* 717 (1987).

Epstein, Isidore, *Judaism: A Historical Presentation* (1959).

Fein, Bruce, "Supreme Court Report: Scalia's Way," *A.B.A. Journal*, Feb. 1990, p. 38.

Femminella, Francis X., "The Ethnic Ideological Themes of Italian-Americans," in Juliani (A.I.H.A.).

———, (ed.), *Italians and Irish in America* (1985). (A.I.H.A. 1983)

Ferber, Nat Joseph, *A New American: From the Life Story of Salvatore A. Cotillo, Supreme Court Justice, State of New York* (1938).

Ferraro, Geraldine, *Ferraro, My Story* (1985).

Ferraro, Thomas J., "Blood in the Marketplace: The Business of Family in the Godfather Narratives," in Werner Sollors (ed.), *The Invention of Ethnicity* (1989).

Fingarette, Herbert, *Self Deception* (1969).

Finney, Charles Grandison: See Edman, *Great Gospel Sermons*, Timothy Smith.

Fiorenza, Elisabeth Schussler, *In Memory of Her: A Feminist Theological Reconstruction of Christian Origins* (1985).

Fish, Stanley, *Doing What Comes Naturally: Change, Rhetoric, and the Practice of Theory in Literary and Legal Studies* (1989).

Flood, Charles Bracelen, *Lee: The Last Years* (1981).

Frank, John P., "The Legal Ethics of Louis D. Brandeis," 17 *Stanford Law Review* 683 (1965) (ALE).

Franklin, John Hope, and August Meier (eds.), *Black Leaders of the Twentieth Century* (1982).

Freedman, Monroe H., *Lawyers' Ethics in an Adversary System* (1975).

———, "Legal Ethics and the Suffering Client," 36 *Catholic University Law Review* 331 (1987).

———, "Personal Responsibility in a Professional System," 27 *Catholic University Law Review* 191 (1978).

———, "Two Fables," *A.B.A. Journal*, May 1, 1988, p. 57.

———, *Understanding Lawyers' Ethics* (1990).

Freeman, Douglas Southall, *R. E. Lee: A Biography* (1935).

Gabaccia, Donna R., *Immigrant Women in the United States: A Selectively Annotated Multidisciplinary Bibliography* (1989).

Gallagher, Dorothy, *All The Right Enemies: The Life and Murder of Carlo Tresca* (1988).

Gallo, Pat (ed.), *The Urban Experience of Italian-Americans* (1977). (A.I.H.A. 1975).

Gambino, Richard, *Blood of My Blood: The Dilemma of the Italian Americans* (1974).

———, "Italian Americans Today," in Moquin and Van Doren.

Gaustad, Edwin Scott, *Dissent in American Religion* (1973).

———, *The Great Awakening in New England* (1957).

Geach, P. T., *The Virtues* (1977).

Gelpi, Donald L. (ed.), *Beyond Individualism: Toward a Retrieval of Moral Discourse in America* (1989).

Gesualdi, Louis J., "A Documentation of Criticisms Concerning Amoral Familism," in Juliani (A.I.H.A. 1980).

Gilligan, Carol, *In a Different Voice: Psychological Theory and Women's Development* (1982).

Glazer, Nathan, and Daniel Patrick Moynihan, *Beyond the Melting Pot: The Negroes, Puerto Ricans, Jews, Italians, and Irish of New York City* (1963).

Glendon, Mary Ann, *Abortion and Divorce in Western Law* (1987).

Goldberg, Michael, *Jews and Christians, Getting Our Stories Straight: The Exodus and the Passion-Resurrection* (1985).

——, *Theology and Narrative: A Critical Introduction* (1982).

Graber, Glenn C., and David C. Thomasma, *Theory and Practice in Medical Ethics* (1989).

Great Gospel Sermons (1949).

Green, Rose Basile, *The Italian-American Novel: A Document of the Interaction of Two Cultures* (1974).

Greenhouse, Carol J., *Praying for Justice: Faith, Order, and Community in an American Town* (1986).

Gregory, David L., "Catholic Labor Theory and the Transformation of Work," 45 *Washington and Lee Law Review* 119 (1988).

Gustafson, James M., *Christian Ethics and the Community* (1971).

——, *Ethics from a Theocentric Perspective* (1981, 1984).

——, *Protestant and Roman Catholic Ethics* (1978).

Hall, Stephen S., "Italian-Americans Coming Into Their Own," *New York Times Magazine*, May 15, 1983, p. 28.

Haring, Bernard, *The Law of Christ* (1963).

Harney, Elizabeth Haney, "What Is Feminist Ethics? A Proposal for Continuing Discussion," 8 *Journal of Religious Ethics* 115 (1980).

Harriman, Mary Case, "Miss Fixit," *New Yorker*, Jan. 30, 1937, pp. 21–25; Feb. 6, 1937, pp. 22–25 (on Fanny Holtzmann) (ALE).

Harris, Lis, *Holy Days: The World of a Hasidic Family* (1985).

Harrison, Barbara Grizzuti, *Italian Days* (1989).

Hartt, Julian N., *A Christian Critique of American Culture: An Essay in Practical Theology* (1967).

Hatch, Nathan, *The Professions in American History* (1987).

Hauerwas, Stanley, *A Community of Character: Toward a Constructive Christian Social Ethic* (1981).

———, *Character and the Christian Life: A Study in Theological Ethics* (1975).

———, *Christian Existence Today: Essays on Church, World, and Living in Between* (1988).

———, "Constancy and Forgiveness: The Novel as a School for Virtue," 15 *Notre Dame English Journal* 23 (Summer 1983).

———, et al., "Faith in the Republic: A Frances Lewis Law Center Conversation," 45 *Washington and Lee Law Review* 467 (1988).

———, *Suffering Presence: Theological Reflections on Medicine, the Mentally Handicapped, and the Church* (1986).

———, *Truthfulness and Tragedy: Further Investigations in Christian Ethics* (1977).

———, *Vision and Virtue: Essays in Christian Ethical Reflection* (1974).

———, "Will the Real Sectarian Please Stand Up?" 44 *Theology Today* 87 (1987).

———, and Alasdair MacIntyre (eds.), *Revisions: Changing Perspectives in Moral Philosophy* (1983).

Hazard, Geoffrey C., Jr., *Ethics in the Practice of Law* (1978).

———, and Deborah L. Rhode (eds.), *The Legal Profession: Responsibility and Regulation* (1985).

Henderson, Thomas M., "Immigrant Politician: Salvatore Cotillo, Progressive Ethnic," 13 *International Migration Review* 81 (Spring 1979).

Herberg, Will, *Judaism and Modern Man: An Interpretation of Jewish Religion* (1951).

———, *Protestant-Catholic-Jew: An Essay in American Religious Sociology* (1955).

Herman, Sondra R., "Loving Courtship or the Marriage Market? The Ideal and Its Critics, 1871–1911," 25 *American Quarterly* 235 (May 1973).

Heschel, Abraham J., *Between God and Man: An Interpretation of Judaism* (1959).

———, *The Prophets* (1962).

Hobbs, Steven H., "From the Shoulders of Houston: A Vision for Social and Economic Justice," 32 *Howard Law Review* 505 (1989).

Hodge, Charles, "Review of Hoffman's Course," 9 *Biblical Repertory and Princeton Review* 509 (1837).

Hoffman, David, *A Course of Legal Study* (1817; 2nd ed. 1836). (ALE)

———, *Introductory Lectures and Syllabus of a Course of Lectures* (1837) (includes Kent review of Hoffman's *Course*).

Holden, Pat (ed.), *Women's Religious Experience* (1983).

Holtzmann, Fanny: See Berkman, Harriman

Horwitz, Morton J., *The Transformation of American Law, 1780–1860* (1977).

Hostetler, John A., "The Amish and the Law: A Religious Minority and Its Legal Encounters," 41 *Washington and Lee Law Review* 33 (1984).

Houston, Charles Hamilton: See Hobbs, Kluger, McNeil, Tushnet.

Howe, Mark DeWolfe, Book Review, 60 *Harvard Law Review* 838 (1947) (ALE).

Howells, William Dean, *A Modern Instance* (1881) (Riverside ed. 1957) (ALE).

———, *The Rise of Silas Lapham* (1885) (Signet ed., 1963).

Hubbard, B. A. F., and E. S. Karnofsky, *Plato's Protagoras: A Socratic Commentary* (1982).

Hughes, A., and F. LaVeness, "Congresswoman Geraldine A. Ferraro: An American Legacy," in LaVeness and Sweeney.

Huizinga, Johan, *America: A Dutch Historian's Vision, from Afar and Near* (H. Rowan trans., 1972).

Hurst, James Willard, *The Growth of American Law: The Law Makers* (1950).

———, *Law and Social Process in United States History* (1960).

Johnson, Colleen Leahy, *Growing Up and Growing Old in Italian-American Families* (1985).

Johnson, Lyman, "Corporate Takeovers and Corporations: Who Are They For?" 43 *Washington and Lee Law Review* 781 (1986).

Jones, Harry W., "Lawyers and Justice: The Uneasy Ethics of Partisanship," 23 *Villanova Law Review* 957 (1978) (ALE).

Jones, L. Gregory, "Should Christians Affirm Rawls' Justice as Fairness? A Response to Professor Beckley," 16 *Journal of Religious Ethics* 251 (Fall 1988).

Jones, Thomas Goode, "Code of Ethics Adopted by [the] Alabama State Bar Association," 118 *Alabama Reports* xxiii (1899) (ALE).

Jonsen, Albert R., *Responsibility in Modern Religious Ethics* (1968).

Juliani, Richard N. (ed.), *The Family and Community Life of Italian Americans* (1983) (A.I.H.A. 1980).

Jung, C. G., *Analytical Psychology: Its Theory and Practice* (1968).

———, "The Psychology of the Transference," in vol. 16, *Collected Works* (2nd ed., 1966).

———, *Psychological Reflections* (J. Jacobi ed., 1953).

"Jurisprudence—Naturalization—Moral Standard," 33 *Marquette Law Review* 202 (1950).

Kant, Immanuel, *Foundations of the Metaphysics of Morals* (1785) (Lewis White Beck trans., 1969).

Kerber, Linda K., and Jane DeHart-Mathews (eds.), *Women's America: Refocusing the Past* (2nd ed., 1982).

Kluger, Richard, *Simple Justice: The History of Brown v. Board of Education and Black America's Struggle for Equality* (1975).

Kommers, Donald P., "Liberty and Community in Constitutional Law: The Abortion Cases in Comparative Perspective," 1985 *Brigham Young University Law Review* 371.

Krase, Jerome, "The Italian-American Community," in Juliani (A.I.H.A. 1980).

———, and William Egelman (eds.), *The Melting Pot and Beyond: Italian Americans in the Year 2000* (1987) (A.I.H.A. 1985).

Kronman, Anthony T., "Living in the Law," 54 *University of Chicago Law Review* 835 (1987).

———, "Precedent and Tradition," 99 *Yale Law Journal* 1029 (1990).

LaGumina, Salvatore J., "John Pastore," in Krase and Egelman. (A.I.H.A. 1985).

———, "Marconiville, U.S.A.," in Juliani (A.I.H.A. 1985).

———, "The Political Profession," in Pane (A.I.H.A. 1979).

———, *From Steerage to Suburb: Long Island Italians* (1988).

LaSorte, Michael, *La Merica: Images of Italian Greenhorn Experience* (1985).

LaVeness, Frank P., and Jane P. Sweeney (eds.), *Women Leaders in Contemporary U.S. Politics* (1987).

Lee, Robert E.: See Coulling, Flood, Freeman.

Letwin, Shirley Robin, *The Gentleman in Trollope: Individuality and Moral Conduct* (1982).

Levinson, Sanford, *Constitutional Faith* (1988). (See also Hauerwas, "Faith.")

Lewis, C. S., *Christian Reflections* (1967).

Lindbeck, George A., *The Nature of Doctrine: Religion and Theology in a Postliberal Age* (1984).

Long, Edward L., *A Survey of Recent Christian Ethics* (1982).

Lopreato, Joseph, *Italian Americans* (1970).

———, *Peasants No More: Social Class and Social Change in an Underdeveloped Society* (1967).

Louden, Robert B., "Aristotle's Practical Particularism," 6 *Ancient Philosophy* 123 (1988).

———, "Rights Infatuation and The Impoverishment of Moral Theory," 17 *Journal of Value Inquiry* 7 (1983).

Luban, David (ed.), *The Good Lawyer: Lawyers' Roles and Lawyers' Ethics* (1983).

———, "The Noblesse Oblige Tradition in the Practice of Law," 41 *Vanderbilt Law Review* 717 (1988).

———, "Paternalism and the Legal Profession," 1981 *Wisconsin Law Review* 454.

MacIntyre, Alasdair, *After Virtue: A Study in Moral Theory* (2nd ed., 1984).

———, *Three Rival Versions of Moral Enquiry* (1990).

———, *Whose Justice? Which Rationality?* (1988).

Maglione, Connie A., and Carmen Anthony Fiore, *Voices of the Daughters* (1989).

Maimonides, Moses, *Mishneh Torah* (Code of Maimonides) (Hershman trans., 1949).

Mann, Thomas, *Death in Venice* (1930) (Vintage ed., H. T. Lowe-Porter trans., 1954).

Mariano, John Horace, *The Italian Contribution to American Democracy* (1921) (Arno ed., 1975).

———, *The Italian Immigrant and Our Courts* (1925).

Maritain, Jacques, *The Range of Reason* (1952).

Martori, Joe, *Street Fights: A Novel Based on a True Story* (1987).

Marty, Martin E., *Righteous Empire: The Protestant Experience in America* (1970).

Mason, Philip, *The English Gentleman: The Rise and Fall of an Ideal* (1982).

Matsuda, Mari J., "Liberal Jurisprudence and Abstracted Visions of Human Nature: A Feminist Critique of Rawls' Theory of Justice," 16 *New Mexico Law Review* 613 (1986).

May, William F., *The Physician's Covenant: Images of the Healer in Medical Ethics* (1983).

McClendon, James Wm., Jr., *Biography as Theology: How Life Stories Can Remake Today's Theology* (1974).

———, *Systematic Theology: Ethics* (1986).

McCormick, Richard A., *Health and Medicine in the Catholic Tradition: Tradition in Transition* (1984). (See also Graber and Thomasma.)

McNeil, G. R., "Charles Hamilton Houston: Social Engineer for Civil Rights," in Franklin and Meier. (ALE)

McNemar, Richard, *The Kentucky Revival* (1808).

Meilaender, Gilbert C., *Friendship: A Study in Theological Ethics* (1981).

———, "The Singularity of Christian Ethics," 17 *Journal of Religious Ethics* 95 (Fall 1989). (On the two moral orders; see also Oakeshott.)

———, *The Theory and Practice of Virtue* (1984).

Menkel-Meadow, Carrie, "Portia in a Different Voice: Speculations on a Woman's Lawyering Process," 1 *Berkeley Women's Law Journal* 39 (1985).

Meloni, Alberto C., "Italy Invades the Bloody Third: The Early History of Milwaukee's Italians," 10 *Milwaukee History* 47 (1987).

Merola, Mario, *Big City D.A.* (1988).

Meyer, Gerald, *Vito Marcantonio: Radical Politician, 1902–1954* (1989).

Miller, Arthur, *A View from the Bridge* (Bantam ed., 1961).

Miller, R., and T. Marzik (eds.), *Immigrants and Religion in Urban America* (1977).

Millon, David, "The Sherman Act and the Balance of Power," 61 *Southern California Law Review* 1219 (1988).

Moquin, Wayne, and Charles Van Doren (eds.), *A Documentary History of the Italian Americans* (1974).

Murdoch, Iris, "On 'God' and 'Good,' " in Hauerwas and MacIntyre.

———, *The Sovereignty of Good* (1970).

Musmanno, Michael A., *The Story of the Italians in America* (1965).

Nagareda, Richard, "The Appellate Jurisprudence of Justice Antonin Scalia," 54 *University of Chicago Law Review* 705 (1987).

Nelli, Humbert S., *From Immigrants to Ethnics: The Italian Americans* (1983).

———, "Italians," in *Harvard Encyclopedia of Ethnic Groups* (1980), at 545.

Neuhaus, Richard John (ed.), *Law and the Ordering of Our Life Together* (1989).

———, *The Naked Public Square: Religion and Democracy in America* (1984).

Newman, John Henry, *The Idea of a University* (1852). (Oxford ed., 1976).

Niebuhr, H. Richard, *The Responsible Self: An Essay in Christian Moral Philosophy* (1963).

Niebuhr, Reinhold, *The Irony of American History* (1952).

———, *Moral Man and Immoral Society: A Study in Ethics and Politics* (1932). (Scribner's ed., 1960).

Notarianni, Philip F., and Richard Raspa, "The Italian Community of Helper, Utah," in Juliani (A.I.H.A. 1980).

Novak, Michael, *In Praise of Cynicism* (1977) (ALE).

———, "Catholics and Power," *Notre Dame Magazine*, Feb. 1980, p. 12 (ALE).

Oakeshott, Michael Joseph, *Rationalism in Politics, and Other Essays* (1962).

Okin, Susan Moller, *Justice, Gender and the Family* (1989).

O'Meara, Joseph, and Thomas L. Shaffer, "Obscenity in the Supreme Court: A Note on Jacobellis v. Ohio," 40 *Notre Dame Lawyer* 1 (1964).

Oppenheim, Frank M., "A Roycean Response to the Challenge of Individualism," in Gelpi.

Pane, Remigio U., *Italian Americans in the Professions* (1983) (A.I.H.A. 1979).

Paolini, J., Jr., "An American Italian: The Life and Times of Luigi DePasquale (1892–1958)," in Krase and Egelman. (A.I.H.A. 1985).

Parker, Alan A., "Not Only a Great Man, But a Decent Man" (on Rep. Peter W. Rodino, Jr.), *Trial*, Feb. 1986, p. 11.

Passamaneck, Stephen M., and Louis M. Brown, "The Rabbis— Preventive Law Lawyers," 8 *Israel Law Review* 538 (1973).

Patai, Raphael, *The Jewish Mind* (1977).

Patterson, Haywood, and Earl Conrad, *Scottsboro Boy* (1973).

Pelikan, Jaroslav, *The Christian Tradition: A History of the Development of Doctrine* (1971).

Pepper, Stephen, "The Lawyer's Amoral Ethical Role: A Defense, a Problem, and Some Possibilities," 1986 *American Bar Foundation Research Journal* 613, 657.

Perlmann, Joel, *Ethnic Differences: Schooling and Social Structure Among the Irish, Italians, Jews, and Blacks in an American City, 1880–1935* (1988).

Pincoffs, Edmund, "Quandary Ethics," in Hauerwas and MacIntyre.

Plato, *The Collected Dialogues* (Edith Hamilton and Huntington Cairns eds., 1961). (See also Hubbard and Karnofsky.)

Post, Stephen, "Communion and True Self-Love," 16 *Journal of Religious Ethics* 345 (Fall 1988).

Powell, H. Jefferson, *Persons in God* (unpub. 1988).

Pugliese, Peter F., "Americans of Italian Descent in the Judiciary of Pennsylvania," in Pane (A.I.H.A. 1979).

Quilici, George L., *The Italian American Lawyers of Chicago* (1968).

Rawls, John, *A Theory of Justice* (1971).

Redmount, Robert S., "Attorney Personalities and Some Psychological Aspects of Legal Consultation," 109 *University of Pennsylvania Law Review* 972 (1961).

——— , "Psychological Views in Jurisprudential Theories," 107 *University of Pennsylvania Law Review* 472 (1959).

Rhode, Deborah L., "Class Conflicts in Class Actions," 34 *Stanford Law Review* 1183 (1982).

——— , "Ethical Perspectives on Legal Practice," 37 *Stanford Law Review* 589 (1985).

——— , "Feminist Critical Theories," 42 *Stanford Law Review* 617 (1990).

——— , *Justice and Gender* (1989).

——— , "Why the ABA Bothers: A Functional Perspective on Professional Codes," 59 *Texas Law Review* 689 (1981).

Rodes, Robert E., Jr. *The Legal Enterprise* (1976).

——— , *Law and Liberation* (1986).

——— , "Pluralist Christendom and the Christian Civil Magistrate," 8 *Capital University Law Review* 413 (1979).

——— , "Sub deo et Lege, a Study of Free Exercise," 4 *Religion and the Public Order* 3 (1968).

———, *Lay Authority and Reformation in the English Church: Edward I to the Civil War* (1982).

———, *Ecclesiastical Administration in Medieval England: The Anglo-Saxons to the Reformation* (1977).

Rose, Phyllis, *Parallel Lives: Five Victorian Marriages* (1983).

Rotunda, Ronald D., "Lawyers and Professionalism: A Commentary on the Report of the American Bar Association Commission on Professionalism," 18 *Loyola University* [Chicago] *Law Journal* 1149 (1987).

———, "Professionals, Pragmatists, or Predators?" 75 *Illinois Bar Journal* 420, 482, 540 (1987).

———, "The Word 'Profession' Is Only a Label—and Not a Very Useful One," *Learning and the Law,* vol. 4, no. 2, p. 16 (Summer 1977).

Ruether, Rosemary Radford, *New Woman, New Earth: Sexist Ideologies and Human Liberation* (1975).

Royce, Josiah, *The Basic Writings of Josiah Royce* (J. J. McDermott, ed., 1969).

Saladino, Salvatore Maximillian, *Italy from Unification to 1919: Growth and Decay of a Liberal Regime* (1970).

Sandel, Michael J., *Liberalism and the Limits of Justice* (1982).

Sandler, Gilbert, *The Neighborhood: The Story of Baltimore's Little Italy* (1974).

Santini, Rosemary, "An American Dream," in Barolini, *Dream Book*.

Sartorio, Enrico C., *Social and Religious Life of Italians in America* (1918).

Scarpaci, Jean A. (ed.), *The Interaction of Italians and Jews in America* (1974). (A.I.H.A.)

Schiro, George, *Americans by Choice: History of the Italians in Utica* (1975).

Schlesinger, Arthur Meier, *Prelude to Independence: The Newspaper War on Britain, 1764–1776* (1966).

Schnackenburg, Rudolf, *The Moral Teaching of the New Testament* (1965).

Schneider, William, "The New Shape of American Politics," *Atlantic Monthly,* Jan. 1987, p. 39.

Schneyer, Theodore, "Moral Philosophy's Standard Misconception of Legal Ethics," 1984 *Wisconsin Law Review* 1529.

Schroeder, Theodore (ed.), *Free Press Anthology* (1909).

Schudson, Michael, *Discovering the News: A Social History of American Newspapers* (1978).

———, "Public, Private, and Professional Lives: The Correspondence of David Dudley Field and Samuel Bowles," 21 *American Journal of Legal History* 191 (1977) (ALE).

Schussler-Fiorenza: See Fiorenza.

Schwartz, Murray L., "The Death and Regeneration of Ethics," 1980 *American Bar Foundation Research Journal* 953.

———, "The Professionalism and Accountability of Lawyers," 66 *California Law Review* 669 (1978).

Shaffer, Thomas L., Book Review (of four studies of narrative), 33 *American Journal of Jurisprudence* 241 (1988).

———, *Faith and the Professions* (1987).

———, "Judges as Prophets," 67 *Texas Law Review* 1327 (1989).

———, "Jurisprudence in the Light of the Hebraic Faith," 1 *Notre Dame Journal of Law, Ethics, and Public Policy* 77 (1984).

———, *On Being a Christian and a Lawyer* (1981).

———, "The Legal Ethics of Radical Individualism," 65 *Texas Law Review* 963 (1987).

———, "The Unique, Novel, and Unsound Adversary Ethic," 41 *Vanderbilt Law Review* 697 (1988).

Sharswood, George, "Essay on Professional Ethics" (1854), in 32 *Reports of the American Bar Association* (1907).

Sherry, Suzanna, "Civic Virtue and the Feminine Voice in Constitutional Adjudication," 72 *Virginia Law Review* 543 (1986).

Simon, William H., "Ethical Discretion in Lawyering," 101 *Harvard Law Review* 1083 (1988).

Simonsen, Judith A., "The Third Ward: Symbol of Ethnic Identity," 10 *Milwaukee History* 61 (1987).

Singer, Isaac Bashevis, and Richard Burgin, *Conversations with Isaac Bashevis Singer* (1985).

Sirey, Aileen Riotto, Anthony Patti, and Lisa Mann, *Ethnotherapy: An Exploration of Italian-American Identity* (1985).

Smith, Timothy L., *Revivalism and Social Reform in Mid-Nineteenth-Century America* (1958).

Snow, C. P., *Strangers and Brothers* (Omnibus ed., 1974).

———, *Trollope: His Life and Art* (1975).

Soloveitchik, Joseph B., "The Lonely Man of Faith," 7 *Tradition* 5 (1965).

Sophocles, "Antigone," in *The Oedipus Cycle* (Dudley Fitts and Robert Fitzgerald, eds., 1977).

Sorrentino, Anthony, "Organizing the Ethnic Community," in Juliani (A.I.H.A. 1980).

Stackhouse, Max L., "Piety, Polity, and Policy," in Carl H. Esbeck (ed.), *Religious Beliefs, Human Rights, and the Moral Foundation of Western Democracy* (1986).

————, *Public Theology and Political Economy: Christian Stewardship in Modern Society* (1987).

Stanley, Justin A., "Professionalism and Commercialism," 50 *Montana Law Review 1* (1989).

Story, Joseph, "Review of Hoffman's *Course*," *North American Review,* Nov. 1817, p. 45.

Stout, Jeffrey, *Ethics After Babel: The Languages of Morals and Their Discontents* (1988).

————, "Idealist Ethics" (on Josiah Royce among others), in Childress and Macquarrie.

Swaine, Robert T., *The Cravath Firm and Its Predecessors* (1946).

Swiderski, Richard M., *Voices: An Anthropologist's Dialogue with an Italian-American Festival* (1987).

"Symposium: The Republican Civic Tradition," 97 *Yale Law Journal* 1493 (1988).

Talmud: *The Soncino Talmud* (A. Cohen trans. 1935).

Thomas, Lewis, *The Lives of a Cell: Notes of a Biology Watcher* (1974).

————, *The Medusa and the Snail: More Notes of a Biology Watcher* (1979).

————, *The Youngest Science: Notes of a Medicine-Watcher* (Bantam ed., 1983).

Thomas, William B., and Kevin J. Moran, "Centralization and Ethnic Coalition Formation in Buffalo, New York, 1918–1922," 23 *Journal of Social History* 137 (1989).

Thompson, Priscilla M., *Arriving in Delaware: The Italian-American Experience* (1989).

Tinder, Glenn, *Tolerance: Toward a New Civility* (1976).

Tocqueville, Alexis de, *Democracy in America* (1835) (Random House ed., 1945).

Tomasi, Silvano M. (ed.), *The Religious Experience of Italian Americans* (1973). (A.I.H.A.)

Toulmin, Stephen, "Ethics and Equity: The Tyranny of Principles," 15 *Gazette* 240 (1981).

Tresca, Carlo: See Gallagher.

Tricarico, Donald, "The Italians of Greenwich Village," in Juliani (A.I.H.A. 1980).

Trilling, Lionel, "Science, Literature, and Culture," 33 *Commentary* 461 (1962).

Tropea, J. L., J. E. Miller, and C. Beattie-Repetti (eds.), *Support and Struggle: Italians and Italian Americans in a Comparative Perspective* (1986). (A.I.H.A.)

Tushnet, Mark V., *The N.A.A.C.P.'s Legal Strategy Against Segregated Education, 1925–1950* (1987). (See Hauerwas, "Faith.")

United States Catholic Conference, *The Challenge of Peace: God's Promise and Our Response—A Pastoral Letter on War and Peace* (1983).

United States Catholic Conference, *Economic Justice for All: Pastoral Letter on Catholic Social Teaching and the U.S. Economy* (1986).

Vecoli, Rudolph J., "Cult and Occult in Italian American Culture," in Miller and Marzik.

——— (ed.), *Italian American Radicalism: Old World Origins and New World Developments* (1972). (A.I.H.A.)

Velikonja, Joseph, "The Periodical Press and Italian Communities," in Juliani (A.I.H.A. 1980).

Venturelli, Peter J., "Tuscan-American Families," in Juliani (A.I.H.A. 1980).

Vezzosi, Elisabetta, "The Dilemma of the Ethnic Community: The Italian Immigrant Woman Between 'Preservation' and 'Americanization' in the Early Twentieth Century," in Tropea, Miller, and Beattie-Repetti (A.I.H.A. 1986).

Viscusi, Robert, "Il Caso Della Casa," in Juliani (A.I.H.A. 1980).

———, "Professions and Faiths," in Pane (A.I.H.A. 1979).

———, "The Semiology of Semen," in Caporale (A.I.H.A. 1982).

Vorspan, Albert, *Giants of Justice* (1960) (ALE).

Walzer, Michael, *Exodus and Revolution* (1985).

———, *Interpretation and Social Criticism* (1987).

Warner, Marina, *The Lost Father* (1989).

Wasserstrom, Richard, "Lawyers as Professionals: Some Moral Issues," 5 *Human Rights* 1 (1975).

Watson, Andrew S., M.D., "Some Psychological Aspects of Teaching Professional Responsibility," 16 *Journal of Legal Education* 1 (1963).

————, "The Quest for Professional Competence: Psychological Aspects of Legal Education," 37 *Cincinnati Law Review* 93 (1968).

Weisz, Howard Ralph, *Irish-American and Italian-American Educational Views and Activities, 1870–1900: A Comparison* (1976).

Welter, Barbara, "The Cult of True Womanhood, 1820–1860," 18 *American Quarterly* 151 (1961).

West, Robin, "Jurisprudence and Gender," 55 *University of Chicago Law Review* 1 (1988).

Wexler, Stephen, "Practicing Law for Poor People," 79 *Yale Law Journal* 1049 (1970). (ALE)

White, James Boyd, *When Words Lose Their Meaning: Constitutions and Reconstitutions of Language, Character, and Community* (1984).

————, "The Ethics of Argument: Plato's *Gorgias* and the Modern Lawyer," 50 *University of Chicago Law Review* 849 (1983).

White, James P., "Professionalism and the Law School," 19 *Cumberland Law Review* 309 (1989).

Wiesel, Elie, *A Jew Today* (1978).

————, *The Gates of the Forest* (Frances Frenaye trans. 1982).

Wijesinha, Rajiva, *The Androgynous Trollope: Attitudes to Women Amongst Early Victorian Novelists* (1982).

Wilson, Diane Vecchio, "Assimilation and Ethnic Consolidation of Italians in Cortland, New York, 1892–1930," in Juliani (A.I.H.A. 1980).

Wolfram, Charles W., *Modern Legal Ethics* (1986).

Woloch, Nancy, *Women and the American Experience* (1984).

Wyatt-Brown, Bertram, *Southern Honor: Ethics and Behavior in the Old South* (1982).

Yoder, John Howard, *The Politics of Jesus* (1972).

————, *The Priestly Kingdom: Social Ethics as Gospel* (1984).

Zizioulas, J. D. "Human Capacity and Human Incapacity: A Theological Exploration of Personhood," 28 *Scottish Journal of Theology* 401 (1975).

Zucchi, John E., "Paesani or Italiani" in Juliani (A.I.H.A. 1980).

Index

Books by Thomas L. Shaffer

Death, Property, and Lawyers (1970)

The Planning and Drafting of Wills and Trusts
(1972, 1979, 1991) (third edition with Carol A. Mooney)

Legal Interviewing and Counseling
(1976, 1987) (second edition with James R. Elkins)

The Mentally Retarded Citizen and the Law (1976)
(co-editor with Michael Kindred, Julius Cohen,
and David Penrod)

Lawyers, Law Students, and People (1977)
(co-author with Robert S. Redmount)

Legal Interviewing and Counseling Cases (1980)
(co-author with Robert S. Redmount)

On Being a Christian and a Lawyer (1980)

American Legal Ethics (1985)

Faith and the Professions (1987)

American Lawyers and Their Communities (1991)

www.ingramcontent.com/pod-product-compliance
Lightning Source LLC
Chambersburg PA
CBHW021552210326
41599CB00010B/416